MAC ANNOYANCES™

How to Fix the Most ANNOYING Things About Your Mac

D0707498

John Rizzo

O'REILLY®

Beijing • Cambridge • Farnham • Köln • Paris • Sebastopol • Taipei • Tokyo

Mac Annoyances™
How to Fix the Most Annoying Things About Your Mac

by John Rizzo

Published by O'Reilly Media, Inc., 1005 Gravenstein Highway North, Sebastopol, CA 95472.

O'Reilly books may be purchased for educational, business, or sales promotional use. Online editions are also available for most titles *(safari.oreilly.com)*. For more information, contact our corporate/institutional sales department: 800-998-9938 or *corporate@oreilly.com*.

Print History:		Editor:	Chuck Toporek
November 2004:	First Edition.	Production Editor:	Sarah Sherman
		Art Director:	Michele Wetherbee
		Cover Design:	Volume Design, Inc.
		Interior Designer:	Patti Capaldi
		Illustration:	© 2004 Hal Mayforth c/o theispot.com

RepKover™
This book uses RepKover™, a durable and flexible lay-flat binding.

0-596-00723-X
[C]

Contents

95 ILIFE ANNOYANCES CH.5

Introduction

I was annoyed when Deep Blue beat Garry Kasparov at chess in May of 1997. Kasparov, previously undefeated, was the best humankind had to offer. Yet, IBM's computer, Deep Blue, still beat the pants off him. Irritated conspiracy theorists contend that Deep Blue was a front, and that—like Dorothy's wizard behind the curtain—Bobby Fisher was actually calling the shots from the back room. If only it were so.

The fact is that computers have been annoying us for decades. Remember how ticked off Dave was when HAL began returning the error message "I'm sorry Dave, I can't do that" (in *2001: A Space Odyssey*)? And let's not forget poor Dr. Smith's frustration with that infernal robot nattering, "Danger, Will Robinson" (in *Lost in Space*). Talk about your kernel panics!

But none is more annoying than the computer sitting on your desk. Just replace HAL with a web browser and replace "I'm sorry, Dave" with "Could not open your page because the server could not be found." Even in today's point-and-click environment of graphical interface widgets and gratuitous animation, software is designed to make the hardware happy. If this weren't the case, the computer would just be an inefficient heating unit, and the keyboard would have no effect whatsoever. The hardware, in turn, is designed to facilitate software. So where does that leave you? Sitting in front of a big screen scratching your head and wondering, "Why won't it do what I want?"

BUT WHY *MAC* ANNOYANCES?

At this point, some of you are probably thinking, "Surely John doesn't mean that my faithful Mac is annoying." Indeed I do. I've been a Mac user for the past 20 years, and I've seen it all—from System 1.0 to the latest and greatest version of Mac OS X. And throughout these years, one pattern has been consistent: the current version of the hardware and software—whatever it is—is just fabulous, innovative, and cutting edge. Then, a new version comes out and we wonder how we ever put up with that last irritating version that was seemingly designed for troglodytes. But *this* new version is great. Then, the next version comes out, and the pattern repeats.

I don't want to give the idea that the evolution of the Macintosh has been a steady march of progress. It hasn't. New versions of Mac hardware and software often fix older bugs and annoying features, but they also often create new and unexpected headaches. This means you won't find the answer to all of your Mac's irritations by buying a new Mac or upgrading your software. I suspect that this will always be the case, even when we are asking our robot butlers to go put our flying Jetsons cars in our sky garages.

Let's get one thing straight. In this book, I'm not bashing Apple or Microsoft (well, maybe Microsoft just a little). I like the Mac. It's my machine of choice. I think Macs are less annoying than Windows machines, hands down. But with Macs, you expect more. You expect perfection. You're buying the best personal computer in the world, and you don't expect to be annoyed. We don't expect it to take a "Genius" in an Apple Store to fix a problem.

WHO SHOULD READ THIS BOOK

If your Mac has ever made your blood boil, this book is for you. Consider *Mac Annoyances* as your portable Genius Bar. And while it won't replace a dead hard drive, this book will tell you how to fix the most annoying problems you'll undoubtedly encounter as a Mac user. You know, the ones that can give you *agita* on a daily basis.

DO YOU HAVE AN ANNOYANCE?

If you have an annoyance that this book does not cover, don't tell my publisher. (They may start asking questions that I'd rather not answer.) Instead, email me. You're more likely to get a response from me if you keep your message short (check out the email guidelines in Chapter 2). I can't promise I'll respond to every person, but I will post the good annoyances on my blog at O'Reilly at *http://www. oreilly.com/catalog/macannoy.*

You can contact me at *johnrizzo@mac.com.*

HOW TO USE THIS BOOK

This book is user friendly, even more so than the Mac. There are no commands to type, no menus to select, and no dialogs to maneuver. Simply hold with one hand and turn pages with the other. Or, if you are already using the other hand to prop yourself up on a moving subway, turn pages with your nose. (Operating this book while driving is not recommended.)

However, the user interface of this book is a bit different than other Mac books. You don't need to read the beginning of a chapter to know what's going on later in the chapter. Read this book like you browse the Web: jump directly to the information you can use and skip the rest.

EXPLOIT THIS BOOK

If you have a particular annoyance, search the index rather than the table of contents. This book has an extensive index that's better suited for the hunt-and-peck user who needs a quick solution. For example, if you need to figure out a way to freeze the panes in Microsoft Excel, you could spend 20 minutes reading through Chapter 4, or you could look under "Excel" in the index, find the sublisting for "freezing panes," note the page number, flip to the page in question, and get your answer.

Go ahead; take advantage of this book. That's what it's here for.

WHAT'S IN THIS BOOK

What you'll find in Mac Annoyances are small bits of problem-solving information, mostly unrelated to each other. These bits are arranged into big clumps (called *chapters*, I believe), such as *Email*, *Microsoft Office*, and *iLife*. Some of these chapters are then subdivided into sections devoted to a specific application, such as Apple's Mail application, Microsoft Word, and iTunes.

This book is organized into the following clumps, er, chapters:

Chapter 1, *Mac OS X*

Learn how to deal with the Finder's quirks, fix networking hassles, and make your Mac's look and feel fit *your* needs instead of the other way around.

Chapter 2, *Email*

This chapter includes tips for dealing with spam, attachments, and other hazards. Look for sections on Mail, Entourage, Eudora, and AOL.

Chapter 3, *Internet*

Read this chapter to eliminate infuriating hassles with web browsing, improve Google and Sherlock searches, and beef up instant messaging with iChat and AIM.

Chapter 4, *Microsoft Office*

Office is the mother of all Mac annoyances. Sure, it's a powerful software suite, but only if you can figure out how to make it work for you. This chapter shows you how to get along with Word, Excel, PowerPoint, and Virtual PC.

Chapter 5, *iLife Music and Video*

Here, we get to the fun stuff, the iApps: iTunes, iPhoto, iMovie, iDVD, and GarageBand. (I would have called it *iBand*, but for some reason Apple didn't bother to ask me.) It's even more fun to get around these annoyances.

Chapter 6, *iPod*

iTunes becomes a lot more fun with iPod. That fact that this is the shortest chapter is a tribute to iPod's low annoyance factor.

Chapter 7, *Mac Hardware*

Apple's beautiful hardware is a pleasure to use, especially when it's working as expected. But if it isn't, check out this chapter, which has topics ranging from how to make your Mac faster to deleting annoyances with keyboards, mice, and displays. You'll also find tips for specific PowerBook and iBook models.

WHAT'S NOT IN THIS BOOK

As mentioned earlier, this book is designed to be portable. One way we accomplished this was to leave out chaff. It's all meat (with apologies to our vegetarian readers). There are no annoying instructions on how to use a menu or what Icon View means. I attempt to tell you what you need to know to accomplish the task, but I assume you're a competent Mac user who knows what a toolbar is. Trimming out this stuff means you won't break your back carrying this book.

BUILDING YOUR MAC BOOK LIBRARY?

If you're fairly new to Mac OS X, there are a few books that I'd highly recommend. The first is the perennial favorite, *Mac OS X: The Missing Manual* (O'Reilly), written by David Pogue. This book will help you get up to speed on the ins and outs of Mac OS X, and it's been the best-selling Mac book three years running.

Another useful book to throw in your computer bag is the *Mac OS X Panther Pocket Guide* (O'Reilly), written by my editor, Chuck Toporek. There's a lot of useful information packed into this little book, including a listing of the differences between Mac OS 9's Control Panels and Mac OS X's System Preferences, keyboard shortcuts, and a *Task and Setting Index*, which you can use to configure your Mac. And at $9.95, it's a steal.

On the opposite end of the spectrum, the pages of this book aren't filled with Unix code or instructions on how to grep a regular expression in a bash shell (whatever that means). (Actually, I do know what that means, but the eyes of the average Mac user glaze over when I try to explain it.) To get around certain problems, I do, however, occasionally suggest that you type a few short lines of code in Terminal, an application that lets you get at Mac OS X's Unix command-line interface. Don't worry; no hacker skills required.

> **tip**
>
> If you are interested in learning Mac OS X's Unix side, O'Reilly has some other great books you should check out, including *Learning Unix for Mac OS X Panther* and *Mac OS X Panther for Unix Geeks*. For more information about these books, point your web browser to *http://mac.oreilly.com/*.

USING CODE EXAMPLES

If you do know what you are doing Unix-wise, you may use the few bits code that I've provided in this book in your own programs and documentation. If you are reproducing a small amount of code, you do not need to contact O'Reilly Media for permission. Answering a question by citing this book and quoting example code does not require permission.

However, incorporating a significant amount of example code from this book into your product's documentation *does* require permission. Selling or distributing a CD-ROM of examples from O'Reilly books *does* require permission.

The publisher appreciates, but does not require, attribution. An attribution usually includes the title, author, publisher, and ISBN. For example: "*Mac Annoyances*, by John Rizzo. Copyright 2005 O'Reilly Media, Inc., 0-596-00723-X."

If you feel your use of code examples falls outside fair use or the permission given above, feel free to contact us at *permissions@oreilly.com*.

CONVENTIONS USED IN THIS BOOK

The following typographical conventions are used in this book:

Italic is used for filenames, URLs, paths (such as */Applications/Utilities*), and for emphasis.

`Constant Width Bold` **is used in examples and tables to show commands or other text that should be typed literally by the user.**

`Constant Width Italic` **is used in examples and tables to show text that should be replaced with user-supplied values.**

Forward slashes (/) are used in pathnames to show the location of a document, application, or folder. For example, */Applications/Utilities* indicates that the file is located in the Utilities subfolder of the Applications folder. A tilde (~) represents your home folder. So ~/*Library* means the Library folder in your Home folder. There's no folder called "Home," by the way. This is what we call the folder that is named after your username.

A carriage return (⏎) at the end of a line of code means we didn't have enough room on the page to print it on one line; that is, you should not enter these as two lines of code, but as one continuous line.

Arrows (→) describe menu commands. For example, File → Open means selecting Open from the File menu.

The cloverleaf symbol (⌘) signifies the Command, or Apple key, on your keyboard (look to the left or right of the spacebar for the ⌘ key).

ABOUT THE AUTHOR

John Rizzo bought his first Mac in 1984—complete with 128 KB RAM, a floppy drive (no hard drive), and a dot matrix printer, all for the bargain price of $2500.00. Talk about annoying. When you ran an application, you had to continually swap floppy disks: one for the system software and one for the application.

In 1987, John became technical editor and news writer of *Macintosh Today*, a short-lived weekly news magazine covering Macs. As a startup magazine, *Macintosh Today* was short on staff. It was considered part of the technical editor's duty to serve as the magazine's network administrator, using LocalTalk to hook up the Mac SEs to the powerful Mac II that acted as a server.

Starting in 1988, John served for seven years as an editor and columnist at *Mac User* Magazine, another now-defunct (but long-lived) Mac magazine. His most vivid memory is how he bravely rode out the 1989 Loma Prieta earthquake crouched in a fetal position while Apple monitors crashed to the floor in the next room.

Continuing his pattern of seeking out magazines doomed to die, John was for several years the Mac columnist for *Computer Currents* and was a columnist for *MacWeek* and *eMedia* (all defunct). He also wrote a column for CNET for several years and wrote CNET's reviews of Mac OS X Public Beta, Mac OS X 10.0, 10.1, Jaguar, Panther, and numerous other software and hardware products. John's articles have also appeared in *Macworld*, *Mac Home*, *Mac Addict*, *MacFixIt*, *PC Magazine*, *eWeek.com*, and the *San Francisco Chronicle*. John has been a guest on CNET radio, KPFA-FM, KQED-FM, and other broadcast outlets. He was also once the Ziff Davis system operator of Apple's eWorld online services, which is now.... Well, you get the idea. John has also authored several books about Macs, several of which are not defunct (that is, still in print).

In 1997, John founded *MacWindows.com*, a web site solely devoted to helping users and network administrators use Macs in a Windows world. *MacWindows* is alive and well, and is the Internet's largest repository of cross-platform news and tips.

John started his career as an engineer at Boeing. Once Apple shipped the Mac, he ditched airplanes for a GUI and a mouse.

WE'D LIKE TO HEAR FROM YOU

Please address comments and questions concerning this book to the publisher:

O'Reilly Media, Inc.
1005 Gravenstein Highway North
Sebastopol, CA 95472
(800) 998-9938 (in the US or Canada)
(707) 829-0515 (international or local)
(707) 829-0104 (fax)

We have a web page for this book, where we list errata, examples, and any additional information. You can access this page at:

http://www.oreilly.com/catalog/macannoy

To comment or ask technical questions about this book, send email to:

bookquestions@oreilly.com

For more information about our books, conferences, Resource Centers, and the O'Reilly Network, see our web site at:

http://www.oreilly.com

ACKNOWLEDGMENTS

Thanks to Molly Wood, a talented editor who I've had the good fortune to work with before. Molly has also been an editor at CNET at various times. As always, Molly gave great advice as to the style of this book. She also deserves the credit for getting this project off the ground and for setting the tone.

O'Reilly's Mac editor, Chuck Toporek, helped bring the project in for a landing. He also provided invaluable technical assistance throughout the process. His dedication was boundless, typing with one finger of a stitched-up hand just hours after a painful accident.

Robert Luhn is an O'Reilly honcho who has continued to hire me throughout the years, though I've never figured out why. Robert has been an editor-in-chief extraordinaire at the helm of *PC World* and *Computer Currents*; he also led a CNET department through the dot-com bust.

Steve Bass is a long-time columnist at *PC World*. I've never met Steve, but I owe him thanks for coming up with the original "Annoyances" concept and structure in *PC Annoyances*. He also did a fantastic job. Given how much more annoying Window PCs are than Macs, one can appreciate Steve's monumental achievement. If you also use Windows, go out and buy *PC Annoyances* right now.

Thanks to the O'Reilly team for being such a supportive organization. Also thanks for the cool mug.

Thanks to my wife Chris, who puts up with my writing at all hours of the night.

Finally, thanks to my mom, who has the world's most complete library of my books. Though she doesn't own a computer, Mom never fails to give me great reviews for everything I write.

Mac OS X
ANNOYANCES

Mac OS X? Annoying? To Mac fans, the mere idea that Mac OS X could be annoying is, well, un-Mac-like. After all, don't we all agree that it's the greatest operating system for personal computers? Yet, we still complain. The reason is simple: anything as complex as Mac OS X is bound to have some kinks in it. In fact, while system software updates usually fix problems, they can also add brand-new annoyances themselves. For instance, while the 10.3 update added some great new features, such as Exposé, it also changed the way the toolbar works, requiring you to learn new ways to do things.

Or so it may seem. That's where this chapter comes in.

You may not realize it, but the solutions to many of your everyday Mac OS X annoyances are in the OS itself. Some lie just below the surface, while others are undocumented. Other fixes can quickly be found in low-cost, third-party software that you can download from the Internet. In this chapter, I'll show you workarounds, tricks, tips, and configuration changes to overcome Mac OS X's annoyances.

UPGRADE TO A MODERN MAC OS

The Annoyance: I'm running an older version of Mac OS that is damned annoying...

The Fix: Stop right there—enough said. If you are running anything before Mac OS X 10.2 (Jaguar), you can only benefit from upgrading to the latest version of Mac OS X. If you have Mac OS 9 or earlier, upgrading to Mac OS X means, among other things: *no* more constant rebooting, *no* more applications running out of memory, and fewer headaches in communicating with Windows PCs. Mac OS X also offers much easier connections with cameras, musical instruments, and other peripherals. It is also miles ahead of Mac OS 9 in terms of available software and hardware—GarageBand, iPhoto, and so many other cool applications *only* run on Mac OS X.

If you're already hip to all the Mac OS X benefits, but you're running a version earlier than 10.2, you should upgrade to the latest version, whether it's 10.3, 10.4, or beyond. Mac OS X has matured since version 10.1.*x*. The later versions have fixed many of the interface annoyances of the first few versions, and support more peripherals and more software. Mac OS X Versions 10.2 and later are also smarter than the earlier versions and can keep the system running smoothly with self-repair functions. For example, when you run an installer program for new software or for an upgrade, Mac OS X runs routines that adjust some of the system software to ensure the application launches quickly and runs efficiently. This process is known as *prebinding*, which helps the program communicate with the system software. When you launch an application, Mac OS X checks to see if the software needs tweaking.

The easiest way to upgrade to a current version of Mac OS X is to buy a new Mac with the OS preloaded. Of course, it's quite a bit cheaper to install OS X on your current Mac; just make sure your hardware is up to snuff. First, you need a processor that is a PowerPC G3 or better. Officially, Apple says Mac OS X won't support processor upgrade cards, but in fact, OS X does run smoothly on upgrades. The real issue is that Apple won't provide tech support when you add an upgrade card, which is why the card manufacturers provide the tech support. (See Chapter 7 for more information on upgrade cards.).

You'll also want a *minimum* of 256 MB RAM, and more is better. Yes, Apple says 128 MB is the minimum, but trust me: you won't be happy with the pokey speed that amount of RAM gets you. Mac OS X 10.3 also requires a Mac with a built-in USB port and 2 GB of free hard disk space.

I realize you probably don't have your Mac's hardware specs on the tip of your tongue. Not a problem. Just double-click on the Apple System Profiler (or select it from the Apple menu). It will tell you about your hardware configuration (see Figure 1-1). If you have a version of Mac OS before Mac OS X, and you don't have Apple System Profiler, download it from *http://docs.info.apple. com/article.html?artnum=26161.* (With Panther, it's just called System Profiler and can be found in */Applications/ Utilities.*)

> **t i p**
>
> RAM is pretty cheap, but if you're looking for the absolute best prices in Mac RAM, point your web browser at *www. ramseeker.com* to find comparative pricing from multiple vendors for your exact Mac model.

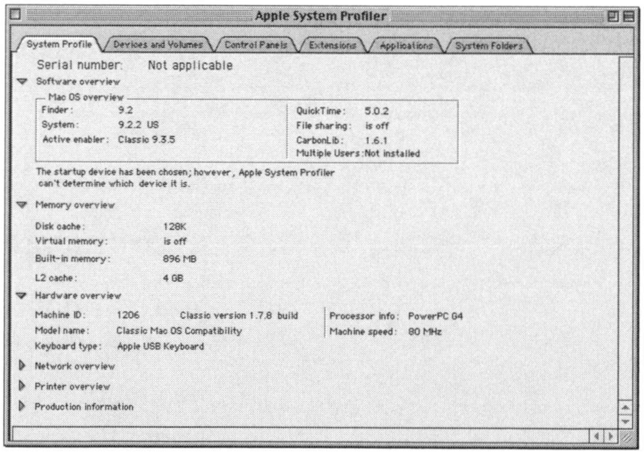

Figure 1-1. Apple System Profiler tells you whether your Mac is ready for Mac OS X by presenting the Mac's specs for processor, RAM, and free hard-disk space. This is the Mac OS 9 version.

MORE USEFUL MAC HELP

The Annoyance: Mac OS X's help system isn't always what I'd call "helpful." It tells me the obvious, like how to turn something on or off, but it often lacks specifics about my own configuration.

The Fix: The theme of the help system seems to be, "Help, schmelp. You'll figure it out." Fortunately, there is additional help available. Use Sherlock to look up Apple's Knowledge Base articles, which often give you the nuts and bolts details that the help system lacks. Apple has published thousands of articles, many of which point out known bugs with certain software and peripherals and provide workarounds or outright fixes.

Sure, you can access the Knowledge Base with a web browser, but why would you do that when you could use Sherlock? Open Sherlock, click the AppleCare icon at the top, and type your search criteria. Press Return or click the magnifying glass icon, and Sherlock presents a list of articles. Single-click an article title, and the article appears in the lower pane of Sherlock, as in Figure 1-2.

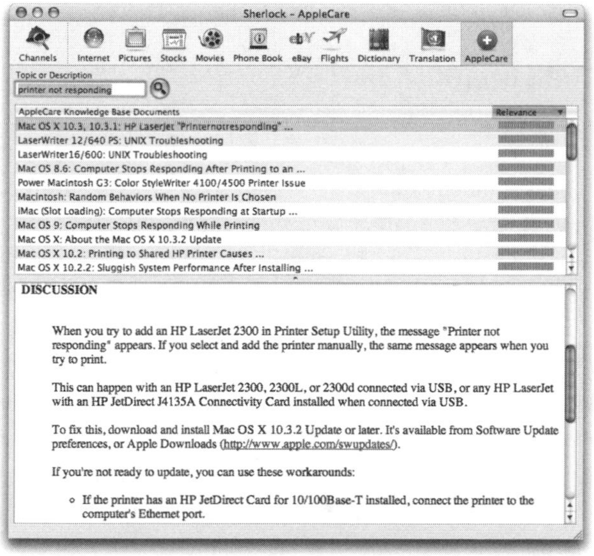

> ### GET INFO
>
> **If Apple's web site doesn't have what you need, don't worry; plenty of other sites can help. Apple's discussion boards (*http://discussions.info.apple.com*) are a good place to search for solutions to problems. For troubleshooting a problem, two of the best web sites are MacInTouch (*http://www.macintouch.com*) and MacFixIt (*http://www.macfixit.com*). O'Reilly's Mac DevCenter (*http://www.macdevcenter.com*) has some great articles describing how to get things done with your Mac, from delving into digital photography and recording music to heavy-duty programming. For collections of handy tips, check out Mac OS X Hints and (*http://www.macosxhints.com*) and OS X FAQ (*http://www.osxfaq.com*).**

Figure 1-2. The AppleCare channel of Sherlock gives you access to technical articles at Apple's Knowledge Base, and you don't have to use a web browser. These articles often have more specific and detailed information than the built-in help system.

Double-clicking hyperlinks in the article launches your default web browser to bring up the linked web page.

For more sources of Mac help, see the Get Info box on this page.

SIDESTEP THE SIDEBAR

The Annoyance: The Finder's sidebar in Mac OS X Panther can be handy, but it eats up screen space. That can be a problem if I want to see the contents of multiple windows at once. Manually opening and closing the sidebar is a pain in the neck—or rather, a pain in my clicking-and-dragging finger. Is there any way to avoid the Finder sidebar altogether?

The Fix: There are two tricks you can use to keep the sidebar closed, while still getting quick and easy access to your folders and files. In fact, these tricks also work in Mac OS X 10.2, which doesn't even have a sidebar. The idea is to make efficient use of the pop-up menus that both the Dock and the Finder's toolbar have—menus that don't take up any screen space when you aren't using them. Check this out:

- Drag your Applications folder and your Home folder (the folder with the same name as your username) from a Finder window into the Dock, next to the Trash icon (the only place the Dock allows folders). Now click one of the folders and hold for a second or two. A menu will pop up, displaying the contents of the folder. Move the cursor to one of the folders in the list, and another menu pops up, displaying its contents, as in Figure 1-3. You can put any folder in the Dock, but I like to use Applications and Home folders, because they contain almost everything that I want to access.

- If you'd rather not clutter up the Dock with a bunch of new icons, drag frequently used folders or files to the toolbar of any Finder window. In Mac OS X 10.3, you have to hold the folder over the toolbar a second or two, wait for the mouse cursor to get a plus sign (+), then drop it. The great thing about the toolbar is that you can add as many files and folders as you want, without shrinking the size of the icons, as with the Dock. When there are too many icons to fit in the toolbar, a double arrow appears. Click it, and your files and folders appear in a drop-down menu, as in Figure 1-4.

Figure 1-4. The Finder toolbar's menu is a handy place to add frequently used folders and files. Items that don't fit on the toolbar are available through a handy pop-up menu.

TURN ON TOOLBAR TITLES

The Annoyance: That's all well and good, but Jaguar's toolbar was better because the icons had titles. In Panther, when I drag two folders to the toolbar, I can't tell which is which, because they both have identical icons.

The Fix: You haven't been fiddling with Panther's settings enough. Apple didn't actually remove toolbar icon titles—they just turned them off. The easiest way to turn them back on is to Control-click the toolbar to bring up its contextual menu. Next select the Icon & Text item, and your toolbar icons now have names.

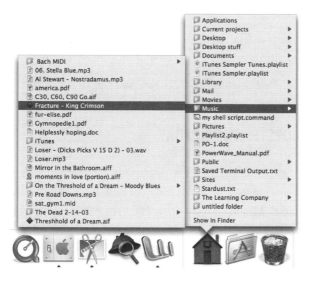

Figure 1-3. You can use the Dock's hierarchical pop-up menu to access your applications, files, and folders.

WHEN DRAGGED FOLDERS DISAPPEAR

The Annoyance: OK, smart guy. I tried to drag my Applications folder from the Finder's sidebar to the Dock—just as you suggested—now it's gone from both. What gives?

The Fix: The folder may be gone from the sidebar, but it's still on your hard drive. When you drag a folder to the Dock, the Finder toolbar, or the Finder's sidebar in Mac OS X 10.3, you *must* drag it from the main part of a Finder window. That is, you cannot drag an item from the Dock to the Finder toolbar or from the sidebar to the Dock. The sidebar, Dock, and toolbar don't hold an actual file or folder, but merely an icon that represents it.

PANTHER ATE MY FAVORITES

The Annoyance: I'm bummed that Apple deleted Favorites from Mac OS X 10.3. Yes, I know, the sidebar is supposed to be the new Favorites, because it appears in Open and Save dialogs. But I had *a lot* of Favorites, and now they're seriously cluttering the sidebar. Also, to be honest, I really miss the heart-shaped icon.

The Fix: The good news is that you can add a Favorites folder, complete with precious heart-shaped icon, to the Finder's sidebar. The good folks in Cupertino stashed away the old one to keep fans of "classic Favorites" happy. You can also add a Favorites icon to the toolbar, though you must also add it to the sidebar to get it into the Open and Save dialogs. To locate the Favorites folder, open a Finder window and click on your Home folder, and then click on the Library folder (~/*Library*). Inside, you will find the good ol' Favorites folder. Now drag the Favorites folder to the Finder's sidebar and/or toolbar. Amazingly, the Favorites icon takes on its old heart-shaped icon.

> **tip**
>
> An easy way to get the Favorites folder (or any folder or file, as a matter of fact) into the sidebar is to select it and press ⌘-T.

The bad news is that there's no way to migrate your old Favorites into the new folder, and there's no Add to Favorites button or menu command. There is, thankfully, a simple method to move items into the Favorites folder: in the Finder, select a file or folder, and press Shift-⌘-T.

HEY, DOCK! MAKE WAY FOR CLASSIC APPS

The Annoyance: Classic applications don't seem to get the whole Dock thing—it's like they don't even know it's there. Classic windows slide underneath the Dock, which means I have to move the window out of the way to get to the scroll arrows or other controls, such as Word's view buttons. It's even more annoying when the Dock's Hidden feature is turned on—I go to scroll, and up jumps the Dock for the interception. Is there any way to make Classic apps any smarter?

The Fix: As we say in my home town of New York, *Fuhgedaboutit*! You can, however, move the Dock to the side of the screen to get it out of the way of your Classic window. Actually, I recommend the side location even if you work mainly with Mac OS X-native applications. Apple's displays have wide form factors, giving you plenty of room to position a fully open document alongside a vertical Dock. I prefer the right side myself, but southpaws may be more comfortable with the left side of the screen.

> **Note the downside: your display height is less than its width, so the Dock is shorter, which means the icons are smaller.**

To make the change, click the Apple menu, click the Dock item, and choose Position on Right (or Left) from the submenu. The Dock is now positioned vertically, with the Trash icon at the bottom.

DUMP THE DOCK

The Annoyance: Call me old-fashioned, but I've never liked the Dock. It takes up too much screen space on my 12-inch iBook. A hidden Dock just gets on my nerves, unexpectedly reappearing when the cursor gets near it.

The Fix: You actually can do without the Dock, using built-in tricks or add-on utilities. First, however, you must get rid of the Dock. Amazingly, you can't actually turn *off* the Dock—an annoying fact in itself—but you can make it barely noticeable. For starters, make the Dock *really* small—a centimeter or two—and then hide it.

To shrink the Dock down to insignificant size, start by removing most of the icons in it—just drag them to the desktop and let go. You can remove everything but the Trash and Finder icons. (Application icons still appear in the Dock when you launch them.) Next, go to the Apple menu and select Dock → Dock Preferences. When System Preferences opens, move the Dock's size slider to Small. The Dock shrinks to the size shown in Figure 1-5. Now you can click "Automatically hide and show the Dock." With this setting, it pops up only if you happen to move your cursor over that square centimeter.

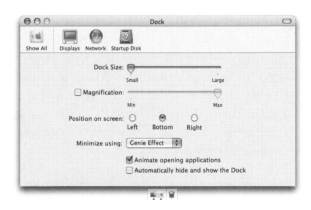

Figure 1-5. By using these settings and removing most of the icons, you can make the Dock teeny tiny. (Did you miss it? Look again; it's just underneath the dialog window.)

Now that the Dock is out of the way, you need a way to switch between open applications. In Mac OS X 10.2 and later, hold the ⌘ key and hit the Tab once. With Panther and later, an Application Switcher (shown in Figure 1-6) stays in the middle of your screen as you hold the ⌘ key, displaying the icons for the applications that are currently open. With the ⌘ key held down, hitting the Tab key selects the next application (⌘-Shift-Tab cycles backwards through the active applications). When you find an application you want to switch to, release the ⌘ key. (In versions earlier than 10.3, you can use the same technique, but you don't see the display. Instead, the icons in the Dock are highlighted when they're selected.)

Figure 1-6. This large transparent switcher dialog appears in the middle of your screen when you hit ⌘-Tab. Hold ⌘ while you hit Tab to select an application, all without the Dock.

At this point, you might be wondering: with the Trash icon glued to the Dock, how do I delete files? Very easily. Click on a file or folder while holding the Control key. In the contextual menu that appears, choose the Move to Trash command. If you're more of a keyboard user, ⌘-Delete moves a selected file to the Trash.

---

tip

If you know Unix, you can set up a *cron* job to automatically empty the Trash so you never have to empty it again.

You can also get third-party Dock replacements that do more than just switch between open applications. In fact, some can act as complete Finder replacements, letting you open anything on your hard drive. Two of the best are inexpensive shareware utilities:

- **DragThing** (*http://www.dragthing.com*) is a highly configurable file launcher that lets you open (and switch between) applications, documents, folders, and URLs using floating "docks" that can be minimized to tabs on the edge of your screen. DragThing can also put a Trash icon on your desktop.

- **LaunchBar** (*http://www.obdev.at/products/launchbar*) takes a different approach, bringing up items with a few strokes on your keyboard. LaunchBar puts a small bar in a corner of your desktop to let you type in few letters—you don't have to spell the name exactly, because in a fraction of a second, a mathematical algorithm guesses what you are looking for.

APPLICATION SWITCHING À LA MAC OS 9

The Annoyance: I've never gotten used to the schizophrenic behavior of application switching when running Classic and Mac OS X native applications together. When I'm running a Classic application, the good ol' application switcher menu is there in the upper-right corner, but it disappears when I switch to a Mac OS X-native program. I wish the app switcher menu would just stay put.

The Fix: You can add a Classic-style application switcher menu to Mac OS X with a shareware program called ASM (*http://www.vercruesse.de*). It also includes the Hide and Show commands of the Mac OS 9 application switcher menu. With ASM installed, an application menu is always there when you switch between Classic and native apps.

REPLACE BRUSHED METAL WITH AQUA

The Annoyance: I'm sick of the brushed metal look. It was okay when iTunes appeared on the scene, but brushed metal has now spread like the Plague to just about every Apple application. The dark, metallic Finder in Mac OS X 10.3 is just too much for me—it's like the dungeon of some 3D game. I wish I could go back to good ol' Aqua.

The Fix: Although iTunes often gets the blame (or credit, depending on your point of view) for starting Apple's brushed-metal design craze, the look actually originated in QuickTime Player 4.0 in 1999. For now, Apple *loves* brushed metal; a Preference setting to switch between Metal and Aqua is not likely to come out of Cupertino. If you want to Aquify Panther, you'll have to take matters into your own hands, with the help of a piece of freeware or shareware.

At the time of this writing, the simplest Aquifier to use is the free Whiteout (*http://www.versiontracker.com/dyn/moreinfo/macosx/21363*). Whiteout works on the Finder and Cocoa applications, such as Safari, iSync, and Address Book, to replace the brushed metal (see Figure 1-7) with off-white Aqua pinstripes (see Figure 1-8). It's not exactly the Jaguar Aqua, however, because it doesn't return the old translucent titlebars. It also doesn't work with Carbon applications, so it can't touch iTunes, iPhoto, or the QuickTime Player.
Pinstripes aren't your only option. If you want more choices in replacing the brushed metal, try the more complicated shareware program ShapeShifter (*http://www.unsanity.com/haxies/shapeshifter*), which lets you change the Mac OS X appearance using free themes that you can download from a variety of sources. I like Panther Aqua No Brushed (*http://www.cepophan.com/themes*), which replaces the brushed metal with a light flat gray. The best way to search for multiple Shape-Shifter themes from different sources is to go to *http://www.MacUpate.com* and search for "ShapeShifter."

Figure 1-7. If you're unhappy with the standard Panther brushed metal, just add Whiteout and...

Figure 1-8. ...voila! Aqua pinstripes replace the brushed metal. If you use ShapeShifter, you now have other interface options as well.

BRING BACK COMPUTER VIEW

The Annoyance: I hate it when Apple deletes features for no good reason. The Finder's Computer view disappeared when I upgraded to Panther. I love the Computer view, which lets me see multiple drives, mounted disk images, and my mounted iPod, all without having to look on the desktop. Yes, I know that the Go menu's Computer command brings up this view, but the command doesn't appear in the sidebar or in new Finder windows.

The Fix: Actually, Apple didn't delete the Computer view in Mac OS X 10.3; they just disabled it. Fortunately, it's easy to turn back on. With the Finder as the front application, go to the Finder menu and select Preferences (⌘-,). Click the sidebar icon. Under "Show these items in the sidebar," click the checkbox next to Computer.

Now, if you want the Computer view to be the default when you create new Finder windows, click the General icon at the top of Finder Preferences. Now, choose Computer from the pop-up menu labeled "New Finder windows open with."

DECIPHER KEYBOARD SYMBOLS

The Annoyance: The menus are full of keyboard equivalents for commands, but I don't know what the symbols mean. Sure, the cloverleaf symbol (⌘) is obviously the Command key, but the other symbols are just hieroglyphics.

The Fix: In the help system, Mac OS X provides a Rosetta Stone for these mysterious ciphers. In the Finder, just choose Mac Help from the Help menu. In Panther, search for "symbols for special keys". In Jaguar, search for "keyboard shortcut symbols". Table 1-1 lists some of the keyboard symbols you'll frequently encounter.

Table 1-1. Menu symbols and the keys used for them

Symbol	Key
⇧	Shift
⌥	Option
⌃	Control
⌘	Command (Apple key)
⌫	Delete
⌦	Forward delete

COOL KEYBOARD COMMANDS

Everyone knows that menus are full of equivalent keyboard commands, but did you know that some keyboard commands are not listed in the menus? Some of these are listed in an Apple Knowledge Base. To see this list, connect to the Internet and go to Sherlock's AppleCare channel. Type 75459 in the search field and hit Return. Here you'll find dozens of keyboard commands for Mac OS X actions. Here are some of my favorites:

☒ **Select a file or folder and hit ⌘-A. This takes you to the folder that contains your selected file or folder.**

☒ **In the Finder's List View, you can expand and collapse a folder without clicking on the little triangle (known as a *disclosure triangle*). ⌘-Right Arrow expands a selected folder, and ⌘-Left Arrow collapses it. Add the Option key, and you can expand or collapse all nested subfolders.**

☒ **⌘-W closes the foremost window, in any application as well as in the Finder. If you're using a web browser with tabs, this command closes the current tab.**

☒ **Shift-⌘ is handy for emptying the Trash without going to the Finder menu.**

Some key commands aren't even listed in Knowledge Base Article 75459. For instance, have you ever wanted to get to the Search field of the Finder toolbar without clicking on it? There is an undocumented key command that activates the Search field: hit Option-⌘-F and begin typing. This works only in Mac OS X Panther and later.

DON'T SEARCH WITHOUT ME

The Annoyance: In Panther, the Search field in the Finder's toolbar returns results before I'm finished typing. This was pretty cool at first, but then I realized that it's an annoyance if you type the wrong character and have to backspace. Each time I backspace, the Finder keeps searching and locking up the Mac for a few seconds at time. Can't Mac OS X wait until I finish typing before it starts searching?

The Fix: Unfortunately, if you continue to use the Search field, be prepared to be constantly annoyed: Mac OS X won't wait until you finish typing. However, if you can't stand being annoyed, ditch the Search command and use the Find command; the Find command waits until you hit Return or Enter before searching. In the Finder, just hit the ⌘-F to bring up the Find dialog, and you can search anywhere on your Mac.

If you're a point-and-click kind of user, you can replace the toolbar's Search field with a Find Command button. With a Finder window open and in the foreground, go to the View menu and select Customize Toolbar. A dialog sheet slide down from the titlebar, as in Figure 1-9. When this dialog is visible, you can drag anything off the toolbar, so drag the Search field off to get rid of it. Now, drag the Find icon to the toolbar.

Removing the Search field makes room for other icons. So while you're at it, you can add any of the other toolbar icons from the dialog or move the existing ones around. When you're finished, click the Done button.

By the way, Jaguar (Mac OS X 10.2) doesn't have the search-as-you-type feature, so this procedure isn't necessary.

> **t i p**
>
> Can't see the toolbar in a Finder window? Click the clear, oblong button in the upper-right corner of the window. This toggles the toolbar and sidebar on and off.

Figure 1-9. Here, I've already added the Find icon, and I am in the process of removing the Search field.

FORCE QUIT FASTER

The Annoyance: I know I can bring up the Force Quit dialog box with the Option-⌘-Esc keys. But is there any way to force quit a misbehaving application without using the Force Quit dialog to choose the application? Bringing up the Force Quit dialog seems like an unnecessary step, and occasionally, things are so messed up that the dialog won't open.

The Fix: You can Option-click any Dock icon to choose Force Quit from the Dock contextual menu that appears. This quits the application immediately, without bringing up the Force Quit dialog. If you add the Shift key to Force Quit's keyboard shortcut (Shift-Option-⌘-Esc), the topmost application is instantly killed off, again, without opening the dialog. *Une danse de la mort*, so to speak.

STREAMLINE SYSTEM PREFERENCES

The Annoyance: The arrangement of items in System Preferences is confusing. The System and Personal categories seem to be a hodgepodge of items, which makes it difficult to find the item I'm looking for. A simple alphabetical list would be simpler. I know I can drag items to the System Preferences toolbar, but dragging *all* of them there doesn't seem any less annoying. Is an alphabetical list too much to ask?

The Fix: You actually have three ways to select an icon alphabetically. The first two methods work in Versions 10.2 and 10.3; the third technique is a Panther-only trick:

Use a menu. System Preferences' View menu lists all of the icons alphabetically—simply choose the one you need.

Reorganize System Preferences icons. The View menu also has an option called Organize Alphabetically. This command displays the System Preference icons in alphabetical order, making them easier to locate (if you're alphabetically oriented)

> **Open System Preferences from the Keyboard**
>
> **Bet you didn't know that holding the Option key while pressing one of the speaker keys opens System Preferences.**

Use System Preferences' Dock menu. In Panther, the Dock menu displays all of the panes—as long as the System Preferences has been launched. You can hide System Preferences (⌘-H) to reduce screen clutter. Then, you can select any System Preference pane no matter what application is in the foreground (see Figure 1-10).

ENLARGE TINY MOVIES

The Annoyance: I like to watch the movie previews in Sherlock's Movies channel, but the movie window is so small, it's hard to distinguish Woody Harrelson from Woody Allen.

The Fix: Mac OS X 10.2 and 10.3 have a little-known zoom feature that you can use to enlarge movie previews or anything else on screen. Turn it on first in the Universal Access pane of System Preferences. Under the Seeing tab, click Turn on Zoom. To zoom in on your movie preview, press Option-⌘- (+). To zoom back out, use Option-⌘- (-).

Figure 1-10. When System Preferences is running, you can bring up any of its panes from its Dock menu.

FAX MULTIPLE FILES WITH ONE PHONE CALL

The Annoyance: I use Panther's built-in fax feature, but it forces me to fax each file separately. It's not only annoying, but it adds to my long distance bill. I'm not interested in creating a beautiful desktop publishing page layout containing everything—I just want to fax multiple documents.

The Fix: You get what you pay for. Though accessible from the Print dialog, Panther's free fax software is rather disappointing, providing minimal features and no hidden extras. However, for a mere $30, you can buy Page Sender from SmileOnMyMac (*http://www.smileonmymac.com*) and use it to combine multiple files into a single fax. It does this by treating additional documents as attachments. Basically, you choose Print for the first document you want to fax and then select Page Sender as your printer in the Print dialog box. Then all you need to do is click the Attachments button to add the other files to the fax. You can even set the order in which the documents will be faxed by dragging them around in the Attachments list (see Figure 1-11).

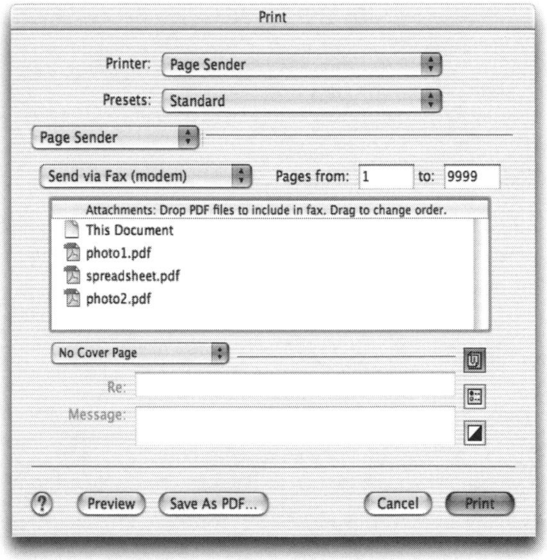

Figure 1-11. Page Sender lets you fax multiple files as attachments to a faxed document, and lets you arrange the order in which the files will be faxed.

EASY SCREEN CAPTURES

Creating an image of what's currently on screen—a screen capture—is useful to send settings to a tech support center or just to show others what you are doing on your Mac.

Mac OS X offers several different ways for you to take a screen shot. The easiest way is to use the keyboard command Shift-⌘-3. This creates a PDF file containing an image of your entire screen. You can find the file, called *Picture1.PDF*, on the desktop; ⌘-Shift-4 turns the cursor into a set of crosshairs (called the marquee tool), which you can use to click-and-drag an area to capture for your screen shot. If you want a screen shot of a single window, add the spacebar to ⌘-Shift-4. (You don't get the drop shadow with this method.)

If you'd rather have a TIFF file instead of a PDF, use the Grab program *(/Applications/Utilities)*. Grab's Capture menu lets you take shots instantaneously, or with a timer, or by selection. If you choose the latter, hit the ⌘-Tab keys to go to the application you want to capture. After the screen capture is created, Grab brings up a dialog to let you save the TIFF file anywhere on your hard disk.

If you want to help the economy by spending money, you could purchase Snapz Pro X from Ambrosia Software ($29, *http://www.ambrosiasw.com/utilities/snapzprox*). If you pony up another $40, you can get a version of Snapz Pro X that records QuickTime movies of your actions. However, if you aren't a publishing professional, save your money. Snapz Pro X's final product isn't much different from Grab's, and the app is much more complicated (annoying, actually). In fact, all of the screenshots in this book were created with Grab.

But there is a catch—the attachment files must be PDF files. This shouldn't stop you, though, because Mac OS X can turn *any* printable file into a PDF. Just open the file, choose Print, and click the Save As PDF button.

Page Sender provides features not found in Panther's fax tool, such as faxing large-format pages, viewing your sent faxes, and using fax numbers from contact programs such as Entourage, Now Contact, and Palm Desktop.

REMOVE AUTO-STARTUP APPLICATIONS

The Annoyance: Some software installers place on my hard drive an application or utility that launches at startup. I've collected an array of these apps that all start up at the same time, which is a nuisance. I want the applications, but I don't like this auto-launch feature.

The Fix: You can tell Mac OS X not to launch these startup items using System Preferences. In Panther, go to the Accounts preference pane and click the Startup Items tab. (In Mac OS X 10.2, go to the Login Items pane to see the list of annoying startup applications.) To prevent one of these applications from launching at startup, select the item and hit the Delete key. This does *not* delete the program; it just deletes its designation as a startup item.

TYPE A PATH IN OPEN AND SAVE DIALOGS

The Annoyance: In Jaguar, I could type a folder's path in the Go To field of the Open and Save dialog to quickly save a file to any folder. But now that I've upgraded to Panther, I'm annoyed that Apple removed the Go To field from all of the Open and Save dialogs. Now, to designate a folder, I have to click and scroll and click and scroll...well, you get the idea.

The Fix: Although the Go To field has been removed from the Panther dialogs, you can still enter a path in the Open and Save dialogs by holding the Shift-⌘-G keys when a dialog is present. This brings up a small "Go to the folder" window where you can type a path. In fact, the new field now also auto-completes your terms. For in-

stance, if you type ~/do and wait a second or two, the system changes that to ~/Documents for you. A handy feature because, as you know, typing isn't considered very "Mac-like."

EASY NAMING IN SAVE DIALOG

The Annoyance: I'm always creating files for a particular project that requires filenames to begin with the same set of numbers and letters and only the last few characters differ—for instance, *SFG_010526_GB2.jpg*, *SFG_010526_ GB3.jpg*, *SFG_010526_ GB4.jpg*, and so on. After a while, it gets to be a pain to keep typing these repetitive filenames, as I'm not the most accurate typist. There's got to be a better way.

The Fix: The Save and Save As dialogs of Panther have a new feature that makes repetitive file naming a walk in the park. First, make sure the dialog is expanded so you can see the columns and the sidebar, as shown in Figure 1-12. Click any grayed-out file, and its name appears in the Save As field. Now, just change the characters at the end of the filename and click on the Save button (or hit Return).

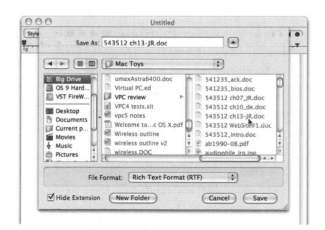

Figure 1-12. Click a grayed-out file in the Save dialog, and its filename is copied to the Save As field.

Having trouble remembering what's in your obscurely named files? You *could* open each file, one by one, to find out, but you'd probably forget again in a week. Instead, why don't you add descriptive comments to each file and then have your comments displayed in the Finder, as shown in Figure 1-13?

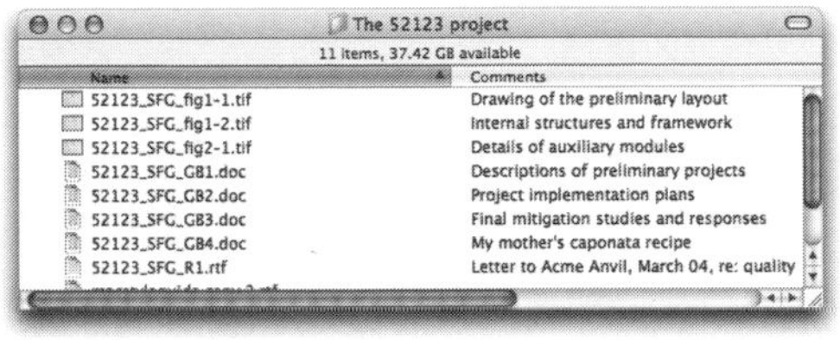

Figure 1-13. To get this view, first tell the Finder to display comments for this folder. Then drag the Comments column next to the Name column.

To add a comment to a file, Control-click (or right-click if you have a two-button mouse) the file and choose Get Info from the Contextual menu. Open the Comments field at the bottom and type in your comment. You want it to be long enough to make sense, but short enough so you can see it in a Finder window. Do this for all the files in a given folder.

Now, select or open the folder whose comments you want to display. Go to the View menu and select Show View Options. Select the checkbox next to Comments and close the View Options dialog. Now, when you open your folder and set it to list view, you find a new Comments column displaying the descriptions of your files. The problem is, the new column appears on the far right, just out of view. Just drag the Comments column next to the Name column to see it.

PANTHER ATE MY KEY CAPS, TOO

The Annoyance: I went and installed Panther, and now I see that Key Caps, a standard Mac utility for many years, is gone. Key Caps was a great little tool for finding out which keys you needed to press to type an umlaut (ü), accent (é), or other special characters, such as the trademark symbol (™) or the British pound sign (£). I'm quite annoyed that Apple dumped Key Caps from Mac OS X.

The Fix: Like some of the other, older features mentioned in this chapter, Key Caps isn't really gone; it's just that its name has changed. However, Apple has hidden it so well that even if you knew the new name—Keyboard Viewer—you wouldn't find it. It's no longer a standalone application, so a search for it would come up empty. The Keyboard Viewer is disabled by default, and enabling it requires close attention. Open System Preferences and click on the icon for the International preference panel and then follow these step:

1. Click the Input Menu tab on the right, and see window like the one in Figure 1-14.

2. Click the checkbox next to "Show input menu in menu bar" at the bottom. This immediately creates a new menu bearing the icon of an American flag on the upper-right side of your screen. (You'll see the French flag, or other flags, if you have other languages set as your default.)

3. The trick now is to add Keyboard Viewer to this menu. In the list of countries, find the Keyboard Viewer, and click its checkbox, as in Figure 1-14.

Now, go to the Input menu (see Figure 1-15) and choose Show Keyboard Viewer. A floating palette with a picture of your keyboard appears. Similar to Key Caps, Keyboard Viewer lets you press one or more modifier keys on your keyboard (Shift, Option, ⌘) to display different characters. The Keyboard Viewer palette is visible and active in any application. To add a special character to your document, hold the appropriate modifier key and click a key on the Keyboard Viewer palette.

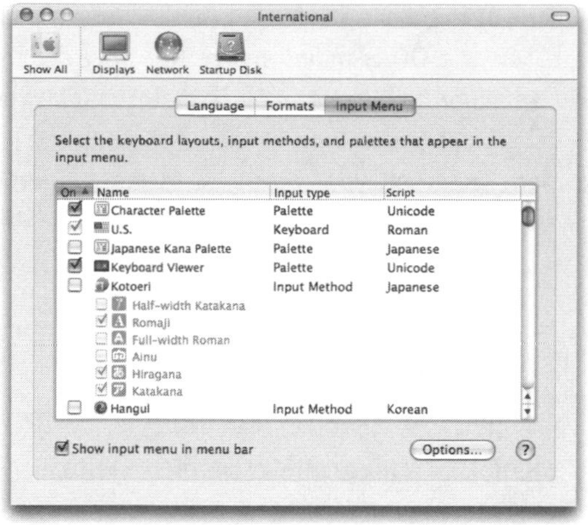

Figure 1-14. Enable the Input menu and the Keyboard Viewer to access Panther's equivalent of Key Caps.

Figure 1-15. The patriotic Input menu lets you show the Keyboard Viewer, which replaced the Key Caps utility in Panther.

REPAIR PERMISSIONS TO FIX FILE GLITCHES

The Annoyance: Argh! Some of my files and applications won't open and are exhibiting other weird behaviors. And my Mac is less responsive than usual. I didn't do anything to cause these problems. At least, I don't think I did.

The Fix: Anything from a bad crash to a routine software installation can cause these problems. Or they can just arise over time. Fortunately, there's a good chance that repairing *file permissions* using Disk Utility will get your Mac working swimmingly again. Even if you are a seasoned Mac user, don't sweat it if you don't know about file permissions. The concept comes from Unix, and because Mac OS X is a Unix operating system, it has file permissions. In Unix, every file is owned by a *user*. You, the carbon-based life form sitting before your Mac, are only one such user. Other users include various Unix entities running on your Mac. The permissions tell the operating system who (or what) is allowed to read, write, and, in the case of programs, execute them. Occasionally, the permissions for various Unix system files get set incorrectly. You can use Disk Utility (Mac OS X 10.2 or later) to reset these permissions back to normal.

Repairing permissions is easy. You don't need to boot from an installation CD, as you would when fixing drive problems. You can run Disk Utility from the startup drive to fix permissions on the same drive:

1. Launch Disk Utility (*/Applications/Utilities*).

2. In the left column, select your startup drive or partition.

3. Click the First Aid tab. (Figure 1-16 shows Panther; the layout in Jaguar is slightly different.)

4. Click the Repair Disk Permissions button in the lower-left of the dialog.

Figure 1-16. Use the Repair Disk Permissions button in Disk Utility to fix file flakiness.

That's it. Disk Utility does its thing for several minutes and then tells you when it's done, and you won't need to restart.

Make it a habit of repairing permissions after you install any software or a software update, even when Software Update does the installing. I suggest that you repair permissions regularly, say, once a month, to keep your Mac running smoothly.

Get Info

Want to know more about Unix file permissions on your Mac? Apple has a Knowledge Base article explaining it, which you can get to by opening Sherlock, clicking the AppleCare icon, typing 106712, and hitting Return. You can also get to the article using this URL in a web browser:

http://docs.info.apple.com/article. html?artnum=106712

MORE UNIX MAINTENANCE

The Annoyance: Okay, so I ran the Repair Disk Permissions and Repair Disk functions of Disk Utility, but my Mac is still a bit tired. I may be having temporal hallucinations, but startup also seems to take longer.

The Fix: The fact that you start up in the morning means that you shut down your Mac at night, a laudable practice that conserves energy and saves you or your company money. However, it also means that the Mac is not running the Unix maintenance tasks that are set to run between midnight and dawn. (These tasks won't run if the Mac is asleep, either.) For instance, there are Unix scripts set to clear out unnecessary system files, make adjustments to certain files, and check log files. For ex-

ample, one of these scripts deletes files in the */tmp* directory every night. Other maintenance tasks are set to run weekly and monthly. If these Unix maintenance scripts aren't running because your Mac is powered off or in sleep mode at night, your Mac's performance could be rather sluggish.

REPAIR DISK VERSUS REPAIR DISK PERMISSIONS

The Repair Disk button of Disk Utility is designed to fix more serious problems with the data structure of your hard disk volume. There are often no symptoms, but if the problems accumulate, you can loose data. Because of this, you should back up your Mac before using Repair Disk.

Running Repair Disk isn't as easy as running Repair Disk Permissions; for one thing, you can't use Disk Repair on the current startup drive. You must restart from another bootable Mac OS X drive, or start up from Mac OS X's install CD, which contains a version of the Disk Utility. To do this, insert Disc 1 into your Mac and restart while holding down the C key; this forces your Mac to start up from the CD. After your Mac starts up, go to the Installer menu (immediately to the right of the Apple menu) and select Disk Utility.

It is useful to run Repair Disk every few months, but because Mac OS X checks the disk every time you startup and shutdown, it isn't necessary to run Repair Disk as often as you should run Repair Disk Permissions. If Repair Disk tells you that there are problems it couldn't fix, you should consider running a third-party utility, such as Disk Warrior from Alsoft (*http://www. alsoft.com*) or Norton Utilities from Symantec (*http://www.symantec.com*).

The fix is to simply run these Unix maintenance routines. The computer geek in me wants you to run these maintenance routines using the cool Unix commands in Terminal (*/Applications/Utilities*). But the Mac user in me would feel guilty if I didn't suggest that you use the $8 Mac program called Macaroni from Atomic Bird (*http://www.atomicbird. com*), which automatically runs these maintenance routines in the background according to daily, weekly, and monthly schedules. Macaroni even checks and repairs file permissions when needed (the task described in the previous annoyance), so that you don't have to use Disk Utility. If your Mac is turned off or asleep when it's time to run a script, Macaroni waits until your Mac is up and running. PowerBook and iBook users don't have to worry about using up precious battery power, as Macaroni won't run unless your Mac is plugged into AC power.

FIX A POOPED-OUT PORT

The Annoyance: My Ethernet port seems to have stopped working. It was working fine for a while, but ever since I installed a minor Mac OS X 10.3.*x* update, System Preferences crashes when I try to bring up the Network pane. I've tried fixing file permissions and running various disk drive utilities. I was optimistic at first because the repair utilities discovered permissions and disk problems. Unfortunately, my Ethernet port still isn't functioning, even after the utilities fixed the problems they found. What am I missing here?

The Fix: You may have a corrupt network configuration file. This type of problem can affect not only Ethernet, but AirPort networking as well. System Preferences may or may not unexpectedly quit, but failure to *even* get on a network when you could before is a symptom of a

---

TECHNICAL TIP: WHY ARE THERE SO MANY LIBRARY FOLDERS?

You may have noticed that there are a lot of Library folders. There's one in your Home folder, another at the root level of the system, and yet another in the */System* folder. The reason is rooted in *user domains*, which is the Unix concept that specifies which users can make changes. The Library folder in your Home folder holds files (preference files, fonts, sounds, and files used by applications) that you have complete control over—this is your domain. You can delete or add anything here (though I highly recommend against deleting anything that you aren't sure about). However, if your Mac has multiple users, the other users won't be able to make changes to this folder.

The Library folder at the root level is accessible to all users, but only a user with an administrator password can add, remove, or alter the files found here.

Application installers don't usually install items here, but they can. The Library folder in the */System* folder, however, is used by the system software; you won't be able to make any changes here.

By the way, if you are using the Go to Folder window to type a path, you should designate each of the three Library folders, as follows:

~/Library
> In your Home folder

/Library
> At the root level

/System/Library
> In the System folder

---

corrupted file. First, throw away a file called *NetworkInterfaces.plist*, which is located in */Library/Preferences/ SystemConfiguration*. Now restart your Mac. Mac OS X looks for the *NetworkInterfaces.plist* file at startup, and if it can't find it (which it won't because you've moved it to the Trash), the system creates a new *NetworkInterfaces. plist* file. Now, when you open the Network preferences panel, you should be able to connect to your network.

MOUNT FILE SERVERS ON THE DESKTOP

The Annoyance: I've been using Mac networks since System 6, but accessing file servers in Mac OS X 10.3.2 is so annoying that I'm almost ready to erase the hard disk and reinstall Mac OS X 10.2. I can't seem to get file servers mounted on the desktop. You would think that a setting that says "Show connected servers on the Desktop" would do what it says, but I've gone to Finder Preferences (the General tab) and selected this. The Finder doesn't seem to respond. Do I need to replace a broken file?

The Fix: This was one of the most annoying aspects of Panther—one that befuddled Mac users on networks everywhere—until Apple fixed it with Version 10.3.3. (In terms of networking, you can think of 10.3.3 as "Panther 1.0.") Upgrading Mac OS X returns your networking back to normal. With Mac OS X 10.3.0, Apple created a file-sharing dichotomy—two completely different user interfaces and behaviors for mounted servers, depending on how you logged on. Here's the basic problem with Versions 10.3.0, 10.3.1, and 10.3.2:

- If you log onto your server by *browsing*—which means going to the sidebar's Network icon and choosing it from a list—the mounted server volumes won't appear on your Desktop, nor will they appear in the sidebar. You must click on the Network icon to access the server.

- However, if you log in by typing a URL in the Go menu's Connect to Server dialog box, the server behaves just as mounted servers have on Macs since the 1980s—as if it were a hard drive. The server appears on the Desktop and in the Finder's sidebar only if you have set it in the Finder's Preference dialog (in the General and sidebar tabs). If you're temporarily stuck with one of these older Panther versions (that is, the powers that be at your office won't let you upgrade), the obvious workaround is to always use the second method to access servers. You can type an IP address or a URL (starting with *afp://* for a Mac server or *smb://* for a Windows server). Once you log in, you can add the server to the Favorites menu in the Connect to Server dialog by clicking the Plus icon.

There is also a workaround for servers that you log onto through the Network icon. Notice that you can't copy-and-drag the icon of the mounted server volume to the Desktop or to the Dock—you receive a message telling you that you don't have the privileges. However, you can make an alias of the network volume and move that to the desktop. Double-clicking this new alias opens the network volume. Furthermore, you can move this alias to the Dock and to the sidebar. And, if you are not currently logged onto the server, double-clicking the alias brings up the logon dialog.

Here's one more oddball behavior: you can log onto a server using *both* methods of the dichotomy simultaneously—the Network icon and the Connect to Server command. It's certainly weird, but it gives you the widest interface options until you can update your system.

BROWSE THE CONNECT TO SERVER DIALOG

The Annoyance: I'm current on my Mac OS X updates, but what I really want in Panther is the ability to browse in the Connect to Server dialog, the way I could in Mac OS X Jaguar. Isn't there a hack that does this?

The Fix: Panther is full of hidden tricks, so it should be of no surprise that there is a very simple hack for browsing the Connect to Server dialog box. A one-line

AppleScript creates a Jaguar-style browsing Connect to Server dialog. To create it, you must open the Script Editor, which is located in the AppleScript folder inside the Applications folder. As in Figure 1-17, type the following line in the Script Editor:

```
open location (choose URL) with error reporting
```

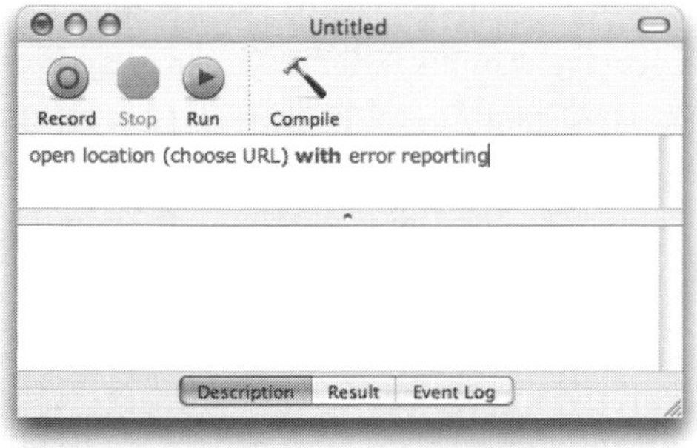

Figure 1-17. This one-line script in Script Editor creates a Connect to Server Dialog that lets you browse for servers (see Figure 1-18).

Now, save the script. Click the Run button to bring up the Connect to Server dialog, shown on the right side of Figure 1-18. Notice that several servers show up in the list. Also notice that there is a Show pop-up menu that lets you browse for specific types of servers, including file servers, web servers, and FTP servers.

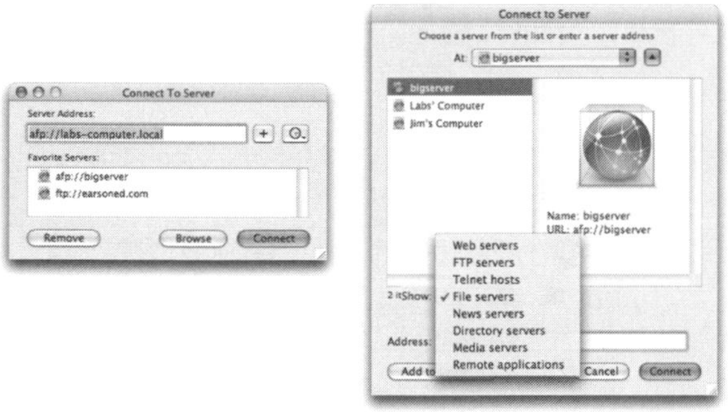

Figure 1-18. To the left is the standard Panther (non-browsing) Connect to Server dialog. To the right is the browsing version created with the AppleScript.

GIMME THOSE WINDOWS SERVERS

The Annoyance: Since upgrading to Panther, I can no longer access files on my company's Windows server. The Network icon shows the server, and I appear to log on and can even see the shares. However, when I open them, there are no files. Other Macs and PCs can see the files just fine. To no avail, I've tried running D Utility and installing Apple's updates.

The Fix: Log on using the Network icon in the sidebar and move the shares on the server into the Trash. Restart your Mac and try logging onto the server. You should now see and access all the server-based files as normal.

This won't delete anything on the server. It does, however, force Mac OS X to go out on the network and recreate the volumes in the Finder.

> **t i p**
>
> By the way, upgrading to 10.3.3 or later also helps you to access Windows servers.

Get Info

Panther has plenty of problems accessing Windows servers. If you're looking for a cross-platform networking solution, check out the MacWindows web site, particularly *www.macwindows.com/panther.html*.

BROWSE FOR APPLETALK FILE SERVERS

The Annoyance: With Mac OS X 10.3, I can no longer browse file servers that use AppleTalk. I go to the Network icon, and they just aren't there. This includes the old Windows NT Server running Services for Macintosh, which doesn't run on TCP/IP, and old Macs with file sharing turned on. AppleTalk is turned on in Network preferences, but still no dice.

The Fix: It certainly is annoying, but with Version 10.3, Mac OS X now separates turning on AppleTalk from turning on AppleTalk *browsing*. In Versions 10.3.0, 10.3.1, and 10.3.2, both are turned off by default. In Version 10.3.3 and later, AppleTalk browsing is turned on by default. To activate AppleTalk browsing, do the following:

1. Open Directory Access (*/Applications/Utilities*).
2. Click the padlock icon in the lower-left corner and type your user password in the dialog that appears.
3. Now add a check in the box next to AppleTalk, under the Services tab.
4. Click the Apply button.
5. Quit Directory Access.

Your old AppleTalk file servers should now be visible when you double-click the Network icon in the sidebar.

SET UP NETWORKING FOR MULTIPLE CITIES

The Annoyance: I travel regularly to multiple cities with my PowerBook and need to connect to the Internet via modem, as well as to various Ethernet and AirPort networks. I've figured out that I can add multiple phone numbers to the modem pane of Internet Connect. I also know that I don't have to carry around a piece of paper with the various settings—I can create multiple port configurations in Network preferences. But then when I get to a city, I have to check and uncheck the various port configurations that apply. Is there an easier way?

The Fix: Create a different *network location* for each city you travel to. In Mac OS X, a single network location can store multiple settings for modem, Ethernet, AirPort, and virtual private networks (VPN). To switch them all, you need only to change the Location item in the Apple menu, as shown in Figure 1-19. All of these port settings switch at once, and the ports (and modem phone numbers) for other cities are hidden. Even if you're only changing the modem settings, it's still easier to switch between them if you create locations, because you never have to open Internet Connect or System Preferences to change the settings.

Figure 1-19. When you choose a location from the Apple menu, all of your network and modem settings switch to the appropriate configurations.

To create a new location, open System Preferences and click the Network icon. In the Location pop-up menu, select New Location. A dialog then appears and asks you to name the location. Give it a simple name, such as the name of a city. Click OK. Now, use the Network pane to create all the configurations you need at that location, including Ethernet, AirPort, and modem. Click Apply Now to save your settings. If you are setting up a modem or virtual private network setting, open the Internet Connect application. Notice that your previous settings appear to be gone. They're just hidden, because you have a new location. Enter any settings you need here.

Keep System Preferences Closed when Networking

If you are running a version of Mac OS X prior to Version 10.3, you should quit the System Preferences application while you are networking. With System Preferences open, networking can slow to a crawl; Panther doesn't have this problem.

CUSTOMIZE SOFTWARE UPDATE

The Annoyance: Updates I don't need—such as an update for an iPod model I don't have—keep showing up in Software Update. Each time, I choose not to install them, and yet they keep coming back. Now, they are starting to pile up in the list of updates. Why doesn't Mac OS X get the hint? Can't I just tell it, "Enough already?"

The Fix: Indeed you can by tweaking settings in the Software Update application. Just visit the Software Update pane of System Preferences and click the Update Now button. After Software Update launches and gives you the list of Updates, select an update you don't want, go to the Update menu, and choose Ignore Update, as in Figure 1-20. (In Jaguar, this menu command is called Hide.) The update then disappears from list of updates. You can do this for as many updates as you like. If you change your mind later, you can choose Reset Ignored Updates from the Software Update menu.

Figure 1-20. Tell Software Update to stop showing you software you don't want to install.

SET AN APPLICATION TO OPEN A FILE

The Annoyance: When I double-click a file, the wrong application opens. This means I have to quit, and then drag-and-drop the file on the correct application icon. It's even more of a pain with a batch of files.

The Fix: You can change which application opens a particular file using the Open With command. After selecting the file with a single click, there are four places you can access this command:

- The File menu.
- The contextual menu (see Figure 1-21), which you bring up by Control-clicking the file.
- The Get Info dialog (see Figure 1-22), which you bring up from the contextual menu or by hitting ⌘-I on the selected file.
- If you select a file in the Finder window, you can use the Action menu in the Finder's toolbar and select "Open With..." from its menu.

In each case, you see a selection of applications installed on your Mac that Mac OS X thinks can open your file. If you don't see your application listed, you can try selecting Other to browse for it.

Figure 1-21. The Open With command of the contextual menu is one way to tell Mac OS X to open a file with another application.

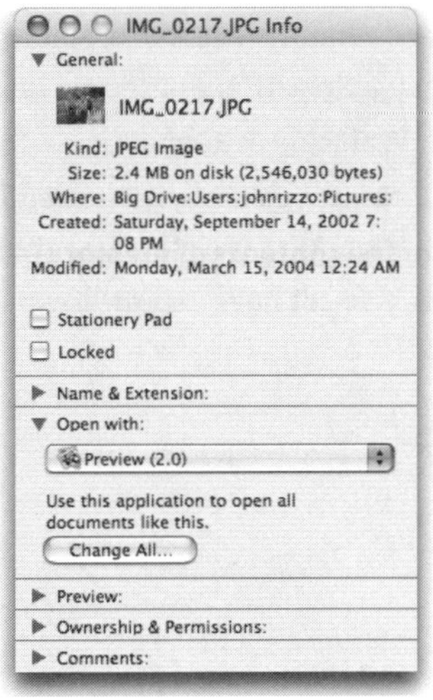

Figure 1-22. The Get Info dialog has a Change All button, which resets all similar files to open with the application you've set.

The Get Info dialog has one additional feature: the Change All command (see Figure 1-22). This lets you reset the default application for all of the files of the same type as the selected file. For instance, if you want all of your JPEG files to open with Preview, you would open the Get Info dialog of a JPEG file, set "Open With..." to Preview, and then click on the Change All button. Now when you go to open a JPEG file—any JPEG file—the image file opens in Preview.

> **t i p**
>
> If you're using the Change All command frequently, a Preference file that stores the setting information can develop errors. You know there's a problem if you try to use the Change All command and it doesn't stick—files are still opening with the wrong application. To fix this problem, delete the *com.apple.Launch-Services.plist* file, which is located in *~/Library/Preferences*. When you delete this file, a new one is created, resetting all of the "Open With..." settings back to the default settings.

CREATE SYMBOLIC LINKS INSTEAD OF ALIASES

The Annoyance: I like to create aliases of folders and place them on the desktop and other locations. This lets me easily get to folders when I need them. But whenever I try to refer to one of these aliases using any command in Terminal, Unix never recognizes the aliases. In the Finder, these aliases have generic icons instead of the fancy icons of the Application and Home folders, which is just plain annoying.

The Fix: The way to fix both of these issues simultaneously is to create symbolic links instead of aliases. Symbolic links are the Unix version of aliases. Like aliases, symbolic links point to another folder or file. Unlike aliases, the symbolic link has the same icon as the original and works in the Unix shell of Terminal (*/Applications/ Utilities*). Here's the drawback: if you move the original folder, the symbolic link breaks.

To create a symbolic link, type the following command in Terminal:

```
$ ln -s [original folder] [location and name of
  symbolic link]
```

For instance, if you want to create a symbolic link to the Applications folder and place it on the desktop, type the following command in Terminal:

```
$ ln -s /Applications ~/Desktop/Applications
```

Remember, that a tilde followed by a forward slash (~/) stands for your Home folder. Also, I called this symbolic link "Applications," but I could have called it "George"—it would still appear on the Desktop with the Applications icon.

MOVE YOUR HOME FOLDER

The Annoyance: I'm running out of room on my hard disk, so I bought a new drive that has a lot more space. However, all of my space-eating files are in my Home folder on the old disk. Is there a way to move the Home folder to the new hard disk? A simple drag-and-drop doesn't work.

The Fix: It's true. Dragging and dropping the Home folder doesn't move some of the invisible files and doesn't properly notify Mac OS X that you've moved it. To make sure all the files are moved, use the Unix command line to make a copy of your Home folder on the new disk (formatted as HFS+). Using NetInfo Manager, you can then tell Mac OS X that you've moved the Home folder.

To copy your Home folder to a new drive, launch Terminal (*/Applications/Utilities*) and enter the following command:

```
$ sudo ditto -rsrc /Users/username /Volumes/ ↵
Newdrive/Users/username
```

Here, use your own Home folder's name instead of *username* and the actual name of your new hard drive instead *Newdrive*. (Also, note the space after the first *username*; this is very important.)

Now, rename your old Home folder with this command:

```
$ sudo mv /Users/corinne /Users/corinneOLD
```

To complete the move, use the NetInfo Manager to tell Mac OS X where the new Home folder is located:

1. Launch NetInfo Manager (*/Applications/Utilities*).

2. Unlock it by clicking the padlock and typing your password in the dialog that appears. (To do this, you need an administration password, which is what you get if you set up your own Mac.)

3. Click the slash (/) in the first column.

4. Click "users" (lowercase) in the second column.

5. Click your username in the third column.

6. Below, in the Property column, click "home", as shown in Figure 1-23.

7. In the Values column, change the name of the home folder to */Volumes/new diskname/folder*. For example, if the new drive was called *Bigdrive*, and your new home folder was called *bobsmith*, the location of your Home folder would be: */Volumes/Bigdrive/bobsmith*

8. Press Enter and Save.

9. Quit NetInfo Manager (⌘-Q).

Figure 1-23. Use NetInfo Manager to tell Mac OS X that you have a new home folder. Here, we've done everything except type the new home folder path.

Now, use the Mac for a while to make sure everything works. Restart, click your Home icon in the sidebar, open files, run iTunes, check things out. If everything seems okay, you can delete the old Home folder. However, you won't be able to do it in the Finder. Instead, fire up Terminal again and delete the old Home folder with the following command:

```
$ sudo rm -r /Users/bobsmithOLD
```

Once again, use your own short user name instead of *bobsmith*.

When you are typing these commands, be sure you pay attention to whether the characters are upper- or lower-cased. Unlike most of the Mac, Terminal commands are case-sensitive.

Email
ANNOYANCES

I can't think of any technological innovation that has more potential for annoyance than email: unreadable attachments, bucket loads of spam, and messages that blather on and on before getting to the point—all this and more, several times a day, every day. Ah, to return to those innocent days before email.

We all know we couldn't live without email, so let's get to the problem-solving portion of the program. With a little know-how, you can work around the most annoying email problems. This chapter begins with fixes for the general problems with email—problems that crop up regardless of which email software you use. It then covers some of the most annoying aspects of some popular email programs, including Mac OS X Mail, Entourage, Eudora, and AOL.

That's not the whole story, though. In this chapter, I go beyond you and *your* annoyances. After all, you may be unwittingly annoying *other people* with the email you send out, which, in turn, makes you look bad. That's why I've also provided tips on how to make your email more effective and less annoying to others.

GENERAL EMAIL ANNOYANCES

SPAM, SPAM, SPAM, SPAM...

The Annoyance: In the good ol' days, I used to complain that I received as much spam as legitimate mail. Ha! Today, I would welcome that amount of spam, as I'm now buried under five times as much junk mail as real email.

The Fix: There are two basic methods that you can apply to the spam spigot to turn the torrent into a trickle. You can run spam-filtering software on your Mac, or you can have your ISP filter your email for you:

Use a Bayesian spam filter on your Mac.

Bayesian analysis is a highly accurate mathematical technique that uses statistics to zero in on spam. The easiest, most effective Bayesian filter is Spam-Sieve ($25, *http://www.c-command.com/spamsieve/*). SpamSieve keeps a database of words that are often used in spam and of words that are used in legitimate messages. It creates this database over time, as you train it—that is, you tell it which messages are spam and which are not. After the training period, the Bayesian filter uses this data to make (highly accurate) guesses as to which incoming messages are spam based on what's in the message. SpamSieve also looks at what's in the headers and the code in HTML messages. (For instance, the term "ff0000" is the HTML code for a bright red color often used in spam messages.) When a Bayesian filter identifies a message as spam, it moves it into a special spam folder. People in your address book are added to a "white list," so their email won't be identified as spam.

Apple Mail also uses Bayesian analysis in its Junk Mail filter. If you are a Mail user, start training it to recognize spam. Mail's built-in filter is pretty good, but SpamSieve is more accurate and catches more spam than Apple Mail. SpamSieve is also safe—in the 11,000 messages SpamSieve has filtered for me, it has only *once* incorrectly identified a legitimate message as spam.

SpamSieve automatically launches when you receive mail from your email software and lets you use your email software's interface to train it. SpamSieve works with Apple Mail, Emailer, Entourage, Eudora (Version 5.2 or later), Mailsmith, and PowerMail—it even works with the old Claris Emailer running in Classic.

Have your ISP block known mail before it gets to you.

Many ISPs, including Earthlink, offer optional (and free) spam filtering that you can turn on and adjust. However, if you're using ISP blocking, I suggest you use the mildest setting to be sure that it doesn't block legitimate mail. (Earthlink calls this "blocking known spam." The more aggressive setting is called "block suspected spam.") There is no training involved here. To access your ISP's spam blocking features, go to the ISP's web site and log in as a user.

OPEN UNOPENABLE ATTACHMENTS

The Annoyance: Sometimes I can't read attachments that come with email messages. I'm not talking about unsolicited twaddle (which, of course, I'm never foolish enough to open), but about attachments from colleagues who assure me that they've forwarded important Word files, spreadsheets, or images. Instead, the attachments either look like monkey-at-a-typewriter gibberish or they won't open at all.

The Fix: The gibberish file you see (like the one in Figure 2-1) is encoded in a format that your email software doesn't understand. Email software encodes attachments into text to help the files survive the journey over the Internet. When you can't open an attachment, it's usually because your email software doesn't support the encoding standard used by the sender's software. Encoding standards include BinHex (used almost exclusively by Macs), MIME/Base64 (a Windows favorite), Uuencode (from the Unix world), as well as others. Another possibility is that your

THE ROOTS OF SPAM FILTERING

Today's state-of-the-art spam filtering comes from the work of a contemporary of Sir Isaac Newton. Reverend Thomas Bayes, a Presbyterian minister and mathematician from Kent, England, created the branch of statistics known as Bayesian analysis. The Royal Society of London published Bayes's paper on statistics, "Essay Towards Solving a Problem in the Doctrine of Chances," posthumously in 1763. In it, Bayes established a mathematical basis for calculating future probability for an event by looking at the number of times the event has and has not already occurred.

Today, programmers use Reverend Bayes's work to block messages pitching ultra-low mortgages, body-part enlargement, and cheap drugs. You can find a good explanation of how it works at software engineer Paul Graham's web site: *http://www.paulgraham.com/spam.html.*

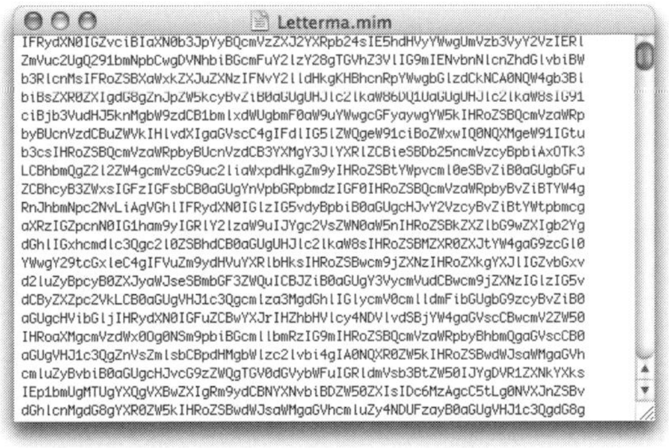

Figure 2-1. A gibberish file is actually a useful file that is encoded. The problem is your email software has failed to decode it.

email software actually does support the encoding standard used, but it just doesn't recognize it. This can happen if the header or other parts of the message get mixed with the encoded attachment. You have several options:

- Your first line of attack is StuffIt Expander (in */Applications/Utilities*). Try dragging the attachment to the StuffIt Expander icon. This often doesn't work, but it's worth a try.

  If you own StuffIt Standard Edition or StuffIt Deluxe, try opening the utility first and then dragging in the attachment.

- If no member of the StuffIt family can decode or recognize the file, you may need to try another utility. Data Viz's file translation utility, MacLinkPlus ($79, *http://www.dataviz.com*), generally does an excellent job at recognizing encoded files, filtering out any worthless text that may have been included, and then decoding the attachments. (Incidentally, MacLinkPlus's main purpose is to convert between different Windows and Mac file formats, so it's handy for that, too.)

  If you want to go a bit cheaper, you can try your luck with various shareware utilities. The $20 Decoder from Etresoft (*http://www.etresoft.com*) can decode a variety of formats; just drag-and-drop the attachment to the Decoder icon.

- You can sometimes clean up an encoded attachment yourself, in order to get StuffIt Expander to recognize it. Open the file in TextEdit or another word processor; delete everything above the line that begins "Content-Type:" (as in Figure 2-2). Save the file as a text-only file and drag it on top of StuffIt Expander. This eliminates the email message, headers, or other extraneous text that may have been added to the attachment and that may be confusing StuffIt Expander.

OPEN WINMAIL.DAT FILES

The Annoyance: Sometimes I receive an attachment called *Winmail.dat* that drives me crazy. I can never open it, not even with the decoding software you just mentioned. When I ask the sender what *Winmail.dat* is, they tell me that they never sent such a file. Am I imagining things?

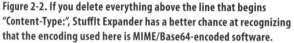

Figure 2-2. If you delete everything above the line that begins "Content-Type:", StuffIt Expander has a better chance at recognizing that the encoding used here is MIME/Base64-encoded software.

The Fix: No, you're just the victim of a Microsoft email system that is making some wacky assumptions. These *Winmail.dat* files come from users of Microsoft Outlook with the Microsoft Exchange server. Don't blame Windows, though—Exchange Server can cause this problem with people sending email from Windows or Mac OS. If certain configurations in Outlook are incorrect, the Exchange server assumes that all outgoing mail is headed for other Outlook users and encodes attachments in a scheme that only Outlook/Exchange understands. This file can be called *Winmail.dat* or can have a type called "application/ms-tnef," which you can see in the file's Get Info dialog.

The whole explanation of the cause is complex, but the fix is easy—just use TNEF's Enough, a fabulous piece of freeware, from Josh Jacob (*http://www.joshjacob.com/macdev/tnef/*). Just drag-and-drop the *Winmail.dat* file on top of TNEF's Enough, and the utility extracts the attachment. If TNEF's Enough can't open the Winmail.dat file, it may also be encoded in another format, such as Uuencode. If that's the case, you must start over, running another decoding utility first before running TNEF's Enough.

SEND WINDOWS-FRIENDLY ATTACHMENTS

The Annoyance: When I send an attachment to colleagues who use Windows, they report back saying that they can't open the files or that when they do, that the files are full of gibberish. Of course, they blame it on the Mac and recommend that I join the rest of the world and buy a PC.

The Fix: You've just touched on one of the most annoying things about most email programs: they're set by default to compress even the smallest attachments, as if we still lived in a world where everyone has a 28.8k baud modem. Windows users usually can't decompress SIT (StuffIt) archives, and most Mac email software defaults to using SIT for compression. To solve the problem, start by turning off that default compression. Most of your attachments don't need compression. Save compression for when you really need it (for files over a couple of megabytes in size). Mail doesn't use compression, but other mail programs do. Here's how to turn off compression in popular email programs:

- In Entourage, go to the Entourage menu and select Mail & News Preferences. Click the Compose Tab. In the Attachments section, set Compression to None.

- In Mailsmith, go to Mailsmith Preferences and click the Enclosures item. Uncheck the box called Compress with StuffIt.

- Eudora doesn't compress by default, but you can turn it on when you add an attachment. Don't do this if you are sending a file to a Windows user.

If you must compress, use the Zip format if you are sending files to Windows users. You can use a utility such as StuffIt Standard Edition ($50, *http://www.stuffit.com*) or ZipIt ($20, *http://www.maczipit.com*).

Hold on, though, you're not done yet. The second reason Windows users can't open your attachment is *encoding*—that is, your Mac is encoding the file in a format that the

WRITE EFFECTIVE (NOT ANNOYING) EMAIL

Email is a great communication tool, but it can also be an annoying distraction. If you want to get your point across, don't aggravate friends and coworkers with email that is unfocused or difficult to read. To write effective email, follow these basic tips:

☒ Use descriptive, short subject lines, such as "Update on Henderson Report." So much spam and virus mail have vague, nondescriptive titles, such "Your Document" or "Web Site." You want to make it easy for your recipients to separate the wheat (your message) from the chaff (everything else).

☒ Get to the point. Email is not the place for grand introductions. Like a newspaper story, the first sentence should convey what your message is about. Minor points should come last.

☒ Use paragraphs—a lot of them. A message in one, long rambling paragraph is hard to read and, therefore, annoying. Don't be afraid to hit the Return key after you finish a thought.

☒ Use capitalization and punctuation. These innovations of civilization were created to make text easier to read. Without them, your message is a chore to get through and, worse, could convey an ambiguous meaning.

☒ Use spellchecking. Bad spelling is often the result of bad typing, but people don't often make that distinction. Spelling errors reflect poorly on you, particularly if you are in a business or academic setting.

☒ Edit your message. Don't hit the send button right away. Take a minute to reread your message and try to shorten it. If the message is important, save it as a draft and come back to it later, or even the next day. Effective email is well written, and writing always benefits from a second look.

Get Info

For a list of compression/decompression and encoding/decoding utilities that can handle Mac, Windows, and Unix formats, see *http://www.macwindows.com/compress.html*.

Windows email software doesn't understand. When sending files to Windows users, I find it best to use MIME Base64 format. If your email software doesn't have MIME Base64 as an option, try AppleDouble encoding.

Entourage, Mailsmith, and Eudora all let you select an encoding format directly from your message window, usually with a pop-up menu or checkbox. The default format is usually the Mac-only BinHex. You can change the default encoding in the Preferences dialog of these applications.

Mail lags behind other email applications in this respect. Before Mac OS X 10.3, Mail was brain-dead in terms of encoding—there was no way to change the default-encoding scheme. Your choices were to use AppleDouble or AppleDouble. However, starting with Panther, Mail has the option of sending "Windows Friendly" attachments. Click Edit → Attachments. In the dialog, select Always

Send Windows Friendly Attachments. In theory, this should apply a global, Windows-friendly compression scheme. However, you can't always count on this setting to deliver attachments that Windows users can open. It's one of the annoying weaknesses of Mail.

HIDE THE RECIPIENTS LIST

The Annoyance: Recently I sent out a very important message to a large group of people. In response, several people complained that I forwarded their email address to "half the known world." What was I supposed to do, send the message to one person at a time?

The Fix: Just as you wouldn't broadcast someone's phone number without her permission, neither should you forward her email address to people she doesn't know. Use BCC (which stands for *blind carbon copy*) to address messages intended for a large group of people, particularly if they don't know each other. The next time someone does this to you, politely point her in the direction of the BCC field.

KEEP YOUR ISP MAILBOX EMPTY

The Annoyance: Email messages don't seem to like me. People keep telling me that they can't send mail to me—their messages get bounced back. One friend told me that a message said that my POP3 mailbox was full. Maybe it's my aftershave?

The Fix: Whoever told you your box was full is a friend, indeed, for giving you the answer to your problem. Your mailbox probably *is* full, because you're forgetting to delete mail from the POP3 email server that holds your messages. Your ISP typically gives you 10 megabytes on its server—when that fills up, further email gets bounced back to the senders. If you have messages containing large attachments, your space on the server fills up even more quickly.

Most email software lets you delete your messages on the server immediately or after a short period. To shorten the

period of time that email is stored on your POP3 server, do the following:

- In Mail, click Mail → Preferences. Select the account from the left column and then click Advanced. Check "Remove copy from server after retrieving message." Choose a new duration from the After One Week pop-up menu (see Figure 2-3). "Right Away" or "After One Day" are good choices.

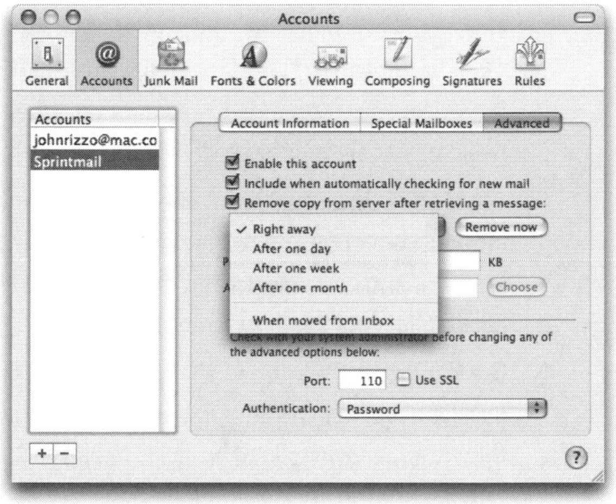

Figure 2-3. You can set Mail to delete messages on a POP3 email server immediately or, if you prefer, over a short period of time. If the period is too long, your mailbox fills up, and new messages bounce back to the senders.

- In Entourage, go to the Tools menu and Click Accounts. In the Mail tab, select the account. Go to the Options tab, find Server options, and choose how long to keep messages on the server.

- In Mailsmith, go to the Window menu and select Accounts. Under the Checking tab, you have two options. The first is to uncheck "Leave Mail on Server." If you want to keep this checked, change the number next to "Delete Mail on Server" to 1 or 2 days.

- In Eudora, select Tools → Options → Incoming mail. Check Delete from server after 0 days. If you like, change 0 to a small number, such as 1, 2, or 3.

A SLICK WAY TO ADD ATTACHMENTS

The Annoyance: I wish there was an easy way to add attachments to an email message. Either I can drag-and-drop everything (which is still a pain, even with Expose), or I can browse through my hard disks using a button.

The Fix: You've been doing it the slow way. You can add an attachment directly from the Finder without even opening your email application—if you have that app's icon parked in the Dock. Just drag-and-drop the file (or folder) to the email app's icon: the application opens and creates a new message window with your file already attached. The trick also works if your application is already open—just buried behind other windows. This method saves many mouse clicks and works with most mail programs, including Mail, Entourage, and Mailsmith.

USE ICHAT FOR BIG ATTACHMENTS

The Annoyance: If I try to send a mail message with a big (I'm talking big—10 MB or more) attachment, it inevitably bounces back. I know I can break up the attachment with StuffIt or some other utility and send it in multiple email messages. That's really clunky, though, and my recipient might not know how to put the pieces back together.

The Fix: We think that email is the best way to send all types of information, but in fact, email really isn't designed to deal with big attachments. Some ISPs limit the size of an attachment you can send or receive, as do local servers on some corporate and university networks.

An easy way to bypass these restrictive email servers is to use iChat (or another IM client that supports file sharing). After establishing a session with another person, just drag your file or folder into the message area of a chat window, and it will be moved to your chat partner's Mac.

> ### KEEP MESSAGES SHORT
>
> Another note on writing effective email: It's *not* the place to write a treatise. Many people consider reading email as something they are forced to do in between doing real work. This means that short messages are read, and long messages are not necessarily. If you must communicate a long thought, attach it as a Word file. Or, here's a thought—*pick up the phone.*
>
> How short it short? A good rule of thumb is that you shouldn't have to use the scroll bar to see the whole message. Another good guideline is to keep your messages to three paragraphs or less, each with three sentences or less. If your message is longer, try cutting it down. You don't have to put every thought or rationale into an email message, and a little editing can make even good writing better.

(If you don't have a chat window open, just drag it to the recipient's name in your Buddy List.) Not everyone can chat, however; some company firewalls may prevent the chat protocols from getting through.

AUTOMATE PREADDRESSED EMAIL

The Annoyance: My boss wants hourly updates on what I'm working on, which is usually, well, writing an hourly update to my boss. I wish there were a way to automate the process so that I could double-click an icon on the desktop and have my email software open with a new, pre-addressed message window.

The Fix: Your wish is your command—an AppleScript command, that is. You can create a very simple script that will automate the process, launching your email application even if it is closed. Open Script Editor, which you can find in */Applications/AppleScript*. In the window that opens, type the following:

```
property target_URL : "mailto:bob@acme.com"
open location target_URL
```

Of course, use your intended recipient's email address instead of *bob@acme.com*. You can also include multiple recipients within the quotes, separated by a comma and space, as in:

```
property target_URL : "mailto:bob@acme.com, ↵
janet@flubber.org"
```

To make sure you haven't mistyped anything, click the Run button. (The text turns from black to colored, as in Figure 2-4.) If your default email software opens and presents you a new email message window, preaddressed with your recipient, then you've typed correctly.

Figure 2-4. This simple AppleScript pre-addresses your email.

Now, go back to Script Editor and choose Save from the File menu. In the dialog that appears, click the File Format popup menu and select Application (as in Figure 2-5). This is an important step, because it causes the script to run when you double-click the script icon (instead of opening Script Editor). Finally, type a name for it—for example, "Email Bob."

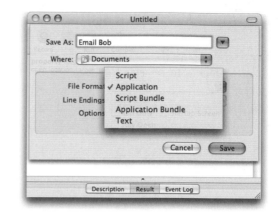

Figure 2-5. The final steps are to designate your AppleScript as an application and to name your file.

You can move this file to any Finder window, and you can add it to the Dock and the Finder's sidebar and toolbar.

CHANGE YOUR DEFAULT EMAIL PROGRAM

The Annoyance: OK, smart guy. I created the above AppleScript, but it launches Mail only, not the email program I actually use. The same is true when I click an email link at a web site. I've searched through System Preferences without finding a clue. How do I tell Panther that I want to use another email application as my default?

The Fix: You used to be able to set your default email client using the Internet pane in System Preferences. However, starting with Mac OS X 10.3, Apple removed that option, and, as strange as it might seem, you must now go to Mail to change your default email app. Follow these steps:

1. Launch Mail.

2. Select Preferences from the Mail menu.

3. Click the General pane.

4. Click the Default Email Reader pop-up menu and choose Select.

5. Browse for your email application in the dialog that appears. Select it and click the Select button.

6. Quit Mail.

With this simple but far-from-obvious change, any Mac OS X application (or AppleScript) that calls for email opens your preferred email app.

USING THE OLD CLARIS EMAILER

The Annoyance: My friends really annoy me when they tell me that I should get with the program and stop using the old Claris Emailer. But I really like Emailer, and the newer features of the current batch of email programs don't really interest me. Should I get a new email program or just new friends?

The Fix: Tell your friends you're driving a classic, not a clunker. Claris Emailer was a premier email client of its time that still holds up against today's software and its more modern features. Even running in Classic, Emailer beats Mail hands down when it comes to speed and is also faster than Mailsmith and Entourage. Apple stopped making Claris Emailer at the height of its popularity in 1998 only because it dissolved the Claris group. If you are still a fan and Emailer is still working, there really isn't any reason to go modern. (Even SpamSieve works with Emailer.)

You should mentally prepare, however, for a time in the future—thanks to say, a new Mac OS X upgrade—when Emailer may stop working. Switching email programs is not a trivial matter. After importing addresses and email messages, there's the job of learning a new program. One way to prepare is to download demo software of modern email applications and test drive them. If you are looking to retain a similar look and feel, Bare Bone Software's Mailsmith (*http://www.mailsmith.com*) and the less capable PowerMail from CTM Development (*http://www.ctmdev.com*) are the closest to Emailer in style. But even

Mailsmith doesn't have some of the little interface niceties of Emailer. For instance, I miss the pop-up menu for filing a message in a different folder.

Get Info

If you want to discuss Emailer with other Emailer users, sign up for Skytouch's Emailer listserve at *http://www.skytouch. com/lists/emailer-talk.html.*

Of course, your friends aren't totally out to lunch, either. The Classic environment in which Emailer runs is less stable than native applications, so you would experience less flakiness by moving to a Mac OS X-native email application. You would also get some newer features, including more options for handling incoming and outgoing HTML mail.

I was an Emailer holdout until the beginning of 2004, when a bad crash toasted Emailer. The crash was not at all connected to Emailer or Classic, but I took it as a sign that I should move on to a Mac OS X-native email application.

EMAIL YOUR RECEIVED FAXES

The Annoyance: Panther is supposed to be able to email faxes that I've received. I've set up this feature in the Print & Fax pane of System Preferences, but my contacts tell me the email never arrives. Isn't this one of the 150 features that Panther added to Mac OS X?

The Fix: Yes, if you have performed a clean install of Panther, emailing faxes should be no sweat. However, if you've upgraded Mac OS X from 10.2.*x* to 10.3, a bug may be preventing the fax-to-email feature. The slash-and-burn solution is to reinstall Panther—but that's a draconian and time-consuming action for such a small attribute.

A much easier solution is to add a piece of free software called FaxEmailHelper (*http://www.rwts.com.au*) by Real World Technology Solutions. The first time you run it, Fax-EmailHelp makes some minor configuration repairs to Mac OS X that fix the faxing bug and a few other bugs, including a problem that prevents some Panther users from sending email faxes through firewalls (see Figure 2-6). FaxEmailHelper also adds a few handy features to help you ensure that the email version of the fax is received. First, it lets you specify an email address that the fax appears to be coming from, instead of Panther's *FaxNotify@your.machine*, which email servers often reject as an invalid address. FaxEmailHelper also lets you

---

WHEN AND HOW NOT TO USE EMAIL

Do you use email for good or to annoy people? A lot of people irritate their email recipients unknowingly, but that's a short-lived excuse. Email can even go beyond annoying to insulting. Here's how to be more selective in what you send:

☒ Don't send email that isn't necessary. Don't Reply to All when all you have to say is "Thanks" or "I agree." Instead, send these kinds of replies to the person for which they are intended.

☒ Don't use email to argue with a group of people. You will never convince anyone of your argument over email, which is a poor medium for debate—that is, email is not *effective* for winning over people to your position. If you want to settle an issue, it is much more effective to phone people or to convene a meeting.

☒ Be careful what you write. If you wouldn't say something to a person's face, don't say it in email. In fact, you should be more cautious than in conversation, as it is very easy to offend people with email, even when you don't mean it. Plain text doesn't convey emotion, context, or facial expressions that might soften your statements. Look for

potential offensive or insensitive remarks and rewrite them.

☒ Don't use harsh language. Strong language and swearing look striking and severe in email. And unlike a verbal utterance, email can be saved, printed, and distributed long after you've cooled down.

☒ If you are making a joke that you think could possibly be taken the wrong way, leave it out. Jokes that work verbally can sound stark and insulting in email. If you must include your joke, at least use an emoticon, such as ;-) as a modifier. Sure, smileys can be annoying, too, but at least they help convey your meaning.

☒ When you send jokes and funny pictures, make sure your recipients actually *want* to receive them. Maybe you like getting forwarded jokes, but I find them distracting. So, if you're sending out jokes to a large group of people, chances are good that someone out there finds it annoying. Ask permission before you add a new person to your "forwards" list or ask your friends, periodically, if they mind receiving mass joke emails.

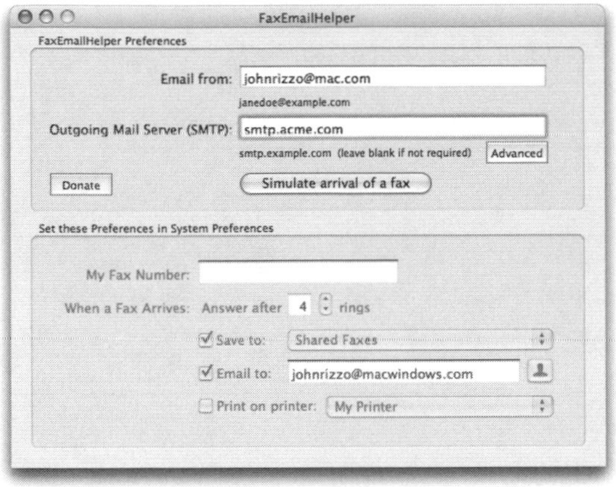

Figure 2-6. FaxEmailHelp fixes some bugs sometimes seen in Panther's fax-to-email feature.

specify an outgoing email SMTP server, instead of Panther's direct forwarding of the email fax, which some ISPs reject as coming from an untrustworthy source. There's also a button to simulate the arrival of a fax to let you test your configuration without having to ask someone to actually send a fax.

APPLE MAIL

COPY JUNK MAIL TRAINING TO ANOTHER MAC

The Annoyance: I just spent several weeks training Apple Mail to filter junk mail like an obedient

---

t i p

To quickly forward a message from Mac OS X's Mail application, use the Shift-⌘-F keyboard shortcut. This creates a new message window, containing the selected message.

If you only want to forward (or reply to) a particular part of an email, select that text first and then hit the Forward (or Reply) button. Only the text you selected in the original email will appear in the new message window.

---

puppy. Now, it works great, and I no longer need to tell it what is junk and what isn't. In the meantime, my wife just got a new Mac, and we'd like to have spam filtering on it as well. Do we have to go through the whole training period again?

The Fix: Fortunately, once you train one Mac to recognize junk mail, you can copy its learning to any Mac you want; just copy one file from your Mac to the same location on the other Mac:~/*Library/Mail/LSMmap* (it can also be called *LSMmap2*).

The Library folder I refer to is the one in the Home folder. Drop the *LSMmap* file into the Mail folder, and the new Mac is instantly trained in the art of spam catching.

STOP JUNK MAIL CRASHES

The Annoyance: Every time I use the Junk mail feature, Mail crashes (or, as it likes to tell me, "unexpectedly quits"). This just started a few days ago, but it's really getting on my nerves.

The Fix: The corruption of a few files causes these crashes. With Mail turned off, try deleting the LSMmap file from the location noted previously. Also delete *Message-Sorting.plist* from the same location. This eliminates crashing, but forces you to retrain your Junk filter. (If you use SpamSieve, described earlier in this chapter, you must reinstall it.)

Receiving a message with a blank To:, From:, or Subject: field has been known to cause this corruption problem. These kinds of messages can be generated by Windows viruses but are usually harmless to Macs. However, the problem with Mail occurs when you try to designate these messages as Junk (it can't seem to process them correctly, and so it just gives up and dies on you). Your best bet is to simply delete such messages. (SpamSieve doesn't have a problem with blank messages, by the way.)

SPOT MYSTERY ATTACHMENTS

The Annoyance: My biggest problem with Mail is that it doesn't seem to tell you if messages have an attachment. I don't want to have to click on each one to see if there's a file attached. In its list of messages, my old email program used to show an icon next to messages with attachments.

The Fix: Actually, Mail *can* display a paper-clip icon next to messages that include an attachment, but for some reason, Apple keeps the feature turned off by default. To turn it on, click View → Columns → Attachments. Mail then adds the Attachments column to the far right of your mailbox windows, using a paper-clip icon as a column heading. This isn't a convenient location for it, so I like to click the paper clip icon at the top of the column and drag it all the way to the left side.

DISABLE AN ACCOUNT

The Annoyance: I have Mail set up with multiple email accounts. When I take my PowerBook on the road, I disable my office account, which is on a local network and unreachable when I travel. Much to my annoyance, Mail continues to check the account anyway, generating error messages.

The Fix: For some reason known only to the mystics, Mail's preferences allow you to disable an account while enabling Mail to continue checking it automatically. As shown in Figure 2-7, you've correctly disabled the account (Preferences → Accounts icon → account name → Advanced tab) but you haven't disabled "Include when automatically checking for new mail."

Figure 2-7. When you disable an account, if you leave the second checkbox checked, Mail continues to check the account when it checks mail automatically, giving you error messages.

DELETE OUTGOING MAIL ACCOUNTS

The Annoyance: I was having trouble with my email account, so I set up multiple outgoing servers to see which setting worked best. I soon discovered that Mail doesn't have any way to remove outgoing mail servers from my account: there's an Add Server command in Preferences but no Remove Server. Now that's just weird.

The Fix: With Mac OS X 10.2.8 and earlier, there is indeed no way to delete an outgoing (SMTP) server from Mail. However, you can manually delete it by editing the preference file, which is a text-based XML file:

1. Quit Mail.
2. Go to the folder ~/*Library/Preferences*.

3. Double-click the file *com.apple.mail.plist*. It will open with Text Edit.

4. Do a search for the string "DeliveryAccounts" using the Find command (⌘-F).

5. Under the DeliveryAccounts title, you should see a list of the outgoing server configurations. You can now delete one or more of these. Each starts with the tag <dict> and ends with </dict>, which you should also delete. For example:

```
<dict>
    <key>AccountType</key>
    <string>SMTPAccount</string>
    <key>Hostname</key>
    <string>smpt.acme.net</string>
    <key>ShouldUSeAuthentication</key>
    <string>Yes</string>
    <key>Username</key>
    <string>jillsmith@acme.net</string>
</dict>
```

After you delete the text, save the file.

Happily, you won't need to do this with a more recent version of Mac OS X. Starting with Version 10.3, Apple added a method to remove outgoing servers:

1. Open Mail Preferences.

2. Click the Accounts icon in the toolbar.

3. Under the Accounts tab, click the Outgoing Mail Server (SMTP) pop-up menu and select Edit Server list.

4. Click a server to remove and click the Remove Server button.

TURN OFF HTML IMAGES IN MAIL

The Annoyance: I just *hate* opening an email and finding an offensive image, big as life, especially when my coworkers and supervisors are loitering behind me. Maybe I should just stop opening email.

The Fix: Many spammers send HTML-formatted email that's essentially a little web page in your inbox, sometimes containing pictures you can do without.

Starting with Panther, Mail lets you prevent images from being displayed in an HTML message you receive. Go to the Mail menu, click Preferences, and click the View icon. Now uncheck "Display images and embedded objects in

HTML messages" (shown in Figure 2-8). Mail now displays only the text portion of HTML messages.

Figure 2-8. Mail lets you turn off the display of images in HTML messages.

There are plenty of other good reasons not to load graphics from HTML messages. See the later sidebar HTML is More than Annoying.

SAVE YOUR MAIL FOR POSTERITY

The Annoyance: My email messages and user addresses are the lifeblood of the work on my Mac. If I lost them, *I'd* be lost. Unfortunately, Mail and Address Book don't keep all their files in one folder. If I want to back up my email and the contacts in Address Book, which files do I need to back up and where are they located?

The Fix: You should back up three components in order to get your Mail up and running again after a problem. These components are your mailboxes, which are filled with messages, your addresses, and the settings for your accounts. You can find all three components in the following places:

- Mailboxes and messages are located in your Home folder at *~/Library/Mail*. Back up the entire Mail folder.

- Your account settings are located in a single file called *com.apple.mail.plist*, in the Home folder at *~/Library/Preferences/com.apple.mail.plist*.

- Mail's addresses are stored in the Address Book. Copy the folder called AddressBook in your Home folder (*~/Library/Application Support/AddressBook*).

HTML MAIL IS MORE THAN ANNOYING

HTML email is a bad idea. You don't want to receive it, and you don't want to send it. HTML, short for Hypertext Markup Language, is the method used to create web pages. As with web pages, HTML email messages can include graphics and colored text and backgrounds. So what's so bad about it? A lot. Let's first consider incoming email.

Think about this: most spam is HTML mail. By not displaying HTML email, you don't have to see most of the spam you receive. 'Nuff said? No? Then how about this: spammers can use HTML email messages to harvest information about your email address.

With HTML, the pictures don't have to be included with the page. Instead, the HTML code includes a command to download the picture from a server. Some spammers use this fact to verify that your email address is valid. You open an HTML email message, and your email software asks the server to send a picture. The server sends you a picture, and the spammer now knows that there is a person behind your email address, which he can now sell to other spammers. Sometimes the "picture" is only a single pixel, so you don't actually see an image in the email message. Here's how to avoid this situation:

- ☒ Bare Bones Software takes pride in the fact that Mailsmith doesn't display HTML—it instead strips out the HTML code, displays only the text, and encloses the full HTML as an attachment, should you want to see it (as you might if it's from someone you know).
- ☒ Mail lets you turn off image rendering (as described in the earlier annoyance Turn Off HTML Images in Mail). When you do, Mail doesn't ask for pictures, so the server won't know anything about you.

- ☒ In Eudora, go to the Special menu and choose Settings. Click the Fonts and Display icon and uncheck "Automatically download HTML graphics." Again, Eudora wont request the graphics.
- ☒ Entourage lets you turn off HTML in the Read tab of Mail & News Preferences. It also has a handy setting: "Allow network access when displaying complex HTML." Turn this off, and Entourage won't ask spam servers to send you graphics.

Sending HTML email is also a bad idea because not all of your recipients' email programs can read it. Some people see your message as a mess, with text interspersed with HTML code. Not all email applications render HTML the same, either. So your beautifully crafted font sizes and colors might look pretty strange to some of your recipients. Depending on your software, you can prevent yourself from sending HTML email: if you are using a web browser such as Netscape Communicator for email, then all of the email you generate is in HTML. You should switch to Mail or to another email application. (Trust me, your overall email experience will improve).

- ☒ Some email programs, including Mail and Mailsmith, do not send HTML email. Consider this a feature.
- ☒ If you use Entourage, open Mail & News Preferences, click the Compose tab, and set Mail Format to Plain Text.
- ☒ In Eudora, go to the Special menu and choose Settings. Scroll through the list and select Styled text. In the Styled Text dialog, choose Plain Text.

FIX MAIL CRASH WITH HP PRINTER SOFTWARE

The Annoyance: Now that I have installed software for my new HP printer, Mail unexpectedly quits. How can these issues possibly be related? I'm not even trying to print from Mail, and yet, there it goes. The HP software is the only software I've installed recently, so I know that's the root of the problem—I just can't figure out why.

The Fix: The problem is with a font—specifically Times RO—that the HP printer software installs. (This can be a problem in the HP OfficeJet 5500 series or in the HP PSC series.) The fix is to simply delete this font. In the Finder, search for Times RO and then drag the file to the Trash.

UPGRADE MAIL'S SPELLCHECKER

The Annoyance: The spellchecker in Mail stinks. It doesn't give me enough spelling suggestions—it often just tells me that I'm wrong. Well, duh. It's kind of like when you tell your doctor, "It hurts when I do this" and she says, "So don't do that."

The Fix: Mac OS X comes with an open source spellchecker called Ispell, which is used for Mail, TextEdit, and other applications that want to take advantage of it. Ispell is a fairly basic spellchecker that doesn't offer a lot in the way of suggestions.

You can replace Ispell with a better open source (and free) spellchecker called CocoAspell (*http://cocoaspell. leuski.net/*). CocoAspell is a Mac OS X version of the Unix Aspell spellchecker. CocoAspell does a significantly better job supplying alternatives to your misspelled word than the built-in Ispell does.

After you install CocoApsell, you have to tell Mail to use it:

1. Open a new message window.
2. Choose the Spelling command from the Edit → Spelling menu.
3. In the dialog that appears, go to the Diction pop-up menu and select an Aspell dictionary, such as "American English (Aspell)."

You need to do this once only, because Mail remembers this setting.

UPGRADE YOUR MAIL PROGRAM

The Annoyance: I really hate the way Mail creates multiple inboxes for each email account. The searching capability is weak, and there aren't many options. (For example, I can't change encoding formats used with attachments.) I also find Mail to be really slow. Oh well, I guess I'll have to wait for Apple to upgrade Mail and hope for the best, right?

The Fix: Actually, it sounds like you're ready for an upgrade to a better mail program. There are nearly two dozen alternatives to Mail, and several of them are significantly better. (This isn't only coming from me—check out the reviews at *Macworld*, *MacAddict*, *MacUserUK*, and other magazines.) Despite the plethora of options, I suggest you first consider two superior email applications. These two programs take radically different approaches, so neither is right for everyone, but you may be happy with one or the other.

Microsoft Entourage

Part of the Microsoft Office suite, Entourage is also available as a standalone mail package (*http://www.microsoft. com/mac*). Truly, Entourage is the Cadillac of Mac email applications. Full featured and sporting a lush user interface, Entourage also includes an integrated calendar and address book that you can share over a network. You can even use Entourage as a client to Microsoft's Exchange Server. This application also includes some good information management tools: buttons for easy navigation between email, address book, calendars, and notes, and a Custom Views feature that lets you combine information from all these areas in different ways. One caveat: all this luxury makes Entourage a big piece of software that doesn't always corner very quickly.

Mailsmith

Mailsmith from Bare Bones Software (*http://www.bare-bones.com/products/mailsmith*) takes the opposite approach of Entourage, aiming its lean-and-mean interface at power users, focusing on performing basic email very well. Mailsmith is faster than Mail and Entourage, and it's flexible. For instance, there's good integration with the Mac OS X Address Book, but Mailsmith doesn't force you to use it—you can use the application's own built-in address book if you find Apple's database lacking. Mailsmith also offers intelligent handling of HTML messages, which I mentioned earlier in the chapter. It strips out the HTML code, displays clean text, and appends the original HTML as an attachment. The powerful filtering capabilities are great for people who need to automatically organize and manage email, and AppleScript support is everywhere. Mailsmith's interface is not as polished as Entourage's interface, and it is a bit rough around the edges. For instance, drag-and-drop is the only way to manually file a message into a folder. (It could benefit from a pop-up menu a la Emailer.)

The rest of the pack

If you want to continue to look for an email package that best fits your needs, there are plenty of choices, each with its own dedicated fan base. Eudora (*http://www.eudora.com*), a popular email application that was once the "power user's" email of choice, is now showing its age. The interface, which hasn't been changed much over the past decade, consists of many separate windows and power features tucked away in obscure menus and commands. Despite the step learning curve, fans like Eudora for its able text tools and huge feature list. You can adjust almost everything in Eudora, assuming you have time to read the 400-page PDF manual.

PowerMail from CTM Development (*http://www.ctmdev.com*) is a much simpler email client with an interface reminiscent of the old Claris Emailer. If you're looking for a quick way to search your email archives, PowerMail is notable for its lightning search engine, which may be faster than that of any Mac OS X mail client.

Nisus Email (*http://www.nisus.com*) is notable for its ability to integrate with a word processor.

ENTOURAGE

SPEED UP ENTOURAGE

The Annoyance: Entourage never really burned rubber, but it was fast enough when I first installed it. Lately, however, I've noticed that Entourage is a lot slower than it used to be. Is this email fatigue?

The Fix: In a way, it actually is email fatigue. Over time, Entourage's database of email becomes cluttered, mixed up, or otherwise inefficient. The fix is to rebuild the database. It's not as technical as it sounds—just hold the Option key as you launch Entourage. A dialog appears (as shown in Figure 2-9) that offers one of two options: Typical Rebuild or Advanced Rebuild. Try the Typical Rebuild first. If you are still experiencing slow performance or problems, then try the Advanced Rebuild. Before you use the Advanced Rebuild option, however, you should back up the Entourage data files.

Archive Entourage

Do you have a log jam of old email that you'd like to move out of Entourage but are not ready to delete? You can archive it with Entourage Email Archive X ($20, *http://www.softhing.com/eeax/info.html*), which lets you move thousands of email messages, attachments, or both. Archiving old messages keeps Entourage's database smaller, which keeps Entourage performance up to par. Entourage Email Archive X gives you a variety of formats to choose from, including several that let you browse them using Entourage or a word processor.

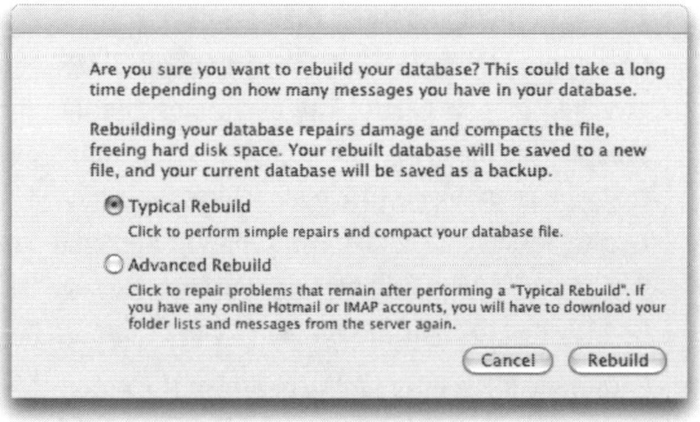

Figure 2-9. When you hold down the Option key while launching Entourage, you get two options for rebuilding the database.

REMOVE RECENTLY DELETED ADDRESSES

The Annoyance: Entourage doesn't seem to understand the meaning of "delete." Say I delete an email address from the Entourage address book. Later, when I'm addressing a new message, a deleted address auto-appears in the To: field. How do I tell Entourage to quit suggesting an address that should no longer exist?

The Fix: Entourage has a feature called Recent Addresses that keeps tabs on addresses you have recently used. Unfortunately, Entourage isn't smart enough to know when you've deleted an address, so it continues to suggest deleted entries. The fix is to delete your dead email addresses from Entourage's Recent Address list. This isn't at all obvious, but it's easy:

1. Go to the Entourage menu and select Mail & News Preferences.
2. Click the Compose tab. Here you should see a section called Recent Addresses at the bottom of the window. This is the source of the annoyance.
3. Click the Clear button to erase the list of recent addresses. Your deleted email addresses should now be gone for good. (Of course, sending more email will replenish the valid recent addresses.)

If the Recent Addresses features is just too annoying to deal with, you can turn it off by unchecking the box next to "Display a list of recently used addresses when addressing messages." Now, Entourage suggests only addresses that are actually in your address book when you address a new message.

CREATE A REMINDER FOR A MESSAGE

The Annoyance: Sometimes, I'll leave a message in my inbox to remind me I still need to deal with it. The problem is, several days later, I forget it's there, because there are dozens of newer messages on top. Obviously, my system doesn't work too well, but isn't Entourage supposed to have a reminder feature that could help?

The Fix: Indeed it does, and you can create a reminder that is linked to the original email message. You do this with Entourage's Flag feature. Once a message is flagged and linked to a reminder, you won't have to keep the message in your inbox; you can file it wherever you want. Here's how to create a reminder:

1. In Entourage, click the Mail button to bring up the Mail window.
2. Click on your Inbox.

3. Click the email message you want to flag.

4. In the toolbar, click the flag icon and hold it down.

5. From the pop-up menu, choose Flag and Follow-up. An event dialog appears (see Figure 2-10).

6. Enter the date and time you want the reminder to appear. You can also type a note to remind yourself what you need to do.

When the time is right, you receive a message on screen (as shown in Figure 2-11). When you click Open Item, the original email message opens.

Figure 2-10. When you create an Entourage reminder linked to an email message, you can set the date for when you want to see the reminder.

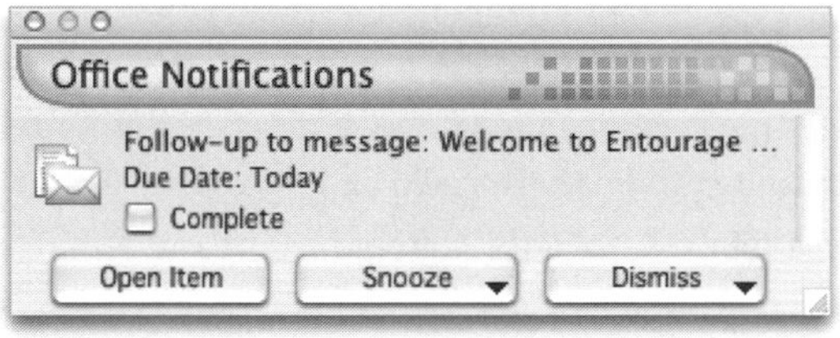

Figure 2-11. This notification is linked to the original email; clicking the Open Item button opens the message.

SYNC ENTOURAGE WITH APPLE ADDRESS BOOK

The Annoyance: I wish Entourage used Mac OS X's Address Book. I have other applications using Address Book, but Entourage has its own. This means I have to type email addresses in two places, which seems pretty dumb in this age of smart software.

The Fix: I'm not a big fan of Apple's Address Book because others (including Entourage's) are more sophisticated, in that they provide more complex searching, sorting, reporting, and sharing. But if you have fax software or other applications tapping into the Apple Address Book, the desire for a single-user database makes sense. The fix is to sync Entourage with Address Book. At this point, iSync doesn't work (another annoyance), but there

---

RECLAIM HARD DISK SPACE

Like Apple Mail and Mailsmith, Entourage stores attached files as part of the email message database. This means if you've copied attachments that you've received to Finder folders, you have two copies. You also have two copies of files that you've sent—your originals and the encoded copies attached to email in your Sent Items folder.

Entourage has a nifty tool to get rid of the redundancy and reclaim the hard disk space—the Remove All Attachments command in the Message window. To use it, first select all of your messages in the Sent Items folder and then choose the command. Next, choose messages that you've read where you've saved the attachments, and then choose Remove All Attachments again.

When you are done, rebuild message database: Quit Entourage, hold the Option key, and relaunch Entourage. Rebuilding condenses the database, which frees up the hard disk space for more interesting items, such as more iTunes or GarageBand songs.

is a free AppleScript written by Paul Berkowitz that does the job. Sync Entourage-Address Book lets you use Entourage as your central database while letting the other applications that use Address Book stay up to speed.

Sync Entourage-Address Book is available at the Script-Builders web site (search for the keyword "Entourage" at *http://www.scriptbuilders.net*). There are different versions for Jaguar and for Panther, so make sure you download the one created for the version of Mac OS X you are using.

EUDORA

TOOLS TO HELP THE EUDORA'S TOOLBAR

The Annoyance: Eudora's toolbar just isn't doing it for me. It doesn't have what I need, and it includes items I don't want. Also, it's funny looking.

The Fix: Though it is ugly, Eudora's toolbar is almost totally customizable. You can add a button to activate for any menu action or command, and even a script. You can also remove buttons:

- To add a new button, hold the ⌘ key while you click between two toolbar buttons. A new button appears. Now choose a menu command (or a script that is listed in a menu).

- To remove a button, ⌘-click on the button and click Remove in the dialog that appears.

- You can also move the toolbar with Option-⌘-drag.

- Finally, if Eudora's toolbar doesn't meet the aesthetic level of the rest of the Mac, try setting the icons to small. Go to the Special menu and select Settings. Click on the Toolbar icon and click only the checkbox next to Small Icons.

SORTING OUT SORTING

The Annoyance: I now have so many email messages in Eudora that when I search or sort, I still must scroll through a million messages. (Well, maybe not quite a million, but far too many.) I could set up a more complex search to narrow it down, but I don't want to work that hard. I wish I could sort by date, and then sort by another column.

The Fix: One of the reasons you still use Eudora (which still looks like it was designed for System 7) is that it can do powerful chores. In this case, you want to perform a complex sort. First, perform a sort the normal way: open a mailbox window and then click a column heading to sort on the column. To sort on a field that is not displayed as a column, choose Sort from the Special menu and choose a field from the submenu. Now, hold the Shift key down while you choose another field from Special → Sort. If you first sort by Date and then Shift-Sort by Sender, the messages are grouped chronologically, and, for each date, listed alphabetically by sender. To sort in the opposite order, hold the Option key while you sort.

GOOGLE SEARCH FROM EUDORA

Want to search Google from within Eudora? Select a word or phrase in an email message and Control-click it to bring up a contextual menu. A menu pops up with a Search Web command. Choosing this command launches your web browser with the Google search results for your term. You need Eudora 6.1 and later for this trick.

If you're running a version of Eudora before 6.1, you can accomplish the same thing by adding a free script called Eudora Google by Jon Schalliol (*http://www.schalliol.com/software*). To use it, select text in an email message and then select Eudora Google from the Scripts menu.

DELETE OLD EUDORA MAILBOXES

The Annoyance: I've created mailboxes specifically for projects, some of which have long since concluded. The old mailboxes are piling up, but amazingly, there's no obvious way to delete them. You'd think that selecting a mailbox and pressing Delete would work, but it doesn't.

The Fix: You're close. You need to go to the Window menu and select Mailboxes. In the Mailboxes window that appears, click the Mailbox you want to remove and select the Delete key. An "are you sure" dialog appears; click the Remove It button.

You can also rename mailboxes by using the old Mac trick of renaming to reorder mailboxes. So if you want your Zombies mailbox to appear first, add a space before the Z in the name.

AOL TOLL-FREE SUPPORT

Ever get tired of wasting hours searching through AOL's FAQs and other web-support pages for an answer? Ever wish you could talk to an actual human being? AOL actually offers toll-free support, 24 hours a day, 7 days a week. You won't find the phone numbers in the support area. To get them, type in the keyword "Call AOL."

Actually, as long as you're reading this, I'll save you the trouble. AOL's number for Mac tech support is 888-265-8007. If you happen to have a Windows PC with AOL on it, the number is 888-346-3704.

AOL

GAG THE TALKING MAILBOX

The Annoyance: I feel like throwing my coffee mug at my Mac every time AOL announces, "You've got mail." I can't just turn off the sound, because I need the sound turned on for other things. I just want AOL to shut up.

The Fix: Hey, you should count your blessings that all software isn't verbally inclined, telling you that "Your file is downloaded," or "You have a spreadsheet." Not consoled? Okay, fine. Here's how to shut AOL up. Log into AOL, go to the toolbar and choose Settings → Preferences. Now, click Toolbar and Sound. Uncheck the box labeled "Enable AOL Sounds," and AOL becomes your silent partner.

DEAL WITH OVERACTIVE AOL SPAM FILTERING

The Annoyance: I've noticed that AOL is now moving legitimate incoming email to the Spam folder. I only know this because I checked my mail with a web browser and found email that I was expecting labeled as spam. Is there any way to see what's in the Spam folder from within the AOL software? More importantly, how do I stop this feature or at least tone it down?

The Fix: To see your Spam folder from within AOL, use the keyword "Spam Folder." This shows you the same Spam folder you saw with your web browser. You can de-spamify a wrongly accused message by selecting it and clicking the button called "This is Not Spam." This moves it back to the inbox.

As to why this is happening, AOL now offers a relatively new feature called Advanced Spam Filtering. That's great, but it's turned on by default and you can't turn it off—at least, not from AOL for Mac OS X. (Note to AOL: *bad idea.*) But you can with AOL for Windows. If you happen to have Microsoft's Virtual PC, you can disable Advanced Spam Filtering with AOL 8 or AOL 9 for Windows. If you don't have Virtual PC, find a friend with Windows.

DOWNLOAD EMAIL FROM MULTIPLE EMAIL ACCOUNTS

The Annoyance: I need a single tool to download email from AOL and another POP email account I have from work. It's a real pain to use different email applications for different accounts.

The Fix: You need AOL Communicator for Mac OS X, a free email application from AOL that lets you download and manage email and address books (as well as instant messaging) from multiple AOL screen name accounts. AOL Communicator handles other (non-AOL) POP and IMAP accounts as well.

AOL offers it for free. To get it, go to Keyword: AOL Communicator. You need Mac OS X 10.2 or later.

Internet
ANNOYANCES

Think back to the early 1970s, when the visionary scientists at the Defense Advanced Research Projects Agency (DARPA) were creating what would become the global "Internet." Did they realize how annoying the Internet would become? Was it a design feature? Probably not. Yet unwieldy lists of bookmarks, irritating banner ads, and searches that yield hundreds of thousands of results make a good case for annoyance by design—not to mention some of the annoying things people say in blogs, discussion forums, and even news sites.

Except for avoiding certain web sites, there's little you can do to avoid annoying content. But starting with the next page, you'll find over 40 tips that will keep your blood pressure under control as you browse the Web, search with Google and Sherlock, and chat up your wired pals. You'll also learn about some browser features that exist outside of Safari—in other web browsers.

WEB BROWSING

CONSIDER YOUR BROWSER OPTIONS

The Annoyance: I hate it when Safari...

The Fix: Before you go any further, did you know that Safari isn't the only browser game in town? Sure, Safari has a lot going for it, and it keeps getting better with each new version. You can workaround a lot of Safari's annoyances, but switching to another browser can alleviate Safari's quirks while giving you features that Safari doesn't have. If you don't care for Safari's macho user interface, upside-down tabs, and lack of advanced cookie settings, take a look at the competition.

Mac OS X. OmniWeb (*http://www.omnigroup.com*) is a very attractive and powerful web browser that actually costs money ($30). Still, it has a number of devoted fans who appreciate the clean interface and powerful, unique features. For instance, it has some of the best bookmark management tools. On the downside, OmniWeb is one of the slower browsers I've tested. If you want tabbed browsing, you need OmniWeb 5 or later.

For fast browsing, check out the free (open source) Mozilla, Firefox, Camino, and Thunderbird. All are hosted at *http://www.mozilla.org*, though they are different projects. Thunderbird is an up-and-comer, a bit earlier in development than the others, but one to watch out for. Another browser, Netscape, is similar in look and feel to Mozilla, but is much bigger and includes a built-in email client, which I don't recommend using. You can find Netscape at *http://channels.netscape.com/ns/browsers/default.jsp*. Firefox has some innovative features, including an extension architecture. All of these browsers are notable for their good performance.

What about Internet Explorer? It's bit behind in the times when it comes to features, but is good for keeping on hand for when nothing else works. I don't recommend the Mac version of Opera (due to its confusing interface and poor performance) or the outdated iCab.

> **WHAT'S WRONG WITH EMAIL IN A BROWSER?**
> Netscape's email client has many of the features that most people need, including spam blocking email searching, and the ability to handle multiple email accounts.
>
> However, there are problems with the email-in-a-browser concept. Every time you need email, you first launch your browser and then switch to the email function, a more complex procedure than with other mail programs. Netscape is also a big, three-in-one application that includes an instant messaging function. This can take a big chunk of your Mac's RAM and processor time, which can slow your Mac down. Netscape also has a more complicated interface than Apple's Mail, Entourage, or Mailsmith; armed with this knowledge, I doubt you'll be compelled to switch to Netscape.

So which web browser is the best? That's almost like asking what's the best flavor of ice cream. At this point, Camino is my favorite (*http://www.mozilla.org/projects/camino/*). Unlike Mozilla, Netscape, Firefox, and Thunderbird, Camino is not available on Windows. Like Safari and OmniWeb, Camino is designed specifically for Mac OS X. Camino follows Apple's own user interface guidelines more closely than Safari. For instance, tabs in Camino look like standard Panther tabs when you run it in Mac OS X 10.3 and standard Jaguar tabs in Mac OS X 10.2. Keychain integration often works better in Camino than in Safari, and many believe that Camino's type rendering is superior to Safari's.

Camino also has some appealing features not found in Safari or Firefox, such as the fabulous Bookmark All Tabs feature (see the later annoyance Bookmark All Tabs) and the power-user keyword features (see the later sidebar Camino Keywords for Faster Browsing). Camino Version 0.8 and later has another feature not found in Safari or

Firefox: the ability to prevent web sites from adjusting the size of your browser window (go to Camino's Preferences, and then to the Web features pane). More features are described throughout the chapter. Camino's performance is also excellent, second only to Safari. One downside: Camino lacks built-in help and a manual, probably due to the fact that Camino hasn't reached full 1.0 version status yet.

BUNCHES OF BROWSERS

There's no risk in trying out different web browsers. You can download multiple browsers and even run them at the same time for a side-by-side comparison. The only thing you can't do, however, is simultaneously run different versions of the same browser (such as Camino's 0.7 and 0.8 Versions) without a little trickery. To get away with this, move the older version out of the Applications folder before installing the newer version. This doesn't work with Netscape and Mozilla, however; these are both variations of the same browser. To run these two together, use Fast User Switching (in Mac OS X 10.3 and later) to switch to a different user, and run Netscape and Mozilla in different users.

CHANGE YOUR DEFAULT BROWSER

The Annoyance: Okay, I give up. I'm not using Safari, but Panther doesn't seem to have a way to let me change my default browser as I could in Jaguar? Is there any way to tell Panther to launch any another browser besides Safari?

The Fix: Well before Mac OS 9, Macs had an Internet preference setting to change your default web browser and email program—a setting Apple removed with Panther.

(Apparently, Apple took a cue from Microsoft in "encouraging" you to use the company browser.) However, you can still change the default web browser; Apple just has made it harder to find. The secret is in Safari's preferences. Go to the General pane and select a browser from the Default Web Browser pop-up menu (as shown in Figure 3-1).

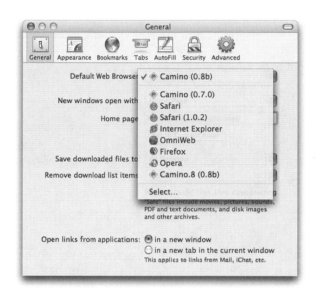

Figure 3-1. Go to the General pane of Safari Preferences to change Panther's default web browser.

OUTSIDE OF SAFARI RIGHT-CLICK TO NAVIGATE

If you have a two- or three-button mouse, Camino and Firefox have a navigation feature that you might go for. Both let you right-click (or Control-click) and choose "Back" and "Forward" from the contextual menu. This little feature doesn't mean much with a one-button mouse, but it can speed up your browsing if your mouse has a second button.

To change your default email application, launch Mail and go to Mail → Preferences. In the General pane, chose a new email app in the Default Email Reader pop-up menu.

BOOKMARK ALL TABS

The Annoyance: I like Safari's Open in Tabs feature for folders of bookmarks. Click on a folder bookmark. The "Open in Tabs" command is under all of the individual bookmarks. This loads each of the bookmarked pages in its own tab. Neat. Only it's a royal pain to create the folders in the first place. You first have to create and name the folder. Then you have to bookmark each web page. Then, in Safari's Bookmarks window, you have to drag each individual bookmark into the folder. Isn't there an easy way?

The Fix: There isn't an easy way in Safari, but in Camino, it's a snap. Camino's version of "Open in Tabs" is a type of bookmark folder called "grouped tabs folder." Its icon is a folder with a picture of a fishtailed bookmark. When you click a grouped tab, the bookmarks all open in their own tabs.

Now, here's the cool part. Creating a grouped tab in Camino is the same as creating a single bookmark except for checking one extra checkbox. Here's how it works:

1. Open all the web pages you want to bookmark in separate tabs.

2. Select the Add Page to Bookmarks command (⌘-D).

3. In the dialog that opens (shown in Figure 3-2) turn on the "Bookmark all tabs." (This is the extra step.)

4. Change the Name of the group to something more descriptive, such as "Handy Mac Sites."

5. Use the Create In pop-up menu to place the new grouped tab in the Bookmark menu or toolbar.

6. Click OK, and you're done.

Figure 3-2. Click the "Bookmark all tabs" checkbox, and Camino creates a grouped tabs folder that opens all of the tabs at once.

Safari Tip

Ever get surfers regret? That's when you wish you hadn't clicked a link or mistyped that URL, because now the page is taking a while to load. There's no need to wait around. Press the Escape key or the Mac's standard Cancel keyboard shortcut (⌘-.), and Safari stops loading the page, presenting only the portion that it has fetched from the web server.

STAY CONNECTED WITH DSL

The Annoyance: I ordered a DSL line so my Mac would always be online. I love the high-speed web surfing, but my iBook keeps asking me if I want to stay connected. If I don't respond, it disconnects me. This made sense when I was connected with a dial-up modem, but now it's just plain annoying.

The Fix: Although it isn't obvious, there is an option you can choose to tell Mac OS X to quit bugging you. Most people would look in the Internet Connect utility, but you won't find it there. Instead, open System Preferences and follow these steps:

1. Go to the Network preference panel.

2. Choose the Ethernet configuration used for your DSL connection. (This can be "Built-in Ethernet" or another configuration, depending on how you have it set up.)

3. Click on the PPPoE tab.

4. Now click the PPPoE Options button near the bottom.

5. In the sheet (as shown in Figure 3-3), uncheck the boxes next to "Prompt every 15 minutes to maintain connection" and "Disconnect if idle for 10 minutes."

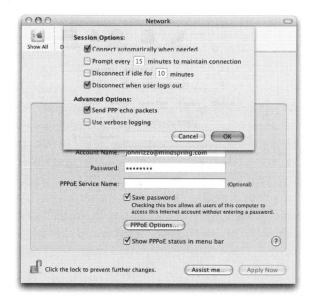

Figure 3-3. Use these settings in System Preferences if you want your DSL connection to stay connected.

While you're at it, check "Connect automatically when needed" and "Disconnect when user logs out." Now, you'll never need to use the Connect command. Just fire up your web browser and surf away.

BLOCKING BANNER ADS

The Annoyance: Web advertisers keep trying to get my attention with an ever-increasing barrage of ads. All the blinking and moving banners and pop-ups make it difficult to read the actual content of the page.

The Fix: I could go into a spiel about how advertising makes free Internet information possible and how the people who run sites like MacInTouch are not getting rich on ads. I could also make a case for the opposite argument: we taxpayers fronted the money to start up the Web, so we shouldn't be bothered by ads. Whatever your view on web advertising, the fact is that blocking ads can cause you aggravation. That's because the technologies used in ads also make web pages function. Attempts to restrict ads can also disable a web page in ways you may not be aware of. For instance, most web browsers let you disable JavaScript, which is often used to presenting banner ads and pop-ups. The problem here is that JavaScript can also provide a host of useful features, such as providing submenus when you move your cursor over a spot, launching audio or video when you click a link, and delivering picture slide shows.

With that warning, here are some tools that allow you to block ads on the Web:

- PithHelmet is Mike Solomon's free utility for Safari running in Mac OS X 10.3 and later. PithHelmet (*http://www.culater.net/software.php*) works as a plug-in for Safari, in that you access its settings from Safari's Preferences. As Figure 3-4 shows, the PithHelmet preferences menu includes a blacklist of ad hosts that provide many of the ads that appear on different web sites. PithHelmet also does general blocking of blocks banner ads, JavaScript, animated GIFs, and Flash ads. However, PithHelmet sometimes blocks images that aren't ads from loading. If you leave the Hide Blocked Content setting turned on, you won't know if you're missing something good. Fortunately, you can exempt any web site from being blocked by Control-clicking (or right-clicking) on the web page (as in the bottom portion of Figure 3-4). If you decide that PithHelmet is not for you, you can uninstall it by following the directions in the Readme file.

Figure 3-4. PithHelmet adds a pane to Safari Preferences to configure ad blocking. A contextual menu (shown at the bottom of this figure) lets you exempt specific sites from blocking.

- Privoxy (*http://www.privoxy.org*) is another free utility blocks banner and pop-up ads, and also helps manage cookies. It's more difficult to set up than PithHelmet, but it works with *any* web browser. Privoxy isn't a Mac-specific piece of software, but it doesn't have its own user interface—use a web browser to configure it. Privoxy is available for many different platforms, so make sure you get the Mac version.

- If you don't use Safari or you don't like depending on unsupported freeware, you can pay $30 for Allume's Internet Cleanup (*http://www.allume.com/mac/clean-up/*). It blocks banner ads and pop-ups, lets you separate tracking cookies from good cookies, and is very easy to use. Internet Cleanup can also block, detect, and eliminate spyware (software that you download

without realizing that it keeps track of your Internet habits). It even tells you if a piece of spyware is trying to connect to the Internet, as well as preventing the connection. Spyware isn't quite the problem on the Mac that it is for Windows, but it does exist.

SELECTIVELY BLOCK POP-UPS

The Annoyance: I don't mind the banner ads so much, but those pesky pop-up ads make me want to give up computing and learn to use a slide rule.

The Fix: The problem isn't blocking pop-up ads, because just about every web browser lets you block pop-ups (the exception being Internet Explorer). The problem is that many web sites use pop-up windows for nonadvertising purposes. For instance, CNN uses pop-ups to display video footage, and Internet radio sites use them to display a music control panel. So rather than just setting your browser to block pop-ups and forgetting about it, get to know how to turn blocking off and on in your browser.

This is very easy in Safari; you can toggle pop-up blocking with ⌘-K or by using "Block Pop-Up Windows" in Safari's application menu. The problem with toggling pop-up blocking is that you might not know when you need to turn pop-ups back on again. You might click a link and nothing happens. Camino Version 0.8 offers a kind of selective pop-up blocking that lets you create a list of sites for which you want to allow pop-ups. This list is called a "whitelist," the opposite of "blacklist." To set up your whitelist, follow these steps:

1. Open Camino's Preferences (⌘-,).

2. Click on the Web Features icon in the toolbar.

3. Turn on the Popup Blocking checkbox.

4. Now click the "Edit Allowed sites" button. In the dialog that appears, you can type in the web addresses for the sites that you want to add to the whitelist.

5. Click the Done button when you've finished entering the web sites that can display pop-up windows on your screen.

You can now leave pop-up blocking turned on all the time, and the pop-ups that you want continue to work for the sites you've specified.

FLASH BE GONE

The Annoyance: Waiting for Shockwave Flash animations to load can be a real waste of time. It's annoying in ads but can be even more annoying on web pages. Some web developers put Flash to good use, but other times its only purpose it seems to serve is to showcase the drawing prowess of the illustrator.

The Fix: Some of the blocking software described in the earlier annoyance Blocking Banner Ads, including PithHelmet, blocks Flash ads. However, if you never want to see Flash again, you can remove the Flash player with the Macromedia Flash Player Uninstaller. Macromedia offers it as a troubleshooting tool, but you can use it to delete all versions of the Flash Player from the web browsers on your Mac. You can download the Uninstaller from Macromedia's site at *http://www.macromedia.com/support/flash/downloads.html*.

SITE-SPECIFIC COOKIE BLOCKING

The Annoyance: It's annoying to spend time filling out a form at a web site, only to have the fruits of my labor rejected. "Turn on your cookies," says the web site. So I open my browser's preferences and turn cookies on. Yet, when I try the web form again, it's still telling me to turn cookies on. What's going on?

The Fix: First, let me say that you cannot have this problem with Safari, due to Safari's lack of advanced security and privacy settings. Safari doesn't let you specify web sites to block or accept cookies from, and there is no setting that asks if you want to accept cookies.

I'd rather have the advanced cookie settings of most other browsers (including Camino, Internet Explorer, OmniWeb, and Opera). However, site-specific cookie blocking can cause this annoyance by telling your browser to block

---

RENDEZVOUS WEB SITES

You may have wondered why Rendezvous (*http://www.apple.com/macosx/rendezvous*) appears in Safari and Camino. Rendezvous isn't used on the Internet but can be used to manage resources on your local network. Some devices on your local network, such as printers, a web cam, or FTP and web servers have a small administrative web site that uses Rendezvous (known to the rest of world as Zeroconf) to automatically configure them. You can access these local sites with Safari or Camino to change settings or do other administration tasks.

To see Rendezvous-enabled web sites on your local network in Safari or Camino, bring up the bookmarks page and select Rendezvous in the left column. Devices that have Rendezvous sites appear in the right column. In Camino, you can also see Rendezvous devices without going to the bookmarks page. To see the list of Rendezvous devices, use Go → Local Network Services.

You can also turn your Mac into a Rendezvous-enabled web server that others can see. Create web pages in your Sites folder (*~/Sites*) and turn on Web Sharing in the Sharing pane of System Preferences.

---

cookies from a specific site. So, even when you turn on acceptance of cookies, your browser is still blocking cookies from this particular site. Here's the fix for most browsers:

1. Open the browser's preferences.

2. Go to the cookies section (often listed under Security or Privacy).

3. Search for the cookie being blocked and delete the cookie preference for that site.

Occasionally, when you return to that web page, you have to click the Back button to let that site send you the cookie again, which you need to accept.

Now, this may seem to be an annoying procedure in itself, and admittedly, it is. However, Camino Version 0.8 and later has a slick feature that lets you change your mind on cookie acceptance without having to delete and recreate the preference:

1. Open Camino's Preferences (⌘-,).

2. Go to the Privacy pane.

3. Click the Edit Site Permissions button (as shown in the top part of Figure 3-5).

4. In the list of cookie permissions, find the web site in question. When you click the arrows to the right of the word "Deny," a little pop-up menu lets you change "Deny" to "Allow" (as shown in the bottom of Figure 3-5).

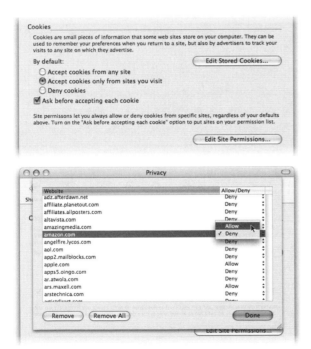

Figure 3-5. In Camino, you can change site-specific cookie blocking between Allow and Deny with the pop-up menu.

VISIT SITES THAT SAFARI CAN'T HANDLE

The Annoyance: Every once in a while, I come across a web page that Safari can't draw correctly. For instance, I click on a button on a music site to open a music player window but the new window is blank. Nothing happens. Safari just won't do its job.

The Fix: This sounds like a job for Internet Explorer, which you will find in the Applications folder (an optional installation in Panther, but installed by default in earlier Mac OS X incarnations). Yes, it's old-fashioned, slow, and lacks many features found in modern browsers (such as tabs and pop-up blocking), but Internet Explorer has one thing going for it—it can render most web pages you throw at it. Most web sites are designed and tested to work with the world's most popular web browser, which is—you got it—Internet Explorer. You probably don't want to make Internet Explorer your default browser, but it is handy to keep around for those times when your default browser just can't handle a web page that you really need access to (such as your bank's web site).

If you deleted IE and want it back, you can download it from *http://www.microsoft.com/mac*.

---

t i p

If you find a page that Safari can't handle, report it to Apple with Safari's bug reporting feature. Go to Safari → Report Bugs to Apple… to open a bug reporting window with the web address of the problematic URL. You can describe the problem and click the Submit button. (You can also add a bug report button next to the Google Search field by going to View → Bug.) Apple's Safari programmers keep a list of all of the problem sites and rank them for testing when developing a new version of Safari. The more people report a particular web site, the better the chance it has of getting on Apple's to-do list of fixes.

FORCE INTERNET EXPLORER TO RELOAD A PAGE

The Annoyance: Internet Explorer's Refresh button doesn't always seem to reload the web page. There are times when I know a web page has been updated, but the Refresh button just brings up the same old page.

The Fix: Internet Explorer's Refresh button isn't really a reload button. That is, it doesn't ask the web server to send you the web page again. Instead, it checks the timestamp of the page on the server. If the timestamp

hasn't changed, Internet Explorer reloads the page from a cache file on your hard disk, not from the web server. To force Internet Explorer to reload a page from the web server, hold down the Option key while clicking the Refresh button.

OUTSIDE OF SAFARI: USE A BROWSER TO SEE WHAT'S ON YOUR IPOD

Camino and OmniWeb both can perform an odd trick. Drag any hard drive to any Camino or OmniWeb window, and the browser creates a web page version of the drive. You can then browse the drive by clicking the links to folders. Folders that are invisible to the Finder become visible in Camino and OmniWeb.

The iPod is a supped-up FireWire drive, so you can also drag its Finder icon to a Camino or OmniWeb window. It displays a normally invisible folder called iPod_Control. Inside this folder is a subfolder called Music. Open Music to reveal a flock of folders called F1, F2, F3, and so on, which contain your music files. Double-click on a music file, and Camino or OmniWeb uses QuickTime to play it. Double-click a text file (such as a note), and OmniWeb displays the text; Camino uses TextEdit to display the text.

OmniWeb, however, can go one step further: when you drag a file or folder to the Desktop, OmniWeb copies it to your Mac's hard drive. This means you can drag any music file from the iPod to your Mac—something that you ordinarily can't do. If you want to copy all of the iPod's music to the Mac, drag the Music folder (again, it's found inside the iPod_Control folder) to the Desktop. The music files are still disorganized into the Fx folders, but dragging them into iTunes copies them into your iTunes Music folder.

FORCE SAFARI AND CAMINO TO RENDER LEGIBLE TEXT

The Annoyance: Safari sometimes renders a web page with type that is too small to read, even when I wear my glasses. This forces me to manually enlarge the type size (several times) using the View menu. You'd think Safari would know when type is too tiny and just render it in some default (and legible) size.

The Fix: It's tempting to blame Windows here, because web page type sizes that look just fine in Windows XP can be completely illegible on a Mac. However, even on a Mac, a font size that's legible on one display might not appear so on another. The fix is to tell your browser what text size is too small. Safari doesn't let you do this, but there is a hack you can use.

The Safari hack is a Unix command that you use in Terminal (*/Applications/Utilities*). Quit Safari, launch Terminal, and enter the following command:

```
$ defaults write com.apple.Safari
WebKitMinimumFontSize 10
```

Once this has been set, Safari renders the usually teeny-tiny text at 10-point type or larger. If that's still too small (or too big), try using 12 (or 9) instead of 10 at the end of the command. You don't have to worry about losing control of the text size—you can still use Safari's Make Text Smaller and Make Text Bigger commands from the View menu.

You don't need a hack for Camino, because it has a handy setting for minimum font size. To set a minimum font size in Camino:

1. Open Camino's Preferences (⌘-,).
2. Click on the Appearance icon in the toolbar.
3. Click the Fonts tab.
4. Now click the advanced button and pick a number in the "Minimum font size" pop-up menu.

CHECK SPELLING WITH YOUR BROWSER

The Annoyance: I love that feeling of accomplishment after posting a pithy comment at a discussion forum or a product description at eBay. That is, until I notice the spelling errors I made, for all the world to see. I wish there was a way to avoid this embarrassment and spell check the text fields of web forms.

The Fix: Safari and OmniWeb both have a Spelling item in the Edit menu that you can use to spell check a text field or spell check as you type. Both options use Mac OS X's built-in spellchecker.

For other browsers, you can add a third-party spellchecker, such as Spell Catcher X from Rainmaker ($40, *http://www.rainmakerinc.com*). Not only does Spell Catcher X work with Mozilla, Firefox, Internet Explorer, Opera, and other browsers, but it does with most Mac OS X applications that don't have spellchecking. Spell Catcher X also improves upon the built-in spellchecking of Safari and OmniWeb as well.

Once installed, Spell Catcher X runs in the background as you type, offering multiple ways to check spelling. You can spellcheck selected text after you finish typing, or you can turn on Interactive Checking to have Spell Catcher change recognizable words (such as Shakespeare) as you type. Another mode is Auto-Show Suggestions, which pops up a dialog (as in Figure 3-6) listing spelling suggestions.

Originally called Thunder 7, Spell Catcher X has been around since the days of System 7 and has been sold by different companies at different times; Rainmaker is the latest owner. Not only is Spell Catcher X handy to use a single spellchecking dictionary for your web browser, email, and word processor, but the features that it offers are also top-notch. These include thesauruses, reference

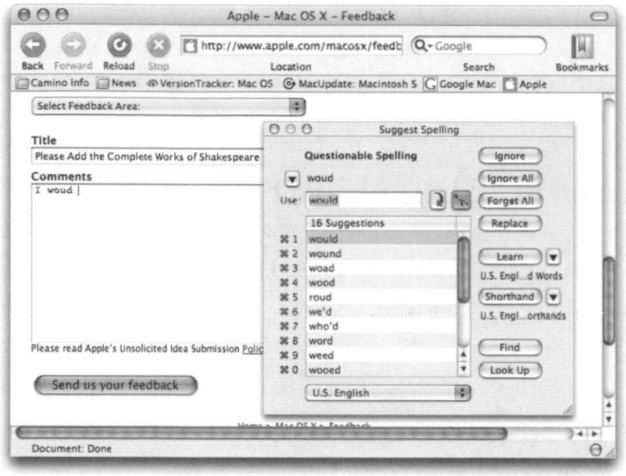

Figure 3-6. With Auto-Show Suggestions turned on, Spell Catcher X brings up a dialog when you mistype a word in a browser (Camino is shown), as well as other applications.

guides for multiple languages, and highly customizable dictionaries. You can even set the spellchecking behavior for different applications.

If Spell Catcher X is more money than you're interested in spending, there is a technique that doesn't cost anything: type your text in TextEdit first, spellcheck it, and cut and paste the text into the web page's text field.

ALPHABETIZE YOUR BOOKMARKS

The Annoyance: What genius decided that browser bookmarks have to be in chronological order—the order in which you bookmarked them? With my Bookmarks menu endlessly scrolling, I can't find anything in there without calling in a search party. Would it kill a browser developer to include an option to alphabetize bookmarks?

The Fix: Once again, this is a matter of which web browser you are using. Several browsers have built-in sorting features. Those that don't offer the ability to search your bookmarks. Here's a rundown of your options:

- Safari doesn't let you alphabetize bookmarks or search them, as many other browsers do. But you can add a free utility, SafariSorter (*http://dearjerry.home.*

> **ACCESS BOOKMARKS OUTSIDE YOUR BROWSER**
> Wouldn't it be cool if you could activate one of your browser's bookmarks without first opening a web browser? Safari Menu, from eDot Solutions (*http://www.edot-studios.com*), is a free utility that adds a menu listing Safari's bookmarks that you can use while you're in any application. There's also a Google command and a "Go to URL" command that brings up a little address window in which to type.
>
> However, Safari Menu is not just for Safari. When you choose a bookmark, Safari Menu launches your default browser. So, if you've set Camino to be your default browser, Safari Menu launches Camino and not Safari (just as you'd like). However, the utility still displays Safari's bookmarks, not that of your browser. The way around this is to export your browser's bookmarks to Safari (Camino has this feature). Or, you can use another utility to synchronize Safari's bookmarks with your default browser. You can do this with the inexpensive shareware application called Bookit ($12), described in the later annoyance One Book File To Rule Them All.

mindspring.com/raisinland/SafariSorter/SafariSorter.html), that alphabetically sorts your bookmarks by name, or by domain names or URLs (as shown in Figure 3-7). You can choose to mix individual bookmarks with bookmark folders or keep them separate. SafariSorter sorts items in the Bookmarks menu and toolbar, or both. The only downside to SafariSorter is that it doesn't sort automatically; if you add a new bookmark, you must run SafariSorter again to sort in that new site.

- Opera 7 (and later) can sort bookmarks by title, URL, and other criteria. To configure Opera to sort your

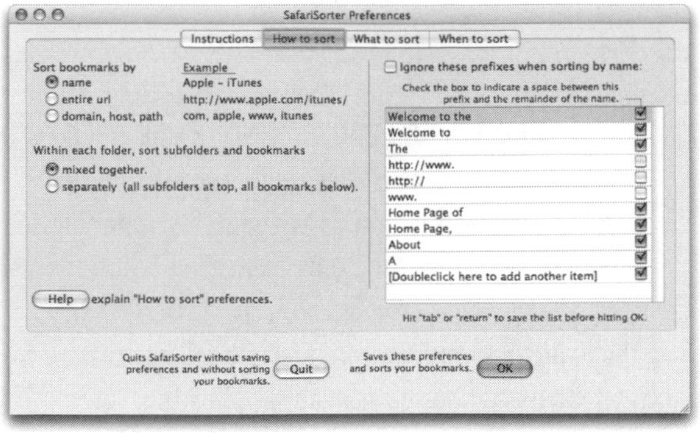

Figure 3-7. SafariSorter's Preferences let you choose how to sort Safari's bookmarks.

bookmarks, click on the Bookmarks icon and then click the View menu above the bookmarks pane. Here, you can select one of the sort criteria and set up Opera so it instantly sorts the items in the Bookmarks menu. Unfortunately, Opera lists all of the folders first, followed by individual bookmarks; you can't mix them up. Opera also has a feature that Safari doesn't: a search field for bookmarks and history.

- OmniWeb 5 also includes built-in bookmark sorting of the Bookmarks window, but not the Bookmarks menu. However, the elegant interface lets you sort a column by clicking on a column heading. One click sorts the column by alphabetical order. A second click reverses the order, and a third click reverts back to the original order. OmniWeb 5 also has a search field in the Bookmarks page.

- Camino can't alphabetize bookmarks either, but it does have a search field for bookmarks and history. Click the Bookmarks icon in the toolbar to switch to the bookmarks window; the search field is in the lower-right corner.

- Firefox also has a search field, but you can't search through the history and bookmarks at the same time.

To access the Bookmarks dialog, select Manage Bookmarks from the Bookmarks menu. To search the History, you must first select History from Firefox's Go menu.

CLEAR DEAD LINKS FROM BOOKMARKS

The Annoyance: You know that drawer you use to throw batteries into? The one where half the batteries are dead, and you have to try them one by one in your flashlight to see if any of them are still good? My Bookmarks menu is kind of like that. However, I don't have the time or patience to try out each one to see if it's dead or even to find the current URLs.

The Fix: OmniWeb is the best browser for keeping your bookmarks current. It automatically checks for dead bookmarks in the background and then reports the results. If it can't connect to a bookmarked web page, it places a yellow exclamation point next to the bookmark, as shown in Figure 3-8. You can try the site yourself by double-clicking the bookmark. If you'd like to see a list of all your dead bookmarks all in one place, click the Unreachable folder in the Collections column. If a web site redirects to a new location, OmniWeb automatically updates the bookmark with the new URL. By the way, the checkmarks next to bookmarks in Figure 3-8 indicate web

Figure 3-8. OmniWeb checks bookmarks automatically and marks dead links with an exclamation point in a yellow triangle icon.

pages that have changed since you last visited them—a handy feature should you want to visits pages only when they're updated. OmniWeb's Dock icon (shown in Figure 3-9) will tell you how many bookmarked web pages have changed.

Figure 3-9. OmniWeb's Dock icon alerts you when it finds bookmarks to web pages that have changed. It lists the number of found pages, as shown here.

For Safari users, there is a utility called Safari Prairiefire ($6, *http://homepage.mac.com/petber/balooba/texts/safari_prairiefire.htm*) that can detect dead bookmarks, though it doesn't come close to OmniWeb's automatic functionality. You use Safari Prairiefire outside of Safari to check the set of bookmarks. It reads Safari's bookmark file and tests each bookmark to see if it's valid and then reports the error codes that it receives. Then, match up the code number with a provided table and decide whether to delete or edit the bookmark. Safari Prairiefire also lets you make changes without actually running Safari, which is a convenient feature.

ONE BOOKMARK FILE TO RULE THEM ALL

The Annoyance: There are so many great web browsers available that I don't want to just settle for one. I like to use the latest versions of different browsers, as well as Internet Explorer. The only problem is that each browser has a different set of bookmarks. Yes, there are utilities to convert bookmarks between some of the browsers, but it's annoying to use multiple utilities to continuously import bookmarks.

The Fix: For those who aren't satisfied with just one browser, Everyday Software's Bookit ($12, *http://www.everydaysoftware.net*) is the answer. Once you've import-

ed the bookmarks from your various browsers, you can use Bookit to edit your list, create and delete folders, and add dividers. Bookit writes identical bookmark files for each of your browsers and can synchronize bookmarks between multiple Macs.

OUTSIDE OF SAFARI:

CAMINO KEYWORDS FOR FASTER BROWSING

Bookmarks start to lose their appeal when you have too many of them. To get around this, Camino and Firefox have a power user feature called "keywords" that lets you get to a web page by typing only a few characters in the address field. If you had a bookmark with a URL as long as your arm you could assign to it a keyword of two or three characters. You do this in the bookmarks page of Camino or Firefox. Find a bookmark, select it, and type ⌘-I. (Camino also has in "i" icon that you can click.) In the dialog that appears, type your keyword. You can now use this keyword in the address field to quickly get to your web page.

Safari doesn't have this feature, but you can add it with the Sagudi utility described in the later section Google.

Bookit has some other bookmark management features as well, such as allowing you to manage bookmarks from a Dock menu or the menu bar. It can also check for dead links (although it can't check for updated links). Bookit also backs up your list of bookmarks, letting you restore older lists if you realize that you've trashed your bookmark list. At the time of this writing, Bookit supports eight browsers: Safari, Camino, OmniWeb, Internet Explorer, Mozilla, Netscape, Opera, and iCal, including the Classic versions of these browsers.

POST A SPAMBOT-PROOF EMAIL ADDRESS

The Annoyance: I like to post one of my email addresses in certain web forums to promote myself and receive feedback. However, my friend says this is a sure-fire way to get deluged with spam (and probably viruses). I certainly don't want more spam, but some of these forums are great opportunities to network. Is there a safe way to do this?

The Fix: Programs called *bots* (short for spambots or webbots) are constantly trawling the Internet for email addresses to add to spam and virus distribution lists. The solution is to use an old low-tech technique called munging that was originally developed for Usenet newsgroups. *Munging* is when you list your email address with inserted words that make sense to a human being, but render the email address useless to a spambot. For example, take this munged address:

luckyjim@earthREMOVE-THISlink.com

Most human readers would recognize that the domain indicated here is *earthlink.com*. Spam programs that try to use this address would get their email returned if you insert the extra words to the *right* of the "at" sign (@). If you munged the left side, as in *luckyREMOVE-THISjim@earthlink.com*, you'd still be safe, but Earthlink (or your ISP) would receive the tons of spam you are avoiding.

Another munging trick is to spell out the "at" sign (@), as in *luckyjim(AT)earthlink.com*. This is a little less intuitive to humans, but makes the address completely invisible to spambots.

PRINT WEB PAGES CLEANLY

The Annoyance: Printing a web page is often a waste of paper. Some pages will have just a line or two of text, while other pages have entire blocks of text chopped off. Other times, the text is so tiny I have to refer to the Mac to figure out what it actually says. And of course, it's a waste of trees to print all those pesky ads.

OUTSIDE OF SAFARI: FIND AS YOU TYPE

You probably know that you can search the text of a web page by typing ⌘-F to bring up a text search dialog box. But did you know that Camino, Firefox, Mozilla, and Netscape allow you to search for text without bringing up the dialog using a feature called "Find As You Type"?

First, click on the web page to make sure the Address field is not active. Now, type a slash (/). The bottom left of the browser window displays the words "Starting find as you type." Next, begin typing the word you're searching for. The browser finds the first instance of the characters you've typed. To search for that same string of characters again, type ⌘-G. If the highlighted word is in a link, you can quickly open it by hitting the Enter key.

The Fix: The basic problem is that most web pages are usually designed for viewing on your screen, not on a printed page. As a result, some web pages are just too wide to fit on a page. If you narrow a page that is designed with a fixed pixel width, the browser cuts off the edge instead of wrapping the text. When this happens, the browser may try to shrink the entire page, resulting in the tiny text syndrome you've encountered. Fortunately, there are a few things you can try:

Look for a Printer-Friendly Version.

News and reviews sites often include a link to a "printer-friendly version" of the page. (At *Macworld.com*, for instance, this link is usually at the end of an article.) This is usually a text version of the page that prints without banner ads or other graphics in a format that fits a standard sheet of paper. If you don't see it, do a text search (⌘-F) for "printer" or "friendly."

Choose Print Preview in the Print dialog box to see what the document will look like. This is a great way to see if the last page is going to contain only a menu from the previous page. Then, enter the page range to leave out the pages that don't have any content.

Some web sites still use frames, a once fashionable element of web page design that divides portions of a web page. An easy way tell if a web page uses frames is to choose Edit → Select All (⌘-A). If the entire page isn't selected, then it is divided into frames. For better results, print the frame separately. This is easy to do in just about every browser. Just Control-click (or right-click) on the frame you want to print and choose Print Frame.

If the web page is particularly wide, you can prevent the tiny text syndrome by switching to landscape mode in Page Setup (in the File menu). Landscape mode is the horizontal page icon.

Mac OS X's ability to save any document as a PDF file sometimes works when you're printing web pages. In the Print dialog box (⌘-P), click the Save As PDF button at the bottom of the window and save the PDF file to your disk. When you open the PDF file, you should see that the web page has been saved as a standard There are drawbacks to this technique: you print all the ads along with the content, and you still might print text that is too small to read—right back where you started. And what's the point of that?

GOOGLE

MAC-SPECIFIC GOOGLING

The Annoyance: What a waste of time it is to filter out the non-Mac chaff from the Mac-specific wheat of Google results. For instance, when I do a search using "Safari" as a term, I get thousands of results that refer to trips to Africa, the beach (as in Surfin' Safari), and all kinds of items that have nothing to do with Safari, the browser.

The Fix: You can weed out everything not Mac-related by going to the Mac-specific Google page at *http://www.google.com/mac*. This is a great place to search for everything Mac and only Mac, including solutions to problems, software and hardware, and peripherals. When you search from this page, every result has something to do with the Mac.

Unfortunately, Safari's Google search field doesn't use this page. However, once you get to Google/Mac, a simple drag-and-drop creates a bookmark in your Bookmarks bar: drag the icon to the left of the URL in the address field to the bookmarks bar. This works with other browsers, including Camino and Internet Explorer.

There is a way to use Safari's address bar to search Google/Mac. All you need to do is add a plug-in. Check out the next annoyance Expand Safari's Googling and Beyond.

EXPAND SAFARI'S GOOGLING AND BEYOND

The Annoyance: Safari's Google search field is nice, but it searches only the main Google area, not Google Mac, Google Images, or Google News. Is there a way to get at other search engines from Safari's search field?

The Fix: You can add a free plug-in that turns Safari's URL text box into a search field that you can use with different search engines. After you install Sogudi (*http://www.atamadison.com/w/kitzkikz.php*), go to the URL field and type in a short hint to specify a search engine, type a space, and then your search terms. For instance, if you want to search Google Images for pictures of Miles Davis, type the following in Safari's address field:

```
img miles davis
```

When you hit Return, Safari brings up a Google results page with pictures of Miles.

Soqudi also has hints for other sites. For instance, to search for the same trumpet player at Amazon.com, type the following in Safari's address field:

    az miles davis

Soqudi doesn't have a built-in shortcut to search the Mac-specific Google engine described earlier; however, you can add it by following these steps:

1. From Safari's Edit menu, add Soqudi.

2. Click the plus sign (+) button to add an item.

3. In the Hint column, type your shorthand for the Google Mac site; in Figure 3-10, I use "gomac".

4. In the destination URL, type the following exactly:

       http://www.google.com/mac?q=@@@&ie=UTF-
       8&oe=UTF-8

5. Click the Save button.

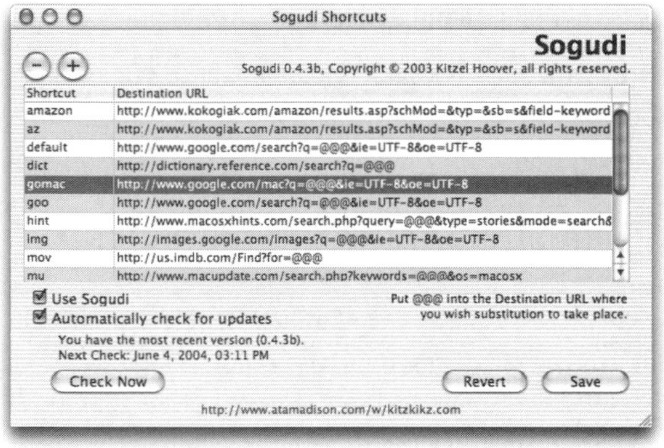

Figure 3-10. Soqudi lets you specify your own shortcuts for search engines. Here I've added a shortcut for the Google Mac page.

With this Soqudi shortcut added, you can search for information about printers that work with Macs by typing "gomac inkjet printer" in Safari's address field.

To create a hint to search Google News, use the same URL shown in step 4, but substitute "news" for "mac", as follows:

    *http://www.google.com/news?q=@@@&ie=UTF-
    8&oe=UTF-8*

By the way, the feature that Soqudi adds to Safari is already built into Camino. See the next annoyance for more about that.

EXPAND CAMINO'S GOOGLING AND BEYOND

The Annoyance: I think it's a rip that Soqudi works only for Safari. What about a quick way to search Google Mac and Google Images for us Camino users?

The Fix: You don't need Soqudi for Camino, because the shortcut function is built right in. In Camino, you can use keywords to search different search engines using the address field. The text strings are also simpler than with Soqudi and Safari, as described here:

1. Click the Bookmarks icon in Camino's toolbar to go to your bookmark page.

2. At the bottom of the window, click the New Bookmark icon.

3. In the dialog box that appears, give it a name like "Google Mac."

4. Select the new bookmark and click the "i" icon to bring up the Info dialog box.

5. Type the URL of a search engine in the Location field. At the end of the URL, type the following without any spaces:

       ?q=%s

   For example, the Google Mac URL would look like this:

       http://www.google.com/mac?q=%s

6. Enter a keyword in the Keyword field. For instance, in Figure 3-11, I used GM (short for Google Mac).

7. Close the Info window.

To use the address field to search, type the keyword followed by your search terms. For example, if you want to search Google Mac for video software, type the following command into the address field and hit Return:

    GM video software

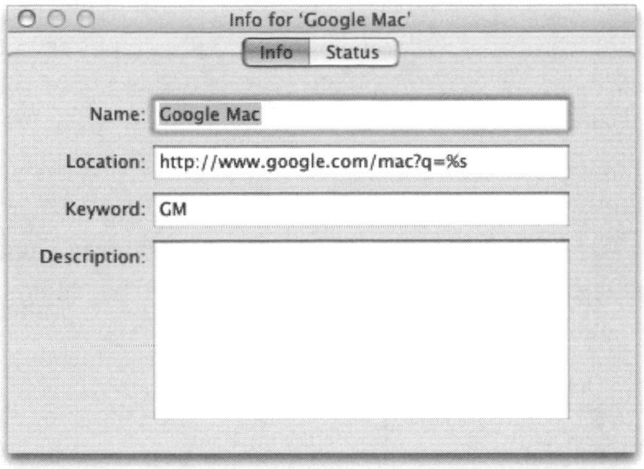

Figure 3-11. You can use Camino's keyword feature to specify a shortcut for search engines. With the setting shown here, we can type "GM," followed by our search terms in the address bar, to search Google Mac.

GOOGLE SEARCH FIELD IN CAMINO

The Annoyance: I like the fact that Safari has a search field, but the most recent version of Camino still lacks one. Is there a way to add a Google search field to Camino?

The Fix: Actually, Camino does have one. Sometimes in Jaguar, Camino's Google field isn't displayed by default, but you can easily turn it on. Go to the View menu and select Customize Toolbar. Drag the Google search field from the dialog box to Camino's toolbar and click Done and you are done.

GOOGLE BY THE NUMBERS

The founders of Google named the web site and company after a very, very large number—the *googol*—in order to reflect the "seemingly infinite amount of information available on the Web."

How big is "seemingly infinite"? A googol is the number 10 to the power of 100, which is 10 multiplied by itself 100 times, or a 1 followed by 100 zeros. This is bigger than the estimated number of atoms in the universe. By comparison, Google has about four billion items in its web index, so Google doesn't even come close to a googol.

The term googol comes from Columbia University mathematician Edward Kasner, who coined the term in the 1930s after asking his 9-year-old nephew, Milton Sirotto, what he would call a very, very large number. Kasner also thought about an even larger number, a googolplex—a 1 followed by a googol of zeros after it.

Google, Inc., refers to its Mountain View, California headquarters as the Googleplex. Pun intended.

Safari's Recent Google Menu

Want to revisit a recent Google search? Click on the magnifying glass in Safari's Google field and hold down the mouse button. A menu that lists your last 10 Google searches pops up. Pick one and Google recreates the search. Safari saves this list after you quit, so it's always there.

KEEP THE ORIGINAL SEARCH RESULTS WHILE VIEWING THE LINKS

The Annoyance: After several Google searches, I finally found the combination of terms that gets me the results I need. Even with Safari's snap-back features, it is still annoying that I have to keep going back to the search list. There must be an easier way to compare pages in the results list.

The Fix: Instead of clicking on Google's search results, get into the habit of Command-clicking on each result and choosing to have that link open in a new tab. (You can do this in any web browser that supports tabs, with the exception of Internet Explorer.) This way, you can keep your results page handy while having multiple tabs or windows open for comparing the results.

REMOVE YOURSELF FROM GOOGLE'S PHONE BOOK

The Annoyance: Once, while goofing off, I typed my phone number (with area code) into Google's search field. Much to my horror, my name, my wife's name, and our address came up. I can imagine phone spammers using software to harvest phone numbers and addresses by feeding Google every possible phone number. Is there a way to keep my contact info off of Google?

The Fix: You can ask Google to remove your phone number from its residential phone book by doing the following:

1. Do a Google search for your phone number.
2. Click the link to "Phonebook results for."
3. Click on the link to PhoneBook Removal Form.
4. Fill out the form at the bottom of the page and click Submit Form.

Sit and stew for up to 48 hours, and then try searching for your phone number again. Google should tell you that your search did not match any documents.

GET BETTER SEARCH RESULTS

The Annoyance: I hate it when Google returns 600,000 results for a search. If I spent only 10 seconds on each result, it would take 70 days—night and day—to browse them all. That's too big a haystack for finding the needle I'm looking for.

The Fix: This is actually your fault—your search is too broad. Adding more words to the search doesn't necessarily help either, because Google returns results that contain only a portion of the additional search terms. One way to make your search more specific is go to Google's Advanced Search page, where you can really get specific. A more convenient method is to use some command symbols in the Google field of your web browser:

Use quotation marks around a phrase.

> This returns results that contain only the exact phrase. As an example, a search for *san francisco board of supervisors* (without quotes) returns 267,000 results. Using quotes, as in *"san francisco board of supervisors"*, yields 12,700 results—95 percent fewer than before. Even better, with the quotation makes, the first five results contained the most relevant sites.

Time Saver: Google any Word in Safari

You can quickly search Google for any word on any web page by highlighting the word and Control-clicking it. Choose Google Search from the contextual menu and a Google results page appears before your eyes.

Use the + sign to force inclusion.

If you want every search result to contain a word or phrase, place a plus sign (+) in front of a search word. Make sure there isn't a space between the + and your word, as in *+printer*.

> ### Time Saver: Search Specific Sites from Google
>
> Locating the search field on some web sites can be a real pain in the you-know-what. You can search a specific web site right from the Google search field by adding the *inurl:* modifier. For instance, to search the Sony web site for MiniDV, use *minidv inurl:www.sony.com* in the Google field.

Use the – sign to exclude words.

When you add a minus sign (–) directly in front of word or phrase, Google won't include that word in any of the results. For instance, to search for pages containing the word *printers* but not *inkjet*, try using *printers –inkjet*.

Use number ranges.

You can narrow your search results by using ranges of numbers—two numbers with two dots between them. For instance, if you were looking for a high-end printer, you could use *printer $500..1000* in the Google field.

Eliminate PDF Files.

Want to get results that don't include PDF files? Just add this after your search terms:

```
-filetype:pdf
```

SHERLOCK

BRING BACK MISSING APPLE CHANNELS IN PANTHER

The Annoyance: After upgrading to Panther, I noticed that Sherlock's Apple channels disappeared. I tried firing up the Mac OS X installer and playing with the Custom Install option, but there was no way to reinstall Sherlock by itself. Is there any way to get the Apple channels back?

The Fix: The upgrade to Panther, and possible other Mac OS X upgrades, has messed up some preference files. This doesn't always happen, but it is just one of the things that can go wrong. You can get the Sherlock channels back by deleting one file and one folder in your Home folder. First, make sure that Sherlock isn't running and then go to ~/*Library/Preferences* and delete the following items:

- The *com.apple.sherlock.plist* file
- The Sherlock folder

When you launch Sherlock, it recreates the files and replaces the missing channels.

GET MORE SHERLOCK CHANNELS

The Annoyance: I like the idea of Sherlock—quick, highly specific web searches, without advertising and none of the pop-ups and browser interface annoyances. However, there are only a few of Sherlock's channels that I actually use. I wish there were more choices, such as a channel for Google or Amazon.

The Fix: Apple occasionally adds channels—they just appear in Sherlock. But if you have Mac OS X 10.3 or later, Sherlock can show you several dozen more channels from other developers. To see which channels are available to you, follow two simple steps while connected to the Internet:

1. Click the Channels icon in the far-left corner of the Sherlock's toolbar.

2. To the left, you should see a pane that's labeled Collections; click the Other Channels folder.

You see a list of several dozen channels, as in Figure 3-12. You can use one of the channels by double-clicking its icon. If you decide that you want to continue using this channel, simply drag it to the Sherlock's toolbar.

Among the other channels are those that search Google and the Google Directory. A channel called Shop is actually an Amazon.com channel, which you can use to search for books, music, movies, and other items Amazon sells. You can also read customer reviews and make purchases. You'll also find several news channels, and a weather

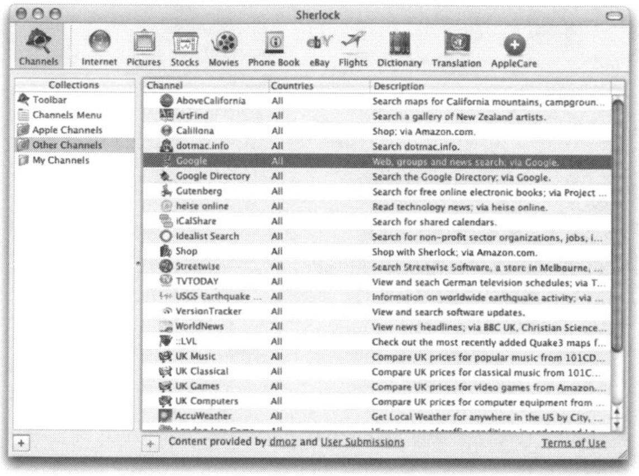

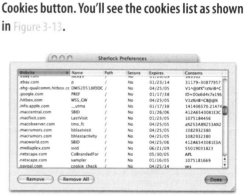

Figure 3-12. Find several new Sherlock channels in the Other Channels folder when you click the Channels toolbar icon.

Retool the Toolbar

To remove a Sherlock channel from the toolbar, hold down the ⌘ key while you drag the icon off the toolbar. You can always bring it back by clicking the Channels icon in the toolbar and dragging it from one of the lists.

SHERLOCK COOKIES

Like any browser, Sherlock is a user interface to the Web. And like a web browser, Sherlock uses cookies to store information such as passwords. Sherlock doesn't have the advertising that you find with a normal browser, so most of Sherlock's cookies are not sinister. However, you can look at Sherlock's cookies, and starting with Panther, delete individual cookies if you so desire. Just open Sherlock's Preferences (⌘-,) and click the Show Cookies button. You'll see the cookies list as shown in Figure 3-13.

Figure 3-13. Sherlock has cookies, too. In Mac OS X 10.3 and later, you can delete individual cookies in Sherlock Preferences.

channel that provides local and national weather. (If you're a techno-geek like me, check out the NASA Science News channel.) Some channels are localized. For instance, I can get scheduling information for Caltrain (a commuter train running up and down the San Francisco peninsula) or see how traffic looks around Trafalgar Square in London. The Other Channels list changes over time, so it's a good idea to check it every once in a while.

GO DIRECTLY TO A SHERLOCK CHANNEL

The Annoyance: Sherlock has too many steps. First you launch it, and then you click a channel and wait for Sherlock to switch.

The Fix: If Sherlock is running, you can quickly get at one of the channels by clicking and holding Sherlock's Dock icon. You can then choose a Sherlock channel from the contextual menu that appears. If you don't see the channel you want, it isn't in Sherlock's toolbar. You can also go directly to a Sherlock channel by creating a URL to that channel, then placing it in the Dock. This is described in the next section Create a Browser Link to a Sherlock Channel.

CREATE A BROWSER LINK TO A SHERLOCK CHANNEL

The Annoyance: Certain Sherlock channels open my web browser to display additional information. Is the reverse true—can my web browser open Sherlock?

The Fix: Your web browser can certainly open Sherlock by using a special Sherlock URL. In Safari (and some other browsers), after you type in the Sherlock URL, you can bookmark the link or drag it to the Dock (near the Trash) to make a single-click link.

The general URL for Sherlock looks like this:

```
sherlock://com.apple.channel?query=your query
```

> **Quick Link**
>
> Why type a URL in a chat dialog when you don't have to? Just drag a link from a web page in browser to iChat's typing area. Hit return and the text becomes a clickable link.

Here, *channel* is the name of the Sherlock channel you want to activate, and your query are your search terms. So, if you want to search the Dictionary channel for "syzygy," type:

```
sherlock://com.apple.dictionary?query=syzygy
```

Sherlock is fussy about capitalization of the name of the channel. If you don't get it right, the URL opens Sherlock but doesn't go to the channel. For most channels, you must use *only* lowercase text to describe the channel in the URL. For instance, to search the AppleCare channel for Knowledge Base articles on the iPod, use this URL:

```
sherlock://com.apple.applecare?query=iPod
```

Similarly, use all lowercase text to references on the eBay channel, as in:

```
sherlock://com.apple.ebay?query=pickle jar
```

There are a few exceptions. For the Stocks channel, use the term "stockQuotes":

```
sherlock://com.apple.stockQuotes?query=IBM
```

The other exception is Panther's Phone Book Channel (called Yellow Pages in Jaguar). The term for both of these is the same, "yellowPages":

```
sherlock://com.apple.yellowPages?query=auto
repair
```

By the way, a search for the Phone Book (or for the Yellow Pages) channel uses the current city you have designated in Sherlock.

ICHAT AND AIM MESSAGING

MOVE BIG FILES WITH ICHAT

The Annoyance: Sometimes I have to send really large files to another person, but my email program reports that the file is too big. I know there are utilities to break up files, but this is a big pain for the person receiving the file.

The Fix: Many people don't realize that transferring large files can be easier and more reliable with iChat than with email. Just start a chat session and drag a file from the Finder to the text message field in an iChat window. You can also drag a file to a name in the Buddy List. It doesn't matter how big the file, because iChat doesn't have a file-size limit to contend with. If you want to open the file that you have just sent, perhaps to discuss it in the chat, click on the link in the chat window. A Finder window pops up displaying the file. When you receive files, iChat saves them by default to your Desktop. You can change the location in iChat's Preferences (⌘-,) in the General pane.

FIXING ISIGHT PROBLEMS WITH ICHAT

The Annoyance: Sometimes when I try to use the iSight camera for a video chat, iChat tells me that I don't have a camera attached or that the iSight is in use by another application. Of course, neither of these is true, but I don't know how to make iChat listen to reason.

The Fix: This problem is usually due to interference from other devices. The FireWire cable that Apple ships with iSight is only lightly shielded, which means it's susceptible to interference from other devices. One solution is to buy a thicker FireWire cable that can block out electromagnetic interference. You can also try to eliminate the sources of interference. For instance, an iPod plugged into the Mac (using an equally thin cable) can sometimes cause problems. Wireless mice can also be a source of problems for an iSight. A desk lamp situated close by is another possibility.

Try shutting these items off, unplugging them, or moving them away from the iSight and its FireWire cable. If this continues to happen, buy the thicker FireWire cable.

BROWSE AND SEARCH SAVED ICHAT LOGS

The Annoyance: I recently discovered that iChat automatically saves the text of my chats. (In iChat's Preferences, go to the Messages pane and click "Automatically save chat transcripts.") However, after I've saved a bunch of chats, it takes quite a bit of time—and a lot of luck—to find a specific piece of a conversation.

The Fix: Get Logorrhea (*http://www.spiny.com/logorrhea*), a free application from Spiny Software. Logorrhea lets you easily browse and search all of iChat's log files at once. Want to see all the chats containing a certain person? Click the Browse tab, and you receive a list of Buddies and dates of the chat sessions. Click on a chat, and you can read the contents. The Search tab lets you search through all of your chat logs for a word or phrase. Click on one of the search results, and the chat opens with all of your search terms highlighted.

ONE MENU FOR MULTIPLE CHAT SETTINGS

The Annoyance: iChat lets me spellcheck from the Edit menu, show fonts from the Format menu, and change the display settings of a chat from the View menu. However, I can never remember which menu has which commands, so I end up taking a tour of all of iChat's menus when I want to use one of the commands.

The Fix: There's only one menu that you really need to remember: the chat window's contextual menu. If you Control-click (or right-click) inside a chat window, you're able to access all of iChat's commands right from that little contextual menu. Short and sweet.

VIDEO CHAT WITH YOUR DV CAMCORDER

The Annoyance: Apple claims that you can use any DV camcorder for video chats with iChat simply by connecting one to the FireWire port. When I tried it on my iBook G3, iChat didn't recognize the camera. Given what Apple said, I will be annoyed if I need to buy an iSight camera.

The Fix: You didn't read the small print that says you need a Mac with a G4 or G5 processor in order to use a DV camcorder with iChat. Apple has programmed iChat to not recognize DV cameras on Macs with a G3 processor. The issue is processing power, or the lack thereof, in a G3 Mac. However, if the G3 processor in your Mac is fast enough (about 500 MHz or faster), you can get around this with a utility called iChatUSBCam ($10, *http://www.ecamm.com/mac/ichatusbcam*). As the name implies, iChatUSBCam also lets you use older USB web cams with iChat.

If you can get the video chat running but the camcorder keeps shutting off, try pulling the tape cartridge out of the camera.

Microsoft Office
ANNOYANCES

Microsoft Office is the software that Mac users love to hate. Word has got to be *the most annoying* application on the Mac. There are times when I feel like I'm fighting with Word rather than using it. Yet, Word is also the Mac's most powerful word processor and the application I depend on the most. Excel and PowerPoint are equally powerful and also annoying in their own ways.

Paradoxically, the power of Office is responsible for both annoyances and solutions to annoyances. For instance, some of Office's annoyances are "features" that just get in your way; Microsoft turns them on by default, seemingly to advertise that the features exist. On the other hand, there are also annoyances that you can get around by using one of the gazillion features buried in the bowels of Office.

I'll show you how you can streamline your use of Word, PowerPoint, and Excel. I'll even provide you with some pointers on using Virtual PC, the Windows emulator included with Microsoft Office Professional. Entourage, the other notable member of the Office suite, is covered earlier in Chapter 2.

WORD

REMOVE OFFICE 2004 TEST DRIVE

The Annoyance: I downloaded the Office 2004 Test Drive from Microsoft to check it out. While it has some nice features, I don't think it's worth the $230 upgrade price for my purposes. So, I ran the Remove Office utility to clear out Test Drive. Now my old copy of Word from Office *v.x* won't launch. When I double-click on a Word document, Word gives me an error message. Call me paranoid, but did Test Drive break my copy of Word X to force me to upgrade?

The Fix: No, there's nothing nefarious going on here. The problem is an annoying oversight in the Remove Office utility. To understand it, let's look at what happened. After you installed Office 2004 (either Test Drive or the full suite), Office told Mac OS X to open Word, Excel, and PowerPoint files using the most current version of these applications. This is normal procedure for most applications. The problem with Remove Office is that it forgets to reset Mac OS X to open Office files with your older version of Office. So, when you double-click on a Word file, Mac OS X looks for Word 2004, can't find it, and spits out an error message.

Fortunately, the fix for this is easy. In the Finder, select any Word file and bring up the Get Info dialog with ⌘-I. In the Open With section, choose your Word application from the pop-up menu. Finally, click the Change All button. To complete the fix, you can do the same with Excel and PowerPoint files.

WHEN TRACK CHANGES GOES BAD

The Annoyance: Whenever I use Word X's Track Changes feature, I feel like I'm competing with Word—and Word usually wins. The Track Changes feature is supposed to color-code the additions and deletions that different people make in a document. But sometimes, as I'm typing, Track Changes changes the name of the editor along with the color of the text, often several times in the

---

> ### DEBUNDLING OFFICE
> Do you like the new features of Word 2004 but think that $329 is a bit too steep for an upgrade? In a break with tradition, Microsoft is offering upgrades to individual Office applications for (just) $109. This lets you use Word 2004 along with your older copies of Excel X and PowerPoint X.
>
> If you're moving to Office for the first time, Microsoft will also sell you the individual applications for $229 each. I know that's not cheap, but it's better than paying $399 for the complete Office suite if all you need is Word. Only Entourage is no longer available by itself. By the way, this is the first time since Word 5.*x* that the Office applications are available separately.

---

middle of a sentence. This can happen when Word changes a straight quote into a curly quote or when it autocorrects spelling. Word will sometimes change the user label for a bit of text to "Unknown." After a while, it's tough to tell who has edited what. For the person who has to accept and reject the changes, the edited document is a multicolored mess.

The Fix: The Track Changes lunacy has been the bane of writers and editors' existence since Word 98 and Word 2001, but has its worst manifestation in Word X. Fortunately, you can tackle this problem by using either of the following approaches:

- Upgrade to Word 2004. Whenever I've attended an advance briefing for a new version of Office during the past few years, I (and many other press people) would beg and plead with Microsoft to fix Track Changes. Finally, Word 2004 not only fixes the nasty Track Changes bugs, but it also makes Track Changes easier to read and easier to accept and reject changes. The Page Layout view drops additions and comments in balloons to the right with connecting dotted lines (shown in Figure 4-1). You can accept or reject changes in each balloon using the icons in the upper-right corner of each balloon—a check for "accept" and an x for "reject." Also, the Reviews toolbar has had a makeover that added clearer options and a new pop-up menu letting you view the document with or without the edits (see Figure 4-2). For professional writers and editors, the rehabilitation of Track Changes may be the most compelling reason to upgrade to Word 2004.

Figure 4-1. Track Changes in Word 2004 places additions and comments in balloons, where you can easily accept or reject them.

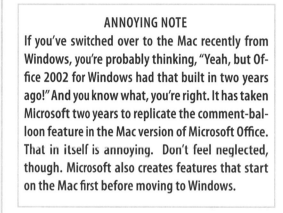

Figure 4-2. The newly revised Reviews toolbar of Word 2004 offers new ways to control the Track Changes feature, including a new pop-up menu that gives you options for viewing the edits.

• Work around the bugs in Word X. Here, you can't really win, so you have to outsmart Word. I've tried all sorts of settings, shutting off every setting I could find, and Track Changes still made me want to hurl my Mac across the room in frustration. (Good thing it was a hefty PowerMac.) But I can suggest a simple workaround to calm your nerves and let you insert a sentence or paragraph while keeping Mr. Unknown at bay.

Open a new blank Word document to use as a scratch sheet. Type your entire new thought on the scratch sheet, make changes to it, and spellcheck it. When you are satisfied, copy the new text and paste it into the document you are already editing. Track changes accepts the new text and attributes it to you, and only you.

> **ANNOYING NOTE**
> If you've switched over to the Mac recently from Windows, you're probably thinking, "Yeah, but Office 2002 for Windows had that built in two years ago!" And you know what, you're right. It has taken Microsoft two years to replicate the comment-balloon feature in the Mac version of Microsoft Office. That in itself is annoying. Don't feel neglected, though. Microsoft also creates features that start on the Mac first before moving to Windows.

TURN OFF HYPERLINKS

The Annoyance: I hate it when Word acts like an obstinate child: I tell it not to do something and it does it anyway. Take, for instance, hyperlinks, those live clickable links to web browsers that Word creates when you type a URL. When I tell Word to turn off hyperlinks, it pays me no mind; the link remains active, and Word continues to create new links.

The Fix: You only *think* that you've turned off hyperlinks. If you want to disable hyperlinks, you must turn them off in not one but two places. You can access both of these places by selecting Tools → AutoCorrect. In this dialog, there are two tabs you need to go to "AutoFormat as you Type" and AutoFormat (*not* AutoCorrect). Under each of these tabs, uncheck "Internet paths with hyperlinks." If you unchecked this only in the AutoFormat tab, Word will continue to convert URL text to actual links.

Once you have directed word to stop creating new hyper-links, you must remove the existing hyperlinks in your document. There are two ways to remove them:

- Insert the cursor at end of a URL and hit the Back-space key.

- Select the URL and hit ⌘-K to remove the hyperlink. Selecting the URL is tricky. If you are skilled, you can click and drag to select. But if you move the mouse over the link, even just a tiny bit, the cursor changes from the arrow to the pointer finger. Clicking with the finger opens the URL in your default web brows-er instead of inserting the cursor. One approach is to click before or after the URL and then use the arrow keys to get to the beginning or end of the URL. Once there, hold down the Shift key and then use the ar-row key once to select the URL. With the URL se-lected, hit ⌘-K and then click on the Remove Link button in the window that appears.

DUMMY TEXT FOR DUMMIES

When you're creating a page layout, it's helpful to fill the page with dummy text. Later, you'll import the real thing. Word has a hidden feature that does this for you. Type `=rand()` and hit Return. Word creates three paragraphs of three sentences each. (The sentences describe the actions of a quick brown fox.)

If you need more text, fill those parentheses with numbers like this:

> `=rand(x,y)`

x is the number of paragraphs and y is the number of sentences per paragraph. The highest number you can use for either x or y is 200.

Doesn't work? You probably have a required Auto-Correct feature turned off. Go to Tools → AutoCorrect and turn on the "Replace text as you type" option.

Similarly, you can use ⌘-K to manually insert hyperlinks when you have hyperlinks turned off. Just type the URL, select it with the mouse and hit ⌘-K to activate that URL in the document.

SPELLCHECK WORDS THAT GET SKIPPED

The Annoyance: Word's spellcheck sometimes forgets how to spell certain words—not just difficult words, either. This tends to happen when people send me their files to work on. I'm not the greatest speller in the world, but it's obvious that some words are not being spellchecked or corrected by Word. It's not that spell-check is turned off—it's still functioning for the most part. I've looked in the spellchecking configurations, but I can't find a setting that would apply. It's a mystery to me.

The Fix: This problem originates with Word's ability to spellcheck in different languages, which is a handy feature for multilingual users. Unbeknownst to you, por-tions of your document have been designated with a lan-guage that Word 2004 calls "No language," or "No proof-ing" in Word X. This "language" basically means that spellcheck skips the word.

The fix is to reset the entire document to the "no lan-guage" or "no proofing" language to English. You won't find this setting in the spellcheck configurations, but in the language settings:

1. First select all of the text in the Word document with ⌘-A.

2. Choose Tools → Language.

3. Choose "English (US)" in the dialog that appears.

4. The Language dialog is slightly different in Word X and Word 2004. (Both are shown in Figure 4-3.) Word 2004 has one extra step: make sure that the checkbox labeled "Do not check spelling or gram-mar" is unchecked.

Now, you may not want to blindly set the entire docu-ment to English. You may have certain parts of the docu-ment that you don't want spellchecked, or you may quote text in another language, e re natas. Exitus acta probat.

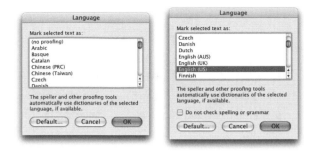

Figure 4-3. With your document's text selected, choose English (US) to get Word to spellcheck selected text. The left Language dialog is from Word X; the right is from Word 2004.

You can use Find and Replace to search for the words set to "no language" ("no proofing") and choose to change selected words to English. This operation is a little different from the previous one, because you won't be searching for text. Instead, you'll search for the "No language" ("No proofing") format and replace it with the English (US) format, as follows:

1. Select Edit → Replace.

2. Make sure the cursor is in the "Find what" field of the Replace dialog.

3. If the Find and Replace dialog isn't already open, expand it by clicking the triangle in the lower-left corner.

4. Choose the Format pop-up menu at the bottom of the dialog (*not* the Format menu in the menu bar) and select Language; the dialog in Figure 4-3 appears.

5. Choose "no language" (Word 2004) or "no proofing" (Word X), and click OK.

6. Now click inside the "Replace with" field.

7. Choose the Format pop-up menu at the bottom of the dialog and select Language.

8. Choose "English (US)" from the list and click OK.

You're now ready to do your search. Click the Find Next button to find the next "no language" word. If this is a word you want to spellcheck, click the Replace button to

designate it as English. If you decide to keep it as "no language," click the Find Next button to find the next word.

SPELLCHECK A SINGLE WORLD

The Annoyance: Word's spellchecker is cumbersome for checking the spelling of just one word. It takes a lot of mouse clicks to use the spellcheck dialog one word at a time. When I'm done, Word adds yet another mouse click by asking me if I want to spell check the entire document. That's a lot of fuss just to spellcheck one stinking word!

The Fix: Skip the dialog for spellchecking single words by using the contextual menu. You'll save mouse clicks and time. Select the word and Control-click (or right-click) to bring up the contextual menu. As you can see from Figure 4-4, you have two places to select a corrected word: from the main body of the contextual menu or from the AutoCorrect submenu. If you select the correct word from the AutoCorrect submenu, Word changes the word for you the next time you misspell it the same way.

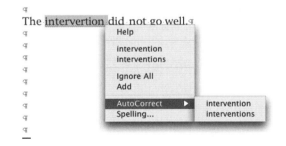

Figure 4-4. You can spellcheck a single word from the contextual menu or choose it from the AutoCorrect submenu to have Word automatically correct the word the next time it appears.

SUPPLEMENT WORD'S SPELLCHECKER

The Annoyance: Word's spellchecker serves me well for the most part, but it doesn't seem to be the brightest bulb in the box when it comes to interpreting the English language. Word tells me I've misspelled a word like *abranchial* (having no gills), but when I go to a *real* dictionary, I find out that I was right all along.

The Fix: The issue of beefing up spellchecking keeps popping up in *Mac Annoyances*. In Chapter 2, I recommend the free iSpell for Mail (see the tip called *Upgrade Mail's Spell Checker*). In Chapter 3, I mention the $40 Spell Catcher for use with a web browser (see the tip called *Spell Check Your Browser*). The latter works with Word, giving you some new features. But if it's spelling new words you're interested in, there is another free resource you can use—a file buried deep within the Unix directories of Mac OS X. To get to it, go to the Finder, select Go → Go to Folder (Shift-⌘-G), and type this path:

```
/usr/share/dict/
```

Here you'll find a text file called *web2*, which is short for *Webster's Second International Dictionary*. This file contains 234,936 words from the 1934 edition of the dictionary, all spelled correctly. The *web2* file contains words unknown to Microsoft Word's spellcheck. For instance, there's *deisidaimonia*, a word of Greek origin used in biblical studies meaning fear of supernatural powers or the dread of demons (not daemons). You'll have to find the definition yourself, as the *web2* file is merely a list of words.

But, wait, there's more. If you use Mac OS X right now, there are two other word files that you can use to aid the spellchecking process, absolutely free! A text file called *web2a* contains 76,205 hyphenated and double words, including such greats as *acetylene tetrabromide*. The other file, called *propernames*, contains 1323 names from around the world, many of which Word's spellcheck doesn't recognize. So if you're writing a letter to your friend, *Krzysztof*, you'll be spared the embarrassment of a misspelling.

> ### EXTRANEOUS GEEK TIP
> ### SEARCH WEB2 FROM TERMINAL
>
> **For those of you working in the Terminal's command line, you can also search** *web2*, *web2a*, **and** *propernames* **using the Unix** `grep` **command, as follows:**
>
> ```
> grep YOURTERM /usr/share/dict/web2
> ```
>
> **To help** `grep` **locate your word, use the portion of the word you think you know how to spell. For instance, search for "undei":**
>
> ```
> grep undei /usr/share/dict/web2
> ```
>
> **This search brings up four words:**
>
> ☒ **undeification**
>
> ☒ **undeified**
>
> ☒ **undeify**
>
> ☒ **undeistical**

You can consult these files when Word doesn't offer the correct spelling for a word. For easy access, drag *web2* to the Dock, near the Trash. When you click *web2*'s icon in the Dock, the file opens in TextEdit, revealing all of the words in the dictionary, neatly placed, one per line. When you find your word, paste it into your Word document, select the word, and open Word's spellcheck dialog. In the "Not in dictionary" field, double-click the word and press the Add button. Words like *deisidaimonia* are now part of Word's custom dictionary.

REMOVE ITEMS FROM THE WORK MENU

The Annoyance: Word's Work menu is great; I can add any open Word document to the menu simply by choosing Add to Work Menu. Choosing one of the files in the list opens the document. But after a few years, the Work menu is as long as my arm, and as far as I can tell, there isn't a "Remove from Work Menu" command or option in any of the menus.

The Fix: You're right, but there is a key command. Press Option-⌘-hyphen, and the cursor turns into a big minus sign. Now go to the Work menu and select a file you want to remove. If you want to remove another document from the Work menu, use the key command again to bring up the big minus sign.

DEEP SIX OFFICE ASSISTANT

The Annoyance: I can't stand that stupid little computer icon that sits on the screen, waving at me, consuming processor power with annoying animation. The idea that I need a cartoon to entertain and distract me from my work is idiotic, to say the least. I tried to turn it off, but it still pops up with wizards.

The Fix: The annoying little 1984 Macintosh with feet is known as the Office Assistant. The little cartoon actually has a name—Max. (You know, Max and Macs, get it? Well, someone in Redmond thought it was funny.) Although Max is easier to get rid of in Word 2004 than in Word X, there are three options for nuking Max in either version:

- Turn off the Office Assistant. Go to the Help menu and unselect "Use Office Assistant," and you'll never have to see it again—except when you use a wizard. In Word 2004, simply closing the Office Assistant window automatically deselects this option for you.

- Turn the Office Assistant off in wizards as well. If you want to tell the Office Assistant not to provide help with wizards, you must first turn the Office Assistant back on, oddly enough. Now, click the assistant to bring up its little balloon, and click the Options button in the balloon. Under the Options tab, unselect the "Help with wizards" checkbox.

- Keep the Office Assistant, but replace Max with something less annoying. **This lets you use** Office Assistant to explain Word's many dialogs, but without the bothersome animation that you despise. Go back to the Office CD. Open the Value Pack folder and double-click the Value Pack Installer. Click the Assistants checkbox and press Continue. Now you can replace Max.

Control-click Max and select Choose Assistant from the contextual menu. You can use the Back and Next buttons to see other Assistants. (In fact, you'll have to use both the Back and Next buttons to view all of them.) Several of these assistants are actually more annoying than Max. For the least distracting choice, I recommend the Office logo (shown in Figure 4-5), which animates only when you open and close it.

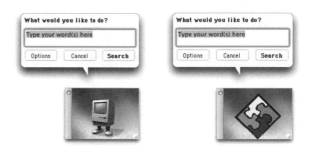

Figure 4-5. The standard Max is shown on the left. A less annoying Office Assistant is on the right.

ANNOYING TIP
MAKE OFFICE ASSISTANT EVEN MORE ANNOYING

Here's a great prank to play on your friends—well, maybe not friends that you want to keep. Give Max sounds. Click the Assistant, click Options, and put a check next to "Make sounds." Max will occasionally spurt clicks and chirps as it animates, making quite a racket during the Rubric's cube sequence.

While you're at it, how about viewing Max's entire repertoire of motions? Control-click Max to bring up his pop-up menu and select "Animate!" (The exclamation point is Microsoft's, not mine.) Each time you do this, Max goes through another animation routine.

ADD A KEYBOARD COMMAND TO COLOR TEXT

The Annoyance: I use color text to represent different stages of my writing. For instance, I use red to indicate text that needs work or possible deletion, blue for text that I've pasted in just for information, and so forth. Unfortunately, Word doesn't offer an easy way to color text. I select the text, hit ⌘-D to bring up the Font dialog, and then select a color from a pop-up menu. Not too hard to do once, but it sure gets old if you need do this every other minute.

The Fix: Although it isn't obvious or easy, you can assign simple keyboard commands to colorize text. The effort is worth it, though, if you need to color text often. Here's how:

1. Go to Tools → Customize.

2. In Word 2004, select the Customize Keyboard submenu. In Word X, click the Keyboard button in the Customize dialog.

3. In the Categories column, choose Format.

4. In the Commands column, click Color.

5. Select a color from the Color pop-up menu that appeared in the previous step.

6. Type a key command that you'd like to use, such as ⌘-1, and it appears in the field called "Press new shortcut key," as shown in Figure 4-6.

> **Warning. . .**
> FontColor may sound like the obvious choice, but it doesn't work for this purpose.

7. If the key command is already used, a "Currently assigned to" message appears, as in Figure 4-6. If the key command is already assigned to another function—particularly one you use regularly—you should type a different key command. If this isn't a command you use, click the Assign button.

8. You can now repeat steps 5 through 7 to add keyboard commands for other colors. Be sure you assign

a key command for black, so you can return the colored text back to its normal color.

9. When you're finished, click OK.

You can now use the key commands to color selected text.

Figure 4-6. Choose Format from Categories and Color from Commands, and you can assign a key command to a color.

> **t i p**
> When assigning your own key commands, try using the Control key instead of Option or ⌘ (such as Control-1 instead of ⌘-1). The Control key isn't used as much as these other keys.

ADD KEYBOARD COMMANDS FOR WORD 2004 AUDIO

The Annoyance: I was excited about the new Audio Notes feature in Word 2004. This lets you to record timestamped audio into the new Notebook Layout view, so you can use it as a dictaphone. Unfortunately, I soon found that using a mouse to control recording (play, stop, pause, and resume) is no better than having a tape recorder on your desk. And it's nearly impossible to type notes based on the audio when you have to constantly reach for the mouse to pause and play.

The Fix: You can create keyboard commands to control Audio notes, which is similar to creating commands for coloring selected texts. The differences with audio control is that you must first create a macro. This is a bit tricky, because Notebook Layout view doesn't let you record macros. You can get around this by typing a line of code in a macro using Visual Basic for Applications. Here's what you do:

1. In your Word document, make sure you are not in Notebook Layout mode by clicking on one of the other view buttons at the lower left of the Word window.

2. Create a new macro by going to Tools → Macro → Macros.

3. Give the macro a name (such as "audionotesplay") and click the Create button. (The name can't have spaces.)

4. Directly above the "End Sub" line, type this line of code:

       WordBasic.AudioNotesPlay
   Note that there are no spaces.

5. Go to the Word menu and select "Close and return to Microsoft Word."

Now, assign a key command to the Play macro. The procedure is similar to that of the previous tip ("Add a Keyboard Command to Color Text").

> **t i p**
>
> If you try to run the macro from the macro window, you'll get an error message. That's okay.

1. Go to Tools → Customize → Customize Keyboard.

2. In the Customize Keyboard dialog, select Macros from the Categories column.

3. Select the new macro ("audionotesplay") from the second column, which is labeled Macros.

4. Enter a key command that you'd like to use (such as ⌘-7).

5. Click OK.

You now have a key command (or "shortcut" in Microsoft language) to start playing your audio note. This command only works when you have a Notebook Layout view.

Now, create commands for Stop, Pause, and Record. To do this, repeat the previous steps with slightly different lines of code:

```
WordBasic.AudioNotesStop
WordBasic.AudioNotesPause
WordBasic.AudioNotesRecord
```

Note that all the macros are stored in the same macro window, but they appear as separate macros in the Customize Keyboard dialog.

COPY AND PASTE FORMATTING

The Annoyance: I find Word's Style menus tedious to use, especially when I have a lot of styles in the list. It takes a lot of scrolling up and down with the mouse in order to zero in on the style that I want. And in a big document, I have to do this over and over again.

The Fix: You could create a macro that has it's own floating palette of styles, but unless you really enjoy Office macro programming, this will be a real chore. Fortunately, there is a much easier way—use the Format Painter tool. This tool lets you copy the formatting of a piece of text and apply only the formatting to another group of text. This means you need only to use a style menu a few times, and then it's just a matter of mouse clicking all the way.

The Format Painter tool is the paintbrush icon in the Standard toolbar, shown in Figure 4-7. (If you don't see it, you can add it via the Tools → Customize dialog. Select Format in the Categories column, and then go to the Commands column and drag Format Painter up to a toolbar.)

Using the Format Painter to copy and paste a format is easy:

1. Click on a word that has a format or style you want to copy.

Figure 4-7. The Format Painter tool lets you copy the formatting of some text and apply it to other text. The I-beam cursor gains a plus sign after you click the tool.

2. Click the Format Painter icon in the toolbar in which you placed it. The I-beam cursor gains a plus sign (+) next to it.

3. Select the text that you want to format.

When you let go of the mouse, the text you selected is reformatted. If you want to use the Format Painter several times in a row, double-click the tool in step 2. When you're done, hit the Escape key to release the tool.

DISCONTINUOUSLY SELECT AND FORMAT

The Annoyance: I need to italicize a number of words scattered throughout a document. Do I really have to format them one at a time, or does one of Word's 8 million features let me do it all at once?

The Fix: Word actually lets you select words (or phrases, or paragraphs) discontinuously, as shown in Figure 4-8. Just hold down the ⌘ key as you select each word or phrase. Now, you can apply the same formatting to all of the selected words at once.

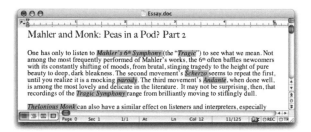

Figure 4-8. Hold the z key as you select words that aren't adjacent. You can then use any formatting command (such as bold or italic) or even spell check the selected words.

WHEN WORD REFUSES TO SAVE

The Annoyance: Sometimes when I go to save a document after working on it for a while, Word says no. More specifically, Word claims that I have too many files open—even when I only have a single document open. The only way out is to quit without saving my latest batch of changes. When I open the file, Word lets me save again. Is Word just tempermental?

The Fix: This is a bug that has been around for years. It's caused by the multitude of invisible work files that Word accumulates as you repeatedly save. (Turning off the fast save option doesn't help.) What you can do to get out of the situation is to do a Save As with a slightly different filename. This retains your changes. Next, trash the original, because it doesn't contain your most recent changes. You can now rename the "Save As" file to the original filename, and everything is copasetic.

MAKE VERTICAL TEXT SELECTIONS

The Annoyance: When I paste in text from an email message, web site, or PDF file, I need to manually reformat it to get rid of text or space running down one side or the other. It would be nice to be able to select a vertical block of text instead of selecting what I want line by line. Is this just wishful thinking?

The Fix: Don't jump to conclusions—Word has such a feature. Just hold the Option key while you drag the cursor, and Word selects exactly where you drag instead of selecting the entire line. (This doesn't work in outline mode, however.) The Delete key removes only the selected area. This technique is also handy when you need to get rid of a bunch of spaces or tabs that someone has included in a document. This is easier when the tabs are visible, as in Figure 4-9. You can turn these on in Word's Preferences by clicking on View and selecting All under "Nonprinting characters."

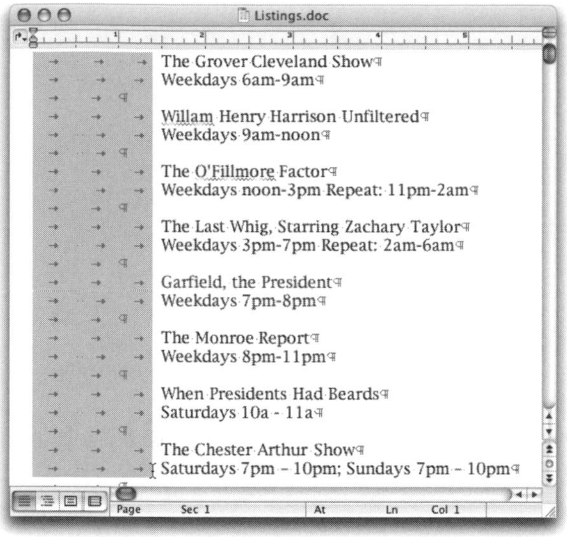

Figure 4-9. Hold the Option key to select vertically to avoid Multiple Selection Syndrome.

STOP WORD FROM CAPITALIZING IWORDS

The Annoyance: Once again, I'm fighting a losing battle, again. I write a sentence like "iPods are great." Word counters by changing this to "IPods are great." Word lets me change this back to "iPod," unless I hit Return right after it. Then it's "IPod" yet again, and the battle continues. How do I get Word to stop capitalizing my iWords?

The Fix: The only way to deal with this annoying "feature" is to turn off Word's auto correct options. This isn't much of a sacrifice if you feel capable of capitalizing your own sentences.

1. Go to Tools → AutoCorrect.
2. Under the AutoCorrect tab, uncheck "Capitalize first letter of sentences."

You may notice that there is an Exceptions button under the AutoCorrect tab, and that it seems to let you define words that Word won't correct. This is a false hope. As long as the Capitalize feature is turned on, Word capitalizes words (even words in the Exceptions lists) at the beginning of a sentence.

RECLAIM WORD'S F9 FROM PANTHER

The Annoyance: I work a lot with documents that have a table of contents. It used to be convenient to update the table of contents by clicking the table and pressing the F9 key. When I updated to Panther, Mac OS X hijacked the F9 key for Exposé (a feature I almost never use). How do I get Mac OS X to give the F9 key back to Word?

The Fix: You could go into Word's Customize dialog (in the Tools menu) and change the TOC-update key combination to something else. But why should you? You're used to using F9 in Word, and you don't use F9 for Expose—it should be Mac OS X that gives up F9, not Word.

Fortunately, this isn't a problem. Open System Preferences and click the Exposé icon. Click the All Windows pop-up menu and select another key or key combination for Exposé. If you just want to turn it off, select the hyphen at the bottom of the pop-up menu.

STOP SLOPPY SEARCHES

The Annoyance: Word's Find feature has recently become sloppy. For instance, when I search for "two" it finds "to" and "too." A search for "hair" brings up "here" and "hear." Has Word stopped paying attention?

The Fix: This is another of Words obscure features: the "Sounds like" search. This feature is disabled by default, but it appears you've turned it on by mistake. To turn it back off, open Word's Find dialog (⌘-F) and click the disclosure triangle in the lower-right corner to expand the dialog, Now, uncheck the "Sounds like" checkbox (shown in Figure 4-10).

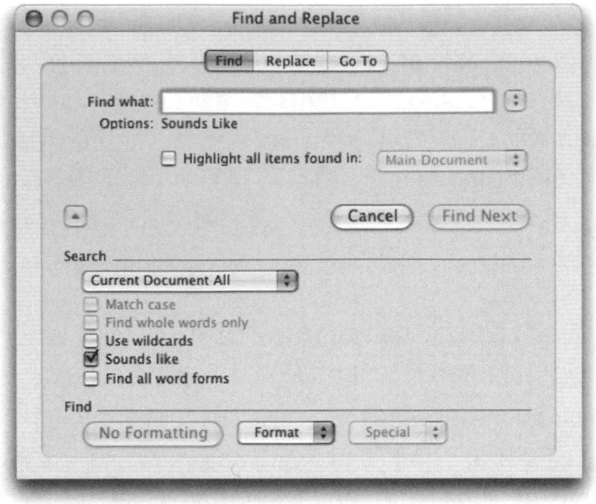

Figure 4-10. With "Sounds like" selected, Word's Find command gets sloppy when it searches, finding words that sound similar to the word you want to actually find.

CUSTOM FORMATTING OF THE TOC

The Annoyance: It's handy having Word generate a table of contents, but it's annoying that I can't select the text of the table of contents (TOC) to reformat it. Word's tacky TOC style clashes with the rest of my beautiful document.

The Fix: There actually *is* a way to change the fonts, the amount indented, and other formatting characteristic in the Word-generated table of contents. You don't do this directly, but by editing the styles that Word uses to generate the TOC. These are identified by the level of indenting used, so that the style for first-level entries is called TOC1, that for the second level is called TOC2, and so on. To edit the TOC styles, do the following:

1. Choose Format→Style. The Style dialog opens.

2. In the Styles column, scroll until you locate TOC1 (shown on the left side of Figure 4-11) Click on it.

3. Click the Modify button. A Modify Style dialog appears (shown on the right side of Figure 4-11).

Figure 4-11. Clicking the Modify button in the Style dialog (left) brings up the Modify Style dialog (right).

4. You can make changes to the font, font size, and color, and can choose bold, italics, or underline. You can also make changes to the alignment.

5. For even more formatting options, make a selection from the Format pop-up menu in the lower-left corner of the dialog. Another dialog opens.

6. When you are finished, click OK in the Modify Style dialog.

7. In the Style dialog, select TOC2 and repeat steps 3 through 6.

8. Repeat for as many levels of the TOC as you need.

9. When you're finished, click the Apply button in the Style dialog.

NAVIGATING BIG DOCUMENTS WITH THUMBNAILS AND BOOKMARKS

The Annoyance: One of the great features of Word is that documents can be really, really long. Navigating huge documents, however, hasn't been easy, because it involves a lot of scrolling and text searching just to get to where you want to be.

The Fix: There are two features you can use for navigating long documents. The first is new to Word 2004. The second is available in both Word X and Word 2004.

The Navigation Pane

With Word 2004, Microsoft took a cue from Preview and Adobe Acrobat and added the ability to navigate around a document by using page thumbnails or a list of pages. Go to View → Navigation Pane, and a vertical list appears, summarizing your document. It works just like in the PDF viewers—you can switch between thumbnails and text (called the Document Map), and click on an image or text line to go right to a page.

Bookmarks

Word X and Word 2004 let you go a step further to set your own bookmarks in spots you think are important. To set a bookmark, place the cursor at a spot you want to bookmark, select Insert → Bookmark, give it a single-word name, and click Add.

The Add button grays out if you use more than one word in the bookmark name, but you can use an underscore to connect words (such as *left_off_here*). You also can't use a number at the beginning of a bookmark name.

Then use the Find dialog (⌘-F) to locate your bookmark. In the dialog, click the "Go to" tab and choose Bookmark from the "Go to what" column. You can then pick the bookmark you want from a pop-up menu, click OK, and bam! You're there.

EMBRACE THE PREVIOUS AND NEXT FIND BUTTONS

The Annoyance: Sometimes when I go to scroll, I accidentally hit one of the double arrows at the bottom of the scrollbar (shown in Figure 4-12). Suddenly, Word takes me to some other place in the document, seemingly at random. Is there any way to shut off this annoying behavior?

The Fix: In this case, you won't be able to beat Word, so you might as well join it. First, the only way to get rid of the double arrows is to turn off the entire vertical scrollbar (in Word's Preferences, click to the View option to the left)—which is a bit draconian for most. Instead, try embracing the Previous Find and Next Find buttons, as they are known; your opinion of them may change after you start using them as they were intended. After you've done a search in the normal manner (with the Find dialog), these buttons act like a Find Again command. The lower double arrow takes you to the next instance of the search term. The upper double arrow searches backward through the document. The great thing about the Previous Find and Next Find buttons is that you don't have to go back to the Find dialog. Just click and go.

Figure 4-12. Clicking the lower double arrow takes you to the next instance of a Find in your document; the upper double arrow searches upward in the document.

DELETE TABLES

The Annoyance: When I select a table and hit the Delete key, the text in the table disappears, but the table itself remains. How do I delete the actual table?

The Fix: Tables obey their own rules. Mostly, this is to enable you to edit text within tables without deleting the tables. There are a few ways to get rid of a table, text and all:

- Select the entire table and then hit the Shift-Delete keys.
- Click somewhere inside the table and go to Table → Delete → Table.
- Include the table as part of a larger selection of text and hit Delete.

RESET DEFAULT PAGE SIZE

The Annoyance: A while ago, I spent some time using Word 2004 to create an invitation to my daughter's birthday party. I created my own custom size in horizontal landscape mode, did the layout, and printed out copies. Now, every time I create a new document in Word, it creates a page using the small, my custom size of the invitation forcing me to manually reset the document to standard letter size. I've tried fiddling with styles and the Page Setup dialog, but I can't figure out how to make Word default to a normal piece of paper.

The Fix: You're looking in the wrong places. When you set up the party invitation, you must have accidentally designated it as the default page layout. Here's how to undo the damage:

1. Go to Format → Document; the Document dialog appears.
2. Click the Page Setup button. (**Don't choose Page Setup from the File menu.**) A Page Setup dialog appears.
3. Click the portrait mode icon.
4. Select US Letter from the Paper Size pop-up menu to set an 8 1/2 × 11 layout.
5. Click OK.

6. Back in the Document dialog, click the Default button.
7. A dialog comes up asking if you want to change the default settings; click Yes.

Your next new Word document will be a normal-sized page.

OPEN OFFICE FILES WITHOUT OFFICE

The Annoyance: I'm an Office holdout. I use it at work but refuse to buy it for use on my Mac at home. (Yes, I'm a tightwad, but there's also the principle of the thing.) I know that TextEdit in Panther can open Word files, but most of the formatting gets lost. I also want to read PowerPoint and Excel files. What are my options?

The Fix: Let's get real for minute: If you need to edit Office files to send back to other Office users, you should have Microsoft Office. But if you need only to read and print Office files, or perhaps extract editable text, you can live without Office. TextEdit does a fair-to-middlin' job, but icWord and icExcel from Panergy Software (*http://www.panergy.com*) will make it easier to work with Office-less paper. There's also good ol' AppleWorks if you have it on your Mac.

Let's compare your options:

TextEdit

If you have Mac OS X 10.2 or earlier, TextEdit won't work with Word files. With Mac OS X 10.3 and later, TextEdit does let you edit Word files and even lets you save in Word format. If you want to view tables in Word documents, you'll need the version of TextEdit that comes with Mac OS X 10.4.

With any of these versions, TextEdit will remove all of the formatting besides the basics (such as bold, italics, and text color), and will remove all styles. If you open a Word document that has revision tracking turned on, you can forget about seeing what's been changed. TextEdit also won't display graphics that have been embedded in the Word file.

You can think of these inexpensive utilities ($20 each or $30 for the pair) as Office readers, much in the same way Acrobat Reader and Preview are PDF readers. icWord can open Word files and present much more of the formatting than TextEdit does, including embedded graphics, paragraphs, tables, and footnotes; icExcel does the same with Excel files. icWord can also open PowerPoint presentations, although the results are not as good as with Word files. You can also search for text, and copy, drag, or paste it to other applications. While you can't edit in icWord or icExcel, you can print and save the file in other (non-Microsoft) formats, such as Rich Text Format (RTF) and AppleWorks. icWord doesn't have the fancy features like revision tracking, but it displays the additions and not the deletions when you import the Word document. (TextEdit shows both additions and deletions next to each other, which is confusing as all heck.) icWord gets the job done for viewing and printing Word documents.

If you have Apple's old all-in-one suite, AppleWorks, give it a try before buying icWord and icExcel. Apple-Works can open and save Word and Excel files using built-in translators. Retention of formatting is fair, but AppleWorks doesn't have a lot of the features of Word and Excel. If you don't have AppleWorks or it doesn't work for you, give icWord a try.

LOSE THE PROJECT GALLERY

The Annoyance: I've been using Word for 10 years, and every time I create a new document, I want a blank Word document, not one of the many templates offered in the Project Gallery. So for Word, the Project Gallery is a useless extra step. When I launch PowerPoint, however, I do use the Project Gallery to create different types of presentations. In Office *v.x*, this was no problem; each application had its own Project Gallery setting. But now that I have Office 2004, a change in one application changes all of them. Can I loose the Gallery in Word 2004 but keep it in PowerPoint 2004?

AN OFFICE NOT READY FOR PRIME TIME: OPENOFFICE FOR MAC OS X

For the more technically inclined (in other words, readers familiar with Unix), there is an alternative to Microsoft Office—OpenOffice for Mac OS X (*http://www.openoffice.org*). OpenOffice is a free, open source suite that includes four main applications that can read and write in Microsoft formats. There's a word processor called Writer, a drawing program called Draw, a spreadsheet called Calc, and a presentation program called Impress.

Before you start your download, there are some major caveats. For one, OpenOffice doesn't have a Mac interface. Instead, it uses X11, a Unix windowing system based on XFree86 (*http://www.xfree86.org*) that runs on top of Mac OS X's Aqua interface. Another issue is that X11 in not installed by default; you'll have to install X11 from Panther's installation CDs. If you're using Jaguar, you can download X11 from Apple (*http://www.apple.com/macosx/features/x11*). Once installed, X11 can be found in the Utilities folder (/Applications/Utilities).

If you're comfortable with Unix and X11, go ahead and give OpenOffice a shot. If not, you may want to hold of for a while. When (and if) OpenOffice is ported to run in Mac OS X's native windowing environment (without X11), it may become a real alternative for the masses.

The Fix: The myriad dialogs of Microsoft Office 2004 offer more than one way to skin a configuration. This is true for the Project Gallery, which you can turn off for all Office applications or just for individual applications. Let's look at turning it off globally:

1. In Word 2004, PowerPoint 2004, or Excel 2004, choose File → Project Gallery (Shift-⌘-P).

2. Click the Customize tab.

3. Now uncheck "Show Project Gallery at startup," as shown in Figure 4-13.

With this setting, you won't see the Project Gallery pop-up at the launch of any Office 2004 application. Now, override this setting individually for any Office application. You'll find the "Show Project Gallery at startup" setting in these places:

- In Word's Preferences (⌘-,), under the General option

- In Excel's Preferences (⌘-,), under the General option

- In PowerPoint's Preferences (⌘-,), under the View option

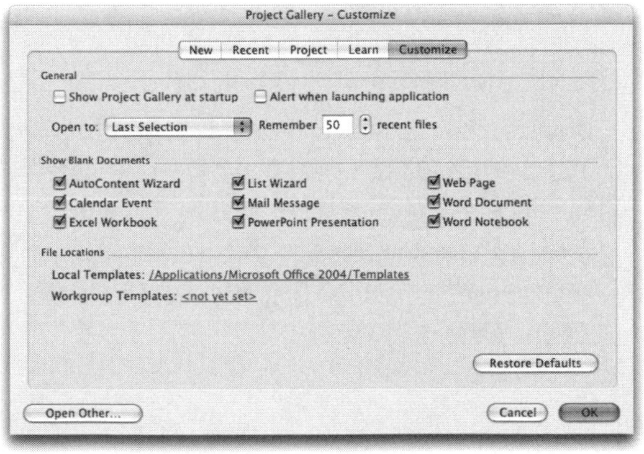

Figure 4-13. Unchecking "Show Project Gallery at startup" in this dialog works for all Office applications.

POWERPOINT

WEIGHT WATCHERS FOR POWERPOINT FILES

The Annoyance: I have a PowerPoint file that's getting too big to email, and I'm not even finished with it. Is there a way that I can bring this bad-boy down in size?

The Fix: It isn't the text that's bloating the PowerPoint file, it's the graphics and video. Working on your images can reduce PowerPoint's file size if you follow these tips:

- Edit your graphics before you import into PowerPoint. Although PowerPoint has some graphic editing tools, you'll end up with smaller files if you edit before you import the image.

- Crop your image before you drag it into PowerPoint. There are many times (most of the time, actually), when you don't need to see the entire image. You can usually cut out the background or crop in close to a portion of your subject. Take a look at photos used in ads or shots on TV. Frequently, close-ups of people don't include the person's entire head. By cropping, you not only get a smaller file size, but the resulting image is often more powerful.

- Keep the number of pixels down. If you aren't printing your presentation, you need only image resolution that is as good as your screen or projector. This falls between 72 dpi and about 96 dpi. If you want good quality printouts, however, skip this tip. Another way to reduce the number of pixels is to use your graphics software to reduce the size (in inches) while keeping the resolution fixed. Using PowerPoint's resize handles does not reduce the PowerPoint file size.

- Convert to grayscale. You can drastically reduce graphics file sizes by going gray. It doesn't work with every image, obviously, but grayscale might even enhance some pictures.

- Use JPEG instead of TIFF for photos. JPEG images are compressed and take a lot less space than TIFF images. As an added bonus, the JPEGs retain enough image quality for printing.
- Use GIF for non-photo images. GIF files can only support 256 colors, which take a lot less disk space than the millions of colors found in most photographs.

If your file is still too big to email, you can separate the graphics from the PowerPoint file and send them separately. In this case, PowerPoint links to the graphics rather than embedding them. To do this, go to File → Save As, select PowerPoint Package from the Format pop-up, and click Save. This copies the linked images, movies, and sounds to a separate folder, which you can then send separately if needed.

FIX FONT PROBLEMS

The Annoyance: After spending hours carefully crafting a presentation, I discover that it looks terrible on other computers. The fonts other users see on their computers aren't the same fonts I used when I built the presentation, and this throws off the whole layout. You might expect this to happen to Windows users, but Mac users also report similar problems.

The Fix: The problem here is that PowerPoint doesn't embed fonts in the presentation. It just tells the operating system to display the fonts. In order for everything to look the same, the people viewing your presentation on their own machine must have the same fonts that you used. And if they don't? PowerPoint takes an educated guess and substitutes another font. PowerPoint's guess may be close-but-no-cigar, which means the substituted font sizes differently from the font you've chosen, causing the layout to look like you threw it together at the last minute.

Here are some strategies for preventing font substitution:

- Only use the fonts that came with Microsoft Office. This is safe for presentations displayed Macs and PCs. Office fonts include Arial, Arial Black, Century Gothic, Comic Sans MS, Copperplate Gothic Bold, Copperplate Gothic Light, Curlz MT, Impact, Lucida

> **USE WORD TO OUTLINE YOUR SLIDES**
> PowerPoint has a pretty good outliner, but it doesn't hold a digital candle to the outliner that has blessed numerous versions of Word for over a decade. Fortunately, it's easy to compose your outline in Word and move it to PowerPoint.
>
> In Word, just choose File → Send to → Microsoft PowerPoint. PowerPoint creates a new file, imports the outline from Word, and creates the presentation's slides for you. (You can also import Word outlines from within PowerPoint by using File → Open, but this is a bit more work.)
>
> This works in the opposite direction, too. If you have a PowerPoint presentation you'd like to export to Word, just select File → Send to → Microsoft Word and PowerPoint creates a brand new outline based on your presentation.

Handwriting, Monotype Sorts, Tahoma, Times New Roman, Verdana, and Wingdings. There are also fonts on the Office CD, in the Value Pack folder, but you can't count on those being installed on other users' computers.

- Use fonts that come with Mac OS X. In addition to Office's fonts, it is safe to use Mac OS X fonts if your presentation will only be displayed on other Macs. Mac OS X's preinstalled fonts include American Typewriter, Baskerville, Big Carlson, Cochin, Copperplate, Didot, Futura, Gill Sans, Helvetica, Herculanum, Marker Felt, Optima, Papyrus, and Zapfino.
- Bring the fonts with you. If you are doing a presentation on another Mac, copy the fonts you used to a CD and install them on the Mac you'll be using to give the presentation. You'll find most fonts in /Library/Fonts. For the most part, you can't move Mac fonts to a Windows machine, and vice versa. After installing the font, you may need to log out (⌘→ Log Out) and log back in again before the font is available to other applications.

- Save your presentation as a PDF file. If your recipients don't need to edit the presentation, and it doesn't include movies or sound, you can convert it to a PDF file, which just about every computer user can read. From the Print dialog box, click the Save As PDF button.

KEEP QUICKTIME MOVIES WHEN MOVING TO PCS

The Annoyance: If I insert a QuickTime movie in a PowerPoint file, it doesn't play when I move the file to a Windows machine. When I run the same file on a Mac, the embedded movie plays just fine. Doesn't Power-Point for Windows support QuickTime?

The Fix: The problem is that PowerPoint for Windows supports older versions of QuickTime only, while the Mac version supports the latest. Specifically, PowerPoint for Windows does not support the newer coder/decoders (known as codecs), such as Sorenson, used to compress the video in more recent versions of QuickTime. To solve this problem, you can use video editing software to replace the codec of the movie with the older Cinepak codec. You do this before embedding the QuickTime movie into the PowerPoint presentation.

You can make this change with QuickTime Pro, which is a $30 upgrade to the version of QuickTime that is part of Mac OS X (see *http://www.apple.com/quicktime/upgrade/*). Once you've purchased and registered QuickTime Pro in the QuickTime preference panel (go to System Preferences → QuickTime, and then click on the Registration button), here's what you do:

1. Open the movie with QuickTime Player.
2. Go to File → Export; a dialog opens.
3. In the Export pop-up menu, select "Movie to Quick-Time movie."
4. Click the Options button; the Movie Settings dialog opens.
5. Click the Settings button; the Compression Settings dialog opens.
6. Select Cinepak from the Video pop-up menu.
7. Click OK in the Compression Settings and Movie Settings dialogs.
8. Click Save in the Export dialog. (Make sure the file-name ends with the *.mov* extension.)

Now, when you insert the QuickTime movie in your Power-Point presentation and send it to a Windows user, they shouldn't have any problems running it on their PC.

KEEP POWERPOINT HIDDEN AT END OF A SHOW

The Annoyance: There's nothing more embarrassing than having my audience see PowerPoint's user interface when I've finished showing my presentation. I'm not doing a demo of PowerPoint, so why should I display the toolbars, formatting palette, and other gizmos? I don't like to leave my final slide up on the screen, because I like to turn up the lights and have the attention focused on me.

The Fix: A single key solves this problem for you. When you get to the last slide, just hit the B key—this turns the screen to black. You can then turn up the lights and turn off the project without exposing PowerPoint's GUI to your audience. You can also hit the B key any time during the presentation—for example, when someone in the audience asks you a question and you need to pause to respond. Pressing the B key again brings you back to the current slide so you can pick up where you left off. Just remember "B" is for "black."

ADD TEMPLATES TO POWERPOINT

The Annoyance: I'm sick and tired of the same old boring templates that came with PowerPoint. They all look kind of, well, "Microsoft-ish." Besides, I want my presentation to stand out, not look like everyone else's.

The Fix: There are plenty of places that you can find templates to add to PowerPoint's repertoire.

Microsoft has a bunch of templates you can download for free (*http://www.microsoft.com/mac/downloads.aspx*). Of course, these are by definition "Microsoft-ish." Another source is PowerBacks (*http://www.powerbacks.com*), which offers several bundles of PowerPoint templates. To give you an idea of the cost, one bundle from PowerBacks includes 1200 PowerPoint templates for a mere $12. They also offer packs of 2400 templates. Not that you would ever need that many templates, but you are more likely to find templates you like from a huge selection of templates than you would with a smaller choice.

Another web site, *http://www.123powerpoint.com/*, offers hundreds of templates that you can purchase and download individually.

If you really want to get away from a Microsoft look and feel, you can abandon PowerPoint altogether and switch over to Apple's own presentation software, Keynote. For more on Keynote, keep reading.

SWITCH TO KEYNOTE

The Annoyance: PowerPoint and I just don't get along. The interface is too complex, and I don't have enough control over the design and placement of text and graphics. The annoyances are just too many to put up with.

The Fix: This sounds like a job for Keynote (*http://www.apple.com/keynote*), Apple's rival presentation application. Apple developed Keynote for Steve Jobs, who uses it whenever he needs to give a keynote address (hence its name). The first thing you'll notice is that Keynote's presentations don't look *anything* like those created with PowerPoint. They look more like the iPhoto books you iDVD layouts that you can produce.

You start out in Keynote by choosing a "theme," as you to do in iDVD. Once you get going, you'll notice how easy

tip

As with PowerPoint, you're bound to get tired of the same old presentation themes that come with Keynote. Fortunately, Keynote Theme Park (*http://www.keynotethemepark.com*) has some great themes you can download for free, and if you're willing to shell out a few bucks, you can opt to pay for one of their ThemePaks.

Keynote presentations are to modify. For instance, you can adjust the placement of text and graphics by gently snapping objects to various grid alignments. Text kerning and anti-aliasing is automatic, and the included fonts are beautiful. You can place photos and movies on a slide and in tables, and you can resize images by simply dragging the image controls. Keynote also has some very cool 2D and 3D transition effects, such as a rotating cube to move between slides.

Keynote can also import from and export to PowerPoint's file format, but not without requiring you to do a little bit of reformatting. If you need to send a presentation to a group of people, you're better off exporting it as a PDF file (via File → Export).

The bottom line is that Keynote is easier to use than PowerPoint and produces more polished-looking slides. If you don't yet have a presentation program, the $99 Keynote gives you more bang for the buck than PowerPoint's $229 bill.

EXCEL

TURN FONT SMOOTHING ON IN EXCEL

The Annoyance: The cell text in Excel X looks odd—kind of jaggy—not smooth like other applications. It's like this on both my Macs. My friend has the new Excel 2004, and to my surprise, the text in his version

Excel looks smooth. Do I need to upgrade to Excel 2004 in order to get text that's easier on the eyes?

The Fix: No, you need only to turn on font smoothing. Both versions of Excel have an odd "feature" that lets you set font smoothing separately from that of Mac OS X's System Preferences. (Why Excel needs it own smoothing control is known only to Microsoft.) The feature is nearly identical in the two versions of Excel, except that in Excel X, font smoothing is turned off by default (smoothing is turned on by default in Excel 2004).

To set smoothing in either version of Excel, go to Excel's preferences (Excel → Preferences, or ⌘-,) and click View. To turn on font smoothing, click on the checkbox next to "Enable Quartz text smoothing," and you're all set.

SWITCH MY ROWS TO COLUMNS (AND VICE VERSA)

The Annoyance: Doh! I just realized that this monster of a spreadsheet I created would work better if the rows were columns and the columns were rows. Copying and pasting each individual cell would waste a whole afternoon. Is there a cure for row-and-column dyslexia?

The Fix: Indeed there is—a slick feature called Transpose. This is my favorite feature of Excel, one that has been around for a long time. Transpose is easy to use—it's just a slight variation on copy and paste. The top of Figure 4-14 shows a spreadsheet stretching out to the right, off of your screen, and into the wild blue yonder—a good candidate for transposing. The 12 months serve as column titles along the top, and city names appear in the first cell of the rows on the left. By reversing the months and cities, you can fit the entire table on your screen.

Here's how to transpose these cells:

1. Select the cells that you want to transpose.
2. Copy the table (⌘-C).
3. Click on the cell to designate it as the top-left cell of the new table.

4. Select Paste Special from the contextual menu (Control-click or right-click a cell).
5. Select Transpose in the Paste Special dialog.
6. Click OK.

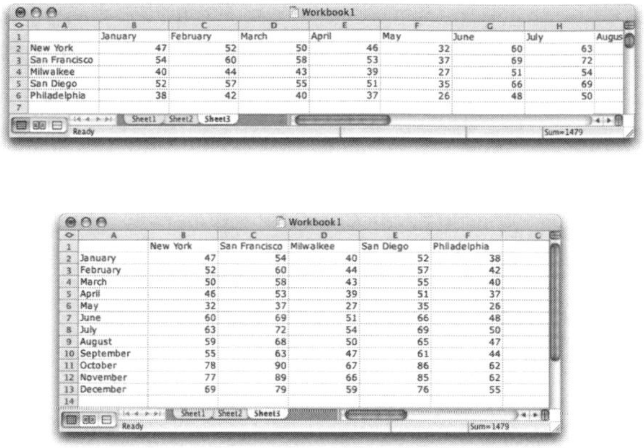

Figure 4-14. The original table (top) runs off the screen to the right. After transposing the rows and column with Paste Special, the table fits in the space (bottom).

REFORMAT NUMBERS AND TEXT

The Annoyance: I hate it when Excel second-guesses me. For instance, I have a spreadsheet that includes product codes that contain slashes (/) in one of the columns. Excel insists on converting the slashes to dates. I know that I can open the Format Cells dialog, click the Numbers tab, and set the cell to good old text, but this is an awful lot of rigamarole to go through. Is there a way to stop Excel from trying to read my mind?

The Fix: There's no need to consult the Format Cells dialog just to change a bunch of numbers or fix some text formatting. You can use certain characters at the beginning of your text string to tell Excel how you want the cell to be formatted. When you hit Return (to go down) or Tab (to got to the cell to the right), the special character disappears, leaving your text or number exactly as you typed it. Here are the more common formatting characters you can use to tell Excel who's boss:

- Need to format something as text? Insert an apostrophe ('). When you use an apostrophe at the beginning of your text string, Excel won't convert it to a number format, even if the number string contains slashes. When you hit Return (or Tab), the apostrophe disappears, and what you type is what you get.

- Need to format something as a fraction? Insert a zero (0) followed by a space ( ) before the fraction. Excel even has the ability to do math on fractions instead of decimals. You don't need to use a 0-space in an equation, however. When the first character in a cell is an equal sign (=), Excel won't try to convert the fractions to dates.

UNDO ACCIDENTAL HYPERLINKS IN EXCEL X

The Annoyance: Like many people, I use Excel X to keep lists and tables. Sometimes I'll use the @ sign to signify a meeting location, such as "Bob @ office." Of course, Excel X automatically converts this to an email link, just as it converted my product numbers with slashes into dates (see the previous annoyance Reformat Numbers and Text). This is quite annoying, because every time I click on the cell, my email program launches with a blank email message window. A similar thing happens if I type in an actual web URL beginning with "http." I can't find any setting to turn this off or to convert the live link to plain text.

The Fix: There isn't any way to turn off this "feature" of Excel X, but there are several ways to work around this annoyance.

- Use an apostrophe before the text as you type it. As described previously, this tells Excel to format the cell as text. Unfortunately, you can't go back and add an apostrophe to get rid of the link.

- Hit ⌘-Z to undo the link. You should use ⌘-Z immediately after Excel converts the text to a live link. If you start typing elsewhere, you'll have to keep hitting ⌘-Z and undo everything you typed after the link.

RENAME AND REMOVE SHEETS

When you create a new Excel spreadsheet, do you ever notice how it always pops up with three sheets (Sheet 1, Sheet 2, and Sheet 3)? While these are fine names for an empty spreadsheet, you might want to rename them to something more descriptive after you've filled in all the blanks.

To rename a sheet, just double-click on one of the tabs and type in something more descriptive.

If you don't need all three sheets in your Excel file, you can delete the ones you don't want by clicking on the unneeded sheet's tab and selecting Delete Sheet from the Edit menu.

This makes it easier to find the sheet you need, and removing empty sheets also makes the Excel file a wee bit smaller in size.

- Convert the link to text with the contextual menu. This is difficult to do, because clicking a cell with a hyperlink launches your email program or web browser. To avoid this, click the cell next to the hyperlink and use the arrow keys to navigate to the linked cell. Press the Control key and select Hyperlink from the contextual menu. In the dialog that appears, click the Remove Link button in the lower left.

Excel 2004 doesn't have this problem, as it takes a more practical approach. Instead of assuming that anything that looks like an Internet address needs to be a hyperlink, Excel assumes that it is just text. If you want a real hyperlink in Excel 2004, enclose the link in quotes and parentheses, and precede it with "=HYPERLINK" all in caps. For instance:

```
=HYPERLINK("http://www.acme.com")
```

When you hit Return (or Tab), the web or email address you've entered becomes an active hyperlink in the Excel spreadsheet. When you click on that link, your default web browser or email program opens up.

AUTOMATICALLY ENTER THE DATE AND TIME

The Annoyance: I need to type the date into quite a few cells in many different spreadsheets several times a day, every single day. Is there any way to automate this tedious task? Can I create an AppleScript or some kind of macro to do this for me?

The Fix: There's no need to resort to programming AppleScripts. Excel has a built-in key command to enter the current date in the selected cell: Control-; (semicolon). Add the Shift key (Control-Shift-;), and Excel inserts the current time.

Excel gets the current date and time from Mac OS X, so your Mac needs to be set to the correct date and time in the Date & Time preference panel (System Preferences → Date & Time).

FREEZE PANES TO NAIL DOWN COLUMN HEADS

The Annoyance: Excel's split pane feature lets me keep the row and column headings visible while scrolling the main table. Unfortunately, the scroll bar at the top can get out of whack, moving the column heads out of view (as in the top of Figure 4-15).

> **tip**
>
> Remember our discussion about discontinuous selecting text in Word? You can do the same in Excel. While holding the ⌘ key, you can select cells, rows, and columns that aren't next each other. You can then apply a formatting change on all of the selections at the same time.

The Fix: Split panes have been in Excel for so long that they're almost a historical feature. More recently,

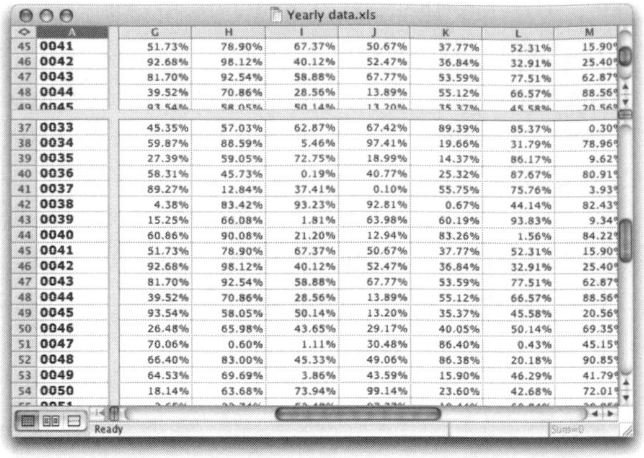

Figure 4-15. When you use the split panes feature, scrolling in the top pane can easily get out of whack.

Microsoft added the Freeze Panes (called "Freeze Pane" in Excel 2004) menu command that accomplishes the same goal, but much more elegantly.

You can see in Figure 4-16 that the Freeze Panes feature doesn't let you scroll the column headings. Instead, Freeze Panes locks the column heads (and rows) in place, while still letting you scroll through the contents of the main table. To use Freeze Panes, make sure the spreadsheet is in Normal view and select Window → Freeze Panes. To unfreeze the panes, click on a cell that will be the top left cell of the main table, and choose Window → Unfreeze Panes from the menu bar.

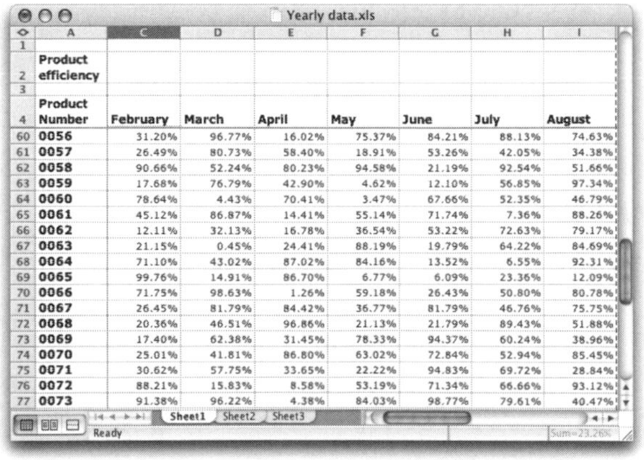

Figure 4-16. The cleaner Freeze Pane keeps the column headings fixed.

DROP AN EXCEL SPREADSHEET INTO A KEYNOTE PRESENTATION

The Annoyance: It's such a pain to get data and charts from an Excel spreadsheet into my Keynote presentations. I like Keynote, but I'm afraid I'll need to go back to PowerPoint because of this.

The Fix: Let's not be hasty, now. While there's no denying that the integration between Excel and Power-Point is much better than between Excel and Keynote, there's no need to dump Keynote. Instead, you can use a handy little utility called XL2K, a free download from *http://homepage.mac.com/imaxinc/index.html.* XL2K moves Excel tables into standard Keynote tables, and moves charts from Excel into standard Keynote Charts. Just select the data, launch XL2K, and choose Table, Chart, or Both. XL2K also lets you choose the chart type. Seconds later, you're looking at a Keynote slide with your Excel numbers and charts.

VIRTUAL PC

SPEED UP VIRTUAL PC

The Annoyance: At first, Virtual PC seemed truly miraculous—it actually lets me run Windows XP on my Mac. Wow! Well, that just turned out to be a theoretical "wow," because my copy of Virtual PC 6 is really too slow to do anything wow-ish with.

The Fix: Virtual PC has had a tough time since Mac OS X came along. In Mac OS 9, Virtual PC could grab hold of almost all of the Mac's processing power—something Mac OS X just won't allow. In addition, several upgrades to Mac OS X make Virtual PC run slower. There are also certain programs, such as some of the features of Norton AntiVirus, that cause Virtual PC to run very slowly. With Version 7, Microsoft optimized Virtual PC for Mac OS X and made the graphics snappier. But even Virtual PC 7 can benefit from these time-tested methods of speeding up Virtual PC:

- Run Windows 2000. This is the fastest version of Windows to run on Virtual PC. (Windows NT is also good, but it's a bit old.) Older versions of Windows have performance problems, because they are not fully 32-bit operating systems. Windows XP runs slower than Windows 2000, because the Windows XP interface is more graphics intensive. Windows 2000 is completely 32-bit, but it doesn't have the overhead of Windows XP.

- Buy more RAM. You need enough memory to simultaneously run two operating systems *and* run Virtual PC at the same time. No matter what Apple and Microsoft say, you need a minimum of 512 MB in a Mac to run Virtual PC. More is definitely better.

- Allocate at least 256 MB RAM to Windows. When you launch Virtual PC, select your copy of Windows in the Virtual PC List window, and then click the Settings button. In the Settings window, click on PC Memory. You can use the slider bar to adjust the amount of RAM for Windows.

- Make sure your Mac is fast enough. Take the minimum processor requirements for Virtual PC very seriously. Processor speed is a huge factor in making everything run smoothly.

- Disable Norton Antivirus Auto-Protect. Not everyone with Norton Antivirus has a problem with Virtual PC, but many people have found that it can bring Virtual PC to a screeching halt. If you have Norton Antivirus installed, you can turn off the Auto-Protect feature in System Preferences.

- Don't run other Mac software—at least, not while you're running Virtual PC. You want to give as much of the Mac's processor to Virtual PC.

- Don't run Classic mode. The Classic environment takes a big chunk of your Mac's processor power. Before you start Virtual PC, go the System Preferences and make sure Classic isn't running.

- Place Virtual PC's virtual drive image file on another hard disk. This can be an external FireWire drive or a second internal drive.

- Turn off VPC Networking. If you aren't networking or accessing the Internet from Windows, you may see some speed gains by shutting off the network in Virtual PC's Settings dialog. (Click Networking and uncheck "Enable Networking.")

Get Info

I run a web site called MacWindows, which is devoted to helping people with Mac/Windows integration problems. Here, you'll find several pages that describe Virtual PC problems and solutions. For Virtual PC 6, point your browser at *http://www. macwindows.com/VPC6.html*. For other versions of Virtual PC, change the 6 in the web address to 3, 4, 5, or 7, respectively.

RUN VIRTUAL PC RUNNING ON A G5

The Annoyance: My copy of Virtual PC doesn't work with my brand spankin' new iMac G5. The very same copy runs just fine on my PowerBook G4. What gives?

The Fix: In order to run Virtual PC on any Mac with a G5 processor, you need Virtual PC 7 or later. All previous versions are incompatible with Macs with G5 processors. There's no working around this except to upgrade.

LOCATE THE VPC 5.0.4 UPDATE

The Annoyance: I've been happily running Virtual PC 5 for many a year. Recently, I had a problem with my hard drive, which I had to reformat. I reinstalled Virtual PC 5 from the CD, but I don't have the 5.0.4 update, which fixed a bunch of bugs. Microsoft offers upgrades to other old applications on its web site, but doesn't offer the Virtual PC 5.0.4 update. Do those misers at Microsoft want me to pay for a later version?

The Fix: Microsoft doesn't offer the 5.0.4 upgrade because they don't own Version 5; they bought Version 6 only. Unfortunately, there is no official source for this important 5.0.4 update. When Connectix was around, it offered the 5.0.4 update at its web site. Connectix shut down it's web site several months after it sold Virtual PC 6 to Microsoft, only offers updates to version 6 and later.

You can find unofficial sources of the 5.0.4 update posted on web sites by individual users who feel they are doing a public service. These sites often aren't up for long, so I can't quote any URLs here. Google is a good way to locate the update using the term "Virtual PC 5.0.4 Update." You're likely to locate a copy. You can also visit a page on my web site, *http://www.macwindows.com/VPC5.html, where I try to keep currently active links to the 5.0.4 update.*

iLife
ANNOYANCES

iLife—Apple's bundle of iTunes, iPhoto, iMovie, iDVD and GarageBand—takes the complex technologies of music, photographs, video, and TV, and simplifies them so that anyone can create or organize content. iLife has revolutionized multimedia and even changed the music industry. So what could be annoying about the favorite software suite of many a Mac user? You might ask this if you haven't been using the "iApps" for any length of time.

Fun, innovative, and often downright amazing, iLife has one trait that causes annoyances to occur almost by definition— its software. While designed to work smoothly together, the iLife apps are actually developed by different groups at Apple, making them susceptible to quirky little hiccups and bugs that can drive you nuts.

This chapter provides over 50 tips and techniques for getting around iLife's most frustrating annoyances. This includes streamlining management of hundreds or thousands of songs or pictures in iTunes and iPhoto, making video editing in iMovie easier, fixing problems with creating DVDs, and dealing with the performance demands of GarageBand. Just one note: the iTunes annoyances in this chapter are annoying when you're sitting in front of your Mac. iTunes annoyances related to the iPod are described in Chapter 6.

ITUNES

BOOKMARK ITUNES MUSIC STORE SEARCH RESULTS

The Annoyance: iTunes doesn't have any way to get back to songs I've previously found at the iTunes Music Store. I like to revisit searches I've previously done to see if Apple has added anything new. If I could bookmark a search, I could quickly check to see what's available, instead of retyping in the same search criteria.

The Fix: While you can't bookmark Music Store searches within iTunes, you can use some of Mac OS X's Internet features to facilitate this function. The easiest method works in Jaguar (Mac OS X 10.2), but not in Panther (10.3). (Don't you hate it when Apple removes features?) The version of iTunes doesn't matter here. In Jaguar, when iTunes returns the results of a search, you can grab the bar called "Search Results for:" and drag it, as shown in Figure 5-1.

![iTunes Music Store search results in Jaguar showing Top Albums with Best of Bowie, Space Oddity by David Bowie, Outside (Bonus Tracks), Hot Space by Queen, and Top Songs list]

Figure 5-1. After an iTunes Music Store search in Jaguar, drag the Search Results bar to the Dock or the Finder to create a URL quick link file.

If you drag this bar directly to the Dock (near the Trash icon), it turns into a URL icon (the icon with the cursor over it in Figure 5-2). When you click on this icon, it launches iTunes and runs your search in the Music Store. If you instead drag the iTunes Search Results bar to the Desktop or a Finder window, the Mac creates a file with an HTTP icon. Again, double-clicking this file icon brings up iTunes and runs the search.

Figure 5-2. In the Dock, the search result has the URL icon (on the left). If you drag the search result first to the desktop and then to the Dock, it has the HTTP icon.

You can keep a folder full of these HTTP icons or drag them to the Dock as well.

Unfortunately, this trick doesn't work if you're using Panther. So, I'll share another, more complicated trick: Use a special type off address to create an iTunes Music Store bookmark in your web browser. When you choose this bookmark, it launches iTunes and displays the results. You could also drag the URL from the web browser to the Dock or the Finder to create icons, similar to those shown in Figure 5-2.

To create a bookmark, type the following text as a single line in the address field of your web browser:

```
itms://phobos.apple.com/WebObjects/MZSearch.woa/
wa/advancedSearchResults? &artistTerm=artists_
name
```

Replace *artists_name* with your search term. This can be one word, such as *Prince* or *Crosby*, or multiple terms separated by a space, as in *David Crosby*. Note that there is also a space between the question mark (?) and the ampersand (&) after Search Results.

If you press the Return key, iTunes opens, displaying the iTunes Music Store search results—a good test to see if you've typed this address correctly. If you are happy with the results, you can switch back to the web browser and bookmark the (blank) web page with the address that you have just typed.

You can create URLs that search several different criteria by changing the terms at the end of the URL:

```
&artistTerm=artists_name
&songTerm=song_title
&albumTerm=album_title
&composerTerm=composer
```

Again, the words after the equals sign are your search terms. For more complex searches—the equivalents of iTunes' Power Searches—you can string these terms together at the end of the address line, using a space in front of the ampersand. For instance, the following example returns any song by David Bowie that contains the word "space" in the name of the song:

```
&artistTerm=bowie &songTerm=space
```

POWER SEARCHING ON THE ITUNES MUSIC STORE

Have you ever conducted a Power Search of the iTunes Music Store? When Music Store is selected in iTunes's Source list, the Search Music Store field has a small triangle near the front. If you click on this triangle, a pop-up menu appears listing the following search criteria options:

- ☒ All (the default)
- ☒ Artists
- ☒ Albums
- ☒ Composers
- ☒ Songs

Select the Power Search option at the bottom of the pop-up menu to bring up a new panel with fields for all of these categories. You can search in multiple categories at once, which helps you zero in on your musical target.

MAKE THE ITUNES 4.5+ ARROWS USEFUL

The Annoyance: iTunes 4.5 added an annoying "feature" designed to help Apple sell more music: the arrows next to every item in the first three columns of my music library. Click on one, and it takes you to relevant information in the iTunes Music Store. Not only do I not need to visit the Music Store this often, but also the ar-

rows mar a previously elegant user interface. Talk about fixing something that ain't broke.

The Fix: There are three ways to deal with the arrow clutter (shown in Figure 5-3). Two of these options actually turn the arrows into a very useful feature: one-click searches that point to your personal music library. The third gets rid of them altogether.

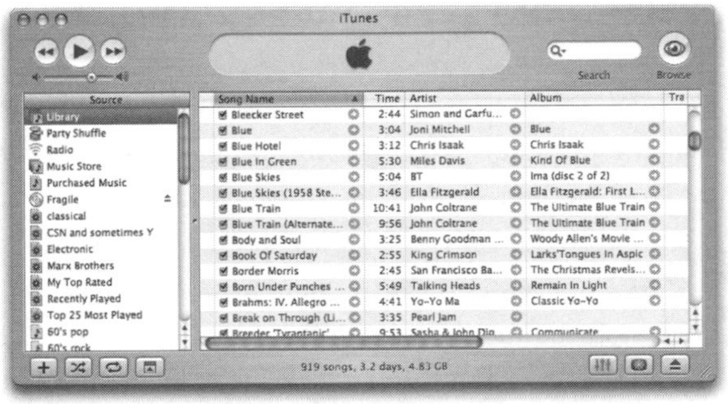

Figure 5-3. The arrows after every item in iTunes 4.5 and later can be annoying clutter when they point to the Music Store, but become one-click searches when you point them towards your own music library.

Hold the Option key when you click an arrow.

This brings you to similar items in your music library instead of the Music Store. For instance, if you Option-click the arrow next to the name of an artist, iTunes shows you all of the items in your library by that artist. The Option key turns a Music Store marketing ploy into a slick, one-click search mechanism for your music library.

Use a shell command to reverse the Option key's behavior.

This makes a simple click on an arrow take you to items in your library and lets you use the Option key to go the Music Store. Just quit iTunes, open Terminal (*/Applications/Utilities*), and enter the following command (don't forget to press the Return key afterwards):

```
defaults write com.apple.iTunes
invertStoreLinks -bool YES
```

The change takes effect the next time you launch iTunes 4.5 or later. This is a slick trick that I use on every Mac that I work on.

Turn off the arrows.

If you still think the arrows are just so much interface clutter, turn them off in iTunes' Preferences (⌘-,). In the General pane, uncheck the "Show links to Music Store" option.

REDUCE ITUNES'S CPU USAGE ON OLDER MACS

The Annoyance: iTunes is a hog when it comes to playing music on my older Mac. I noticed that everything was running slower when I was listening to music, so I checked the Activity Monitor (CPU Monitor in Mac OS X 10.2 and earlier). Sure enough, iTunes causes the processor to be nearly maxed out if I have a few other applications open. Don't tell me I have to buy a new Mac just to listen to iTunes—that would really be annoying.

The Fix: In Mac OS X, iTunes takes enough processing power required for playing music without skipping. (Those who remember iTunes 1 and 2 may remember that merely holding down a menu in Mac OS 9 could make iTunes skip). While newer Macs have more than enough

processor speed for iTunes, older Macs with a 500 MHz or lower processor use a big chunk of your processor's power just to play music.

Fortunately, you can change a few settings to make iTunes a little thriftier with your Mac's processor. Open iTunes Preferences (⌘-,) and go to the Audio pane (called the Effects pane in iTunes 4.5 and earlier). Turning off Sound Enhancer produces the greatest effect, but you can also turn off Sound Check (shown in Figure 5-4).

I would never annoy a reader by suggesting he buy a new Mac solely for iTunes, but you might investigate getting a faster processor, as discussed in Chapter 7.

> Ever want to import just one song from a CD? You have to manually uncheck every song but the one. Annoying, huh? Next time, hold down the ⌘ key when you uncheck a song and *all* of the songs on the CD will uncheck. Then you can re-check the song you want. It works the other way as well—⌘-clicking an empty box checks all of the songs on the CD, in a playlist, or in your entire library.

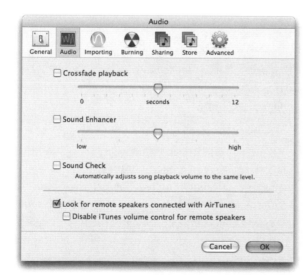

Figure 5-4. Turning off Sound Enhancer and Sound Check in iTunes improves overall performance of slower Macs.

LAUNCH AN INTERNET RADIO WEB SITE FROM ITUNES

The Annoyance: I like the variety and number of radio stations iTunes can play. It's also handy that iTunes displays the URL for the station (as in Figure 5-5). I often like to check out the web sites of some of these stations, but iTunes doesn't let me copy a station's URL in order to paste it into my web browser. Instead, I have to type the URL. Kind of annoying, I'd say.

The Fix: There's no need to copy and paste—iTunes takes you directly to the radio station's web site. Click the top of the iTunes window until the station's URL appears. Press the ⌘ key while clicking on the URL dis-

iTunes
http://www.radioparadise.com
Elapsed Time: 2:28

Figure 5-5. When iTunes shows a URL for a radio station, ⌘-click it to bring up the station's web page in your web browser.

played by iTunes and your web browser launches, displaying the station's web page.

RECORD INTERNET RADIO AUDIO STREAMS

The Annoyance: Sure, iTunes can record music from a CD and play an Internet radio station, but I'd really love it if iTunes could record music from an Internet radio station.

The Fix: When Apple first launched the iTunes Music Store, the music industry was leading an (unsuccessful) effort to kill Internet radio. This is the main reason why iTunes doesn't let you rip Internet radio streams and probably won't any time in the near (or distant) future. However, there are several third-party utilities that can digitally record whatever your Mac is playing.

One of the best utilities is a free application called Wire-Tap from Ambrosia software (*http://www.ambrosiasw.com/utilities/freebies/*). WireTap is a simple floating palette (shown in Figure 5-6) that records any sound generated by your Mac, including iTunes's Internet radio. It also records system beeps and other alert sounds your Mac makes, so if you are recording while you work, you may want to turn these sounds off during recordings. (You can turn these off in the System Preferences Sound pane, under the Sound Effects tab.)

When you hit the Stop button, WireTap creates an AIFF audio file using one of several compression options (including no compression), which you set in WireTap Preferences. To get the best sound, record in uncompressed AIFF and then use iTunes to convert that to either an AAC- or MP3-encoded file. Internet radio has a lower quality than music on CDs, so don't be too concerned about using a high bit rate. If you've recorded a set of

Is Stream Ripping Legal?

Although the record industry doesn't go out of its way to say it, this kind of recording is fair use if you use the recording for your own purposes, just as it is legal to record FM radio onto cassette tapes. You cross the piracy line if you use the recordings to swap for other music files.

Compare Playlists Side by Side

Ever want to view two or more playlists at the same time? You can open any playlist in its own window by double-clicking the icon next to its name in the Source list. (If you double-click the name, you just highlight the name.) Open as many playlists windows as you need. You can even drag items between them, as well as from your iTunes Library.

Figure 5-6. WireTap lets you record Internet radio from iTunes or other applications.

songs, you may want to break them up into individual tracks with a waveform editor, such as the Amadeus from HairerSoft ($30, *http://www.hairersoft.com*).

KEEP ITUNES MUSIC ON ANOTHER HARD DRIVE

The Annoyance: My music collection has outgrown my hard drive—I've run out of disk space. I want to move my music collection to another hard drive. I've tried copying the iTunes Music folder over and deleting the original. Now, iTunes can't find my music and all of the songs in my iTunes Library have a little exclamation mark next to them. Bummer.

The Fix: Don't let iTunes boss you around—you can keep your music wherever you want, including on another hard drive. First, make sure you get the right folder: it's the *entire* iTunes folder in your Music folder in your Home folder (*~/Music*). If you open the iTunes folder and only copy the iTunes Music folder, you miss two important files: *iTunes Music Library* and *iTunes Music Library.xml*, which include the play counts, ratings, and other song info.

Next, tell iTunes that you've moved your music collection:

1. Connect and mount the new hard drive that contains the iTunes folder.

2. Open iTunes Preferences and go to the Advanced pane.

3. Under iTunes Music Location, click the Change button.

4. In the file browser, go to the new hard disk, open the iTunes folder, and select the iTunes Music folder.

5. Click the Choose button. Then click OK to close the Preferences window.

After you've done that, quit and then relaunch iTunes; it should pick up the new location of your iTunes Library and display your songs.

GROUPING FOR MULTIPLE SONG CATEGORIES

The Annoyance: iTunes could use more than one genre to describe a song. For instance, an Ella Fitzgerald song can be jazz and vocal, as well as bebop or ballad—*or* all four. Having to assign one genre over another is inflexible. Sometimes I want to bring up all of the jazz tracks sometimes, and just vocals at other times. Classical music can also have multiple descriptors. For instance, sometimes I want to quickly bring up romantic piano music or modern string quartets. Even pop music can belong to multiple genres, such as dance, hip hop, electronic, or even slow, fast, and guitar.

The Fix: This sounds like a job for the Grouping field, added to iTunes 4.2. You can use Grouping as a kind of sub-genre to build smart playlists. (You could also use Comments, but it's a big field, so I prefer to reserve Comments for detailed notes.) You can add terms to the Grouping field in the same place you edit changes to the name and album. Select a song or group of songs and hit the ⌘-I keys, and then click on the Info tab. You can now type in your terms in the Grouping field.

You can use the Grouping category to add as many sub-genres as you need, separated by commas. For example, for a particular Ella Fitzgerald rendition of "A Night in Tunisia," I might add "vocal, bebop, swinging, piano, combo" to the Grouping field. When you create a smart playlist (by selecting New Smart Playlist from the File menu), you can set one or more of the criteria to Grouping, as shown in Figure 5-7. Be sure to use "Grouping contains" from the pop-up menus and not "Grouping is."

Use Grouping with smart playlists to create cross-genre categories that include jazz, rock, classical, and other types to fit a certain mood. For example, you could add a grouping term called "driving" for the type of tunes you like to listen to while you're behind a wheel or "mellow" for a little dinner music.

A few more things you should know about the Grouping field include:

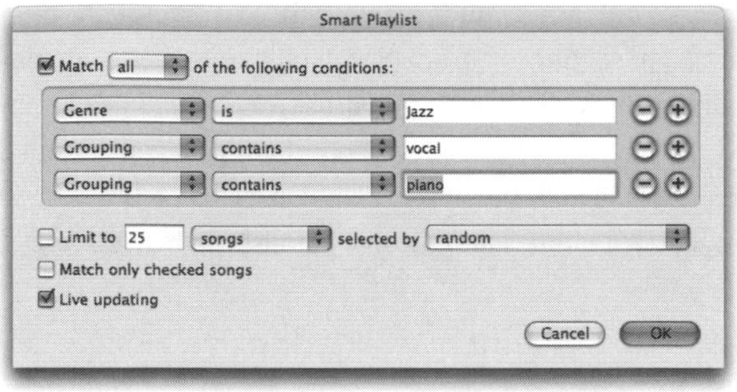

Figure 5-7. This smart playlist collects jazz songs that feature piano and vocal. This works if you use the Grouping field to store sub-genres.

- By Default, the Grouping field is only visible in the Get Info window of a song. However, you can also display a Grouping column in the main pane of iTunes. Just Option-click on the column that you want the Grouping column to come after. A contextual menu appears, listing all of the data categories (shown in Figure 5-8). You can choose Grouping (or any other item) to display its column.

Figure 5-8. Option-click a column, and you receive a list of fields that you can display as a column, including Grouping.

- The Grouping field is stored in MP3 and AAC files, like the title and genre. When you move a music file to another Mac, the Grouping info goes with it.

  In order for your iPod to play smart playlists based on Grouping, you need iPod Update 2004-04-28 or later installed (*http://www.apple.com/ipod/download*). This update works only with third-generation or later iPods. Thes are models with a docking connector on the bottom.

Get Info

Want some ideas about how to create new smart playlists? Want to share a groovin' smart playlist you've created with another iTunes user? Go to *http://smartplaylists.com*; this site lets iTunes users share their smart playlists, as well as tips for creating them.

This is just one way to use the Grouping field. Another way is explained in the next annoyance Use Grouping in Classical Track Naming.

USE GROUPING IN CLASSICAL TRACK NAMING

The Annoyance: iTunes does a good job at organizing pop music, but it's a mess for keeping track of classical music. A classical CD often has three or four pieces of music, each with multiple movements in a separate track. The Internet CD database and the iTunes Music Store usually combine the names of the work and the movement in the "song" title. This leads to some very long titles, such as "Concerto for 2 Violins, Strings, and Continuo in D minor BWV 1043: II. Largo, Ma Non Tanto." Unless the Song Name column is very wide, I can't see which track it is that I'm dealing with.

The Fix: This is another use for the Grouping field—one that is quite different than the one just described. Here, you would move the name of the piece into the Group field and keep the name of the movement in the Song Name field. Figure 5-9 is the "before" example: an album with four pieces of music, each with three movements. (Here, the Song Name column takes up two-thirds of the pane, yet we still can't see the movement names for several of the tracks.)

Figure 5-9. With the name of the piece and the movement both in the Song Name field, it's tough to see what movement each track represents.

In Figure 5-10, I've removed the name of the work from the Song Name, placed it in Grouping, and displayed the Grouping column (as previously described). We can now read all of the movement names.

Figure 5-10. With the redundant name of the work moved to the Grouping field, we can now see the names of the movements.

There is one annoying problem with this approach: if you move these tracks to an iPod, you'll see the movement numbers only, such as "II. Allegro." The fix is to use a playlist to put the whole piece together. You can manually create a playlist, but it's usually easier to create a smart playlist with one line: "Group equals" with the name of the work.

> **ITUNES FOR YOUR HOME STEREO**
> Wouldn't it be great to route your iTunes playlists through your home stereo? It's always been possible—assuming you can run a cable from your Mac to your stereo in another room. Now you can get rid of the wires with AirPort Express with AirTunes ($129, *http://www.apple.com/airportexpress/*). This tiny AirPort base station plugs into a wall outlet near your stereo. Then you can plug your stereo input cable (analog or digital). After some simple setup on the Mac, iTunes will control what comes out of your stereo. Your Mac needs Mac OS X 10.3 or later, iTunes 4.6 or later, and an AirPort or AirPort Extreme card.

ELIMINATE GAPS ON SONGS PLAYBACK

The Annoyance: Some of my CDs contain a string of songs that flow together without a break but are broken up into tracks. (For instance, there's Edvard Greig's *Peer Gynt* and Pink Floyd's *Wish You Were Here*). Unfortunately, after you import these tracks, iTunes plays them back with a small (and annoying) gap in between each track, breaking up the music. Is there any way to get iTunes to play these tracks without that irritating pause?

The Fix: I've discovered two workarounds for this annoyance, each with small problems of its own.

The first workaround uses the crossfade playback feature but with the duration turned down to 0 (iTunes Preferences → Effects → set the Crossfade Effects slider to 0). Although this does improve the transition, those striving for musical purity may not be happy with this solution. The gap is gone, but the two tracks overlap a fraction of a second, which disrupts the rhythm.

For a completely seamless transition, the better solution is to delete the album from iTunes and reimport the CD, using the Join CD Tracks feature (Advanced → Join CD Tracks). This rips a group of selected tracks as a single file, without the annoying gaps between the songs. To use this feature:

- Insert the CD.

- Select the tracks you want to combine.

- Go to the Advanced menu and select Join CD Tracks.

- In the list, the selected tracks now have a single checkbox next to them; press the Import button and the selected tracks will rip as one big file.

Joining tracks also means that you won't be able to bring up the individual songs or sections within. This may not be a problem for some types of classical music and rock albums like Abbey Road. (Do you really want to listen to *Carry That Weight* outside of the Side Two medley?) A more important issue would be if you intend to move this file to an iPod—big files use more of the iPod's battery power, as explained in Chapter 6.

PRINT YOUR OWN ART ON CD COVERS

The Annoyance: iTunes 4.5 added a great new feature—the ability to print CD jewel case covers, listing all of the songs and their durations. The annoying thing is that it only prints the original album cover art, if you happen to have it stored in iTunes. I'd like to use my own photos or drawings for the mix CDs I create; is this possible?

> **SMOOTHER MUSIC STORE PREVIEWS**
>
> Isn't it annoying to click on a 30-second Music Store sample, only to have it stop two or three times before getting through the whole half minute? The problem is a temporarily slow network connection. If this puts a damper on your tunes browsing, you can tell iTunes to download the complete preview before playing it.
>
> Go to iTunes' Preferences (⌘-,), click the Store icon, and select the checkbox next to "Load complete preview before playing." Now when you click a song preview in the iTunes Music Store, you'll have to wait a few seconds as the clip loads before hearing the song preview.

The Fix: Album cover art comes with songs you buy from the iTunes MusicStore, but iTunes also allows you to add art for your CD cover to any song. You can use your own image on a jewel case by treating it as if it were album cover art that you are adding—iTunes can't tell the difference.

1. Select a song in the playlist.

2. Hit ⌘-I click and the Artwork tab.

3. Add your artwork. You can press the Add button to browse for a file or simply drag the file from the Finder to the center area. Even better, drag a photo over from iPhoto.

4. If your song already has album cover art, no problem. You can have multiple pieces of art for any song. In order to print on the jewel case, however, you must move your picture so that it is the first picture on the left, as shown in Figure 5-11.

5. Click OK.

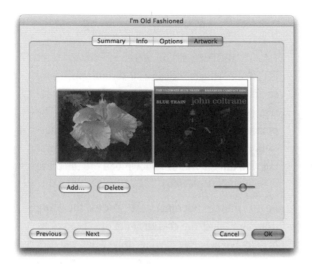

Figure 5-11. You can add your own art to a song by dragging it to the Get Info window of a song. Your added photo needs to sit to the left of any existing album art.

With your art added, you can now print the jewel case:

1. Select the playlist you want to print, and then select the song that has your artwork.

2. Open the Print dialog (⌘-P), which is shown in Figure 5-12.

3. Make sure "CD Jewel case insert" is selected.

4. Go the Theme pop-up menu and select Single Cover. A thumbnail containing your image appears on the right side.

5. Click the Print button.

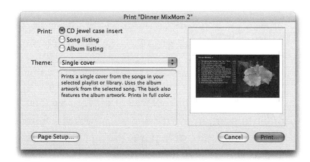

Figure 5-12. When you print your playlist's CD jewel case, your cover image appears in the Print dialog.

After the jewel case cover prints, you might want to delete the art from the song. The cover art increases the size of the song file by as much as half a megabyte. That can add up to a lot of wasted disk space on your Mac and iPod.

IPHOTO

UPGRADE TO IPHOTO 4 OR MORE

The Annoyance: Now that I have few hundred photos, iPhoto 2 is so slow that I'm afraid my kids will graduate before I get to see their school photos.

The Fix: It's time to bite the $50 bullet and buy the latest version of iLife, which is the only way to upgrade to iPhoto 4. iPhoto 4 (there is no Version 3) is a major rewrite that has drastically changed how the application works under the hood. The speed increase is significant. Scrolling, zooming, and sorting all are faster than before, and you can now have up to 25,000 images in your iPhoto library with negligible effect on performance. I haven't tried adding that many images, but adding a few hundred at a time doesn't phase iPhoto 4's database structure.

iPhoto 4 also introduced new features that eliminate some of the annoyances of older versions. For instance, when you created a book in iPhoto 2 or earlier, your only option was to order the hardcover version. Now, you can get a PDF preview of your creation, and you can print it on your own printer. One of the coolest additions to iPhoto 4 is smart albums—the equivalent to iTunes's smart playlists. You can use smart albums to gather together pictures from your entire iPhoto library based on your criteria. Smart albums add a sense of serendipity to slideshows, especially with large photo collections. There's also automatic sorting by year.

That being said, iPhoto 4.0.1 is really the oldest version you should be running. The 4.0.1 update fixed some bugs with smart lists. Minor iPhoto updates are available from Mac OS X's Software Update utility and at *http://www.apple.com/support/downloads/*.

Not sure if the photo you've enhanced or edited in iPhoto is an improvement over the original? With the mouse pointer hovering over the edited image, press the Control key to instantly see the original (untouched) photo again. When you release the Control key, you're back to the edited version. This works with iPhoto's Crop, Enhance, Retouch, Red Eye, B & W (black and white), and Sepia effects, as well as with the Brightness and Contrast controls. Then if you decide you don't like a change you've made, you can simply undo it by using File → Undo (⌘-Z).

SMART SEARCHING WITH SMART ALBUMS

The Annoyance: If iPhoto 4 is supposed to be so great, then why doesn't it have a Search command like the one in iTunes? You can search keywords only using the Show Keyword command in the Photos menu, which has a pretty goofy-looking interface. Now that I have 1000 photos stored, I need a Search command that can search on not just keywords, but on photo titles, album names, comments, and dates.

The Fix: You can easily search iPhoto's library using a smart album you create for this purpose. Choose File → New smart album (Option-⌘-N) from menu bar, name it Search, and then click OK. The new Smart Album appears on the Source list to the left.

When you want to search for something, select your Search album in the Source list and hit the ⌘-I keys to bring up the Smart Album dialog. You can start with using Any Text and Contains from the pop-up menus, and then type in your search term (see Figure 5-13). You can also search by rating, date, roll, and a number of other criteria, including keyword. (Searching for keywords in a smart album uses an interface that is much more logical than the Show Keyword command of the Photo menu.) To add criteria, click the plus (+) icon on the right side of the dialog.

Figure 5-13. Create a Smart Album that you can use for searching. You can then search on any criteria that iPhoto offers.

When you are ready to search, click the OK button; the photos that match the criteria appear in the "Search" Smart Album. As an extra bonus, your search results stay in the Smart Album until you change its criteria. If you want to keep the results, just rename the Smart Album to something else and create a new Smart Album named Search.

In addition to increasing iPhoto's image capacity and speed, Apple added the ability to share your iPhoto libraries on a local network, using the same zero-configuration technology found in iChat.

While sharing photos over a local network isn't something everyone wants or needs, it's so easy to enable in iPhoto 4 that you owe it to yourself to check it out if you have the chance.

To share your iPhoto images on a local network, go to iPhoto's Preferences (⌘-,) and click the Sharing icon. Select the checkbox next to "Share my photos" and choose "Share entire library" or "Share selected albums." There's also an option to require a password here, just in case you don't want everyone on the network gawking at your photos.

Once photo sharing is enabled, other Mac users on the local network who are also using iPhoto 4 can view your photos. To access your shared pictures, all they need to do is open iPhoto 4's Preferences (⌘-,), go to the Sharing pane, and click "Look for shared folders." A new album called Shared Photos appears in the Source list on the left of iPhoto's window.

MOVE IPHOTO'S LIBRARY TO ANOTHER DISK

The Annoyance: I'm an avid amateur photographer, but my hard disk is rapidly running out of space, so I'd like to keep my iPhoto library on an external FireWire drive. iTunes has a setting that lets me move the music library (described in the iTunes section earlier in this chapter), so I expected a similar option in iPhoto. No dice. Am I out of luck here?

The Fix: Chalk this up to iTunes's maturity over the younger iPhoto. Fortunately, you can outsmart iPhoto in this case. iPhoto expects to find its pictures in ~/*Pictures/ iPhoto Library* within your Home folder. If iPhoto can't find the iPhoto Library folder, it asks if you know where it is. You can use this "feature" to trick iPhoto into going to your external hard drive for the image. Here's how:

1. With iPhoto closed, drag your iPhoto Library folder to your external hard disk. The Mac makes a copy of all of the subfolders and files inside.

2. Now go back to the Pictures folder and rename the original iPhoto Library folder to something else. This causes the folder to be unrecognizable to iPhoto.

3. Open iPhoto. After starting up, iPhoto pops up a dialog window, asking if you want to create or find a Library.

4. Click Find Library.

5. Browse through the window and select the iPhoto Library folder on your external drive.

6. Click the Open button.

iPhoto should now display all of your images from your external drive. You can now drag the original iPhoto Library (which you renamed in Step 2) to the Trash.

> **Warning...**
> If you're a paranoid user like me, you might want to first back up your iPhoto Library to a FireWire hard drive, a CD, or a DVD, just in case.

CHANGING DATES AND THE ORDER OF ROLLS

The Annoyance: iPhoto lists rolls according to the date I import them into iPhoto, and then lists those rolls chronologically. This approach is fine for importing photos from a digital camera, but some of my "rolls" didn't come from my camera; I imported them from other

scanned in some pictures from a wedding and gave the roll a date of May 1985, this roll heads to the top of the list if it is the oldest roll.

To change the date of a roll, follow these steps:

1. Launch iPhoto (if it isn't already running).

2. Click the Organize button.

3. Select the Photo Library icon in the Source list.

4. Go to the View menu and select Film Rolls (Shift-⌘-F).

5. Click on the film roll icon that you want to edit.

6. If you don't see a Date field under the Source list, click the "i" icon to display it (as shown in Figure 5-14). You may have to drag the column wider to see the full date and time information displayed in the Date field.

Figure 5-14. When you change the date of a roll in the Date field, iPhoto moves the roll to a different place in the chronological listing.

sources such as scanners, CDs, or email attachments. This means that iPhoto assigns recent dates to my rolls of old family pictures, which is annoyingly confusing.

The Fix: iPhoto 4 made some changes to how roll dating works. iPhoto assigns to a roll the date you imported it, but iPhoto also dates individual photos by the date the image was shot. (It gets this information from the digital camera that you've used.) You can also change the date of any roll without affecting the date of the individual photos. And, changing the roll date changes the order in which its images are displayed. So, if you just

7. Type a different date.

8. You can also change the roll name here. For instance, "Cousin Bill's Wedding" might be a more meaningful name than "Roll 53."

9. Press the Enter key to have the changes take effect. The roll moves to its new place in the chronological listing.

This change doesn't affect the dates of the individual photos in the roll, which can be annoying if you've imported a boxful of old photos. If you also want to change the dates of the photos in the roll, you can change them all at once by following these steps:

1. Shift-click all of the photos in the roll.
2. Select Photos → Batch Change from the menu bar.
3. Now type a date in the dialog that appears (see Figure 5-15).

Figure 5-15. You can change the dates of a group of photos by selecting them, choosing Batch Change from the Photos menu, and typing a new date and/or time.

iPhotoize Your Keynote Presentations

Want an easy way to get multiple iPhoto images into a Keynote presentation? iPhotoToKeynote ($10, *http://www.light-boxsoftware.com/iPhotoToKeynote.php*) is shareware plug-in for iPhoto 4 that adds a Keynote tab to iPhoto's Export dialog. If you click on the Export button, the plug-in launches Keynote and creates a presentation using the photos you've selected.

FIX THE "Y2K" PICTURE DATE PROBLEM

The Annoyance: I have some old family photographs that I've scanned and imported into iPhoto 4. Whenever I try to set the date of a single photo to the early 20th century, such as 1926, iPhoto adds a hundred years (as in 2026). I thought all this Y2K stuff had been solved long ago.

The Fix: While not really a Y2K bug, it is a bit of annoying stupidity on iPhoto's part—you would think that iPhoto should know that no one would want to give a photo a date that is more than 20 years ahead of the date shown in System Preferences. Fortunately, this one is easy to fix. Just tell Mac OS X to use four-digit years instead of two-digit years:

1. Open System Preferences.
2. Go to the International pane.
3. Click the Formats tab.
4. In the Dates section, click the Customize button.
5. Click the checkbox labeled Show Century.

iPhoto now accepts any date you throw at it. There is one side effect to this fix: Mac OS X now displays four-digit years (as in 7/4/2004) in other applications as well, such as Excel spreadsheets.

FIX THE "NOT ENOUGH DISK SPACE" BUG

The Annoyance: Sometimes when I try to export some files from iPhoto 4, it gives me an error message claiming that there isn't enough disk space. My hard disk has 20 GB of free space, but the message appears when I'm only trying to export half a gigabyte worth of photos. I tried to burn the photos to a CD and then to a DVD, but got the same error message. What's going on?

The Fix: According to Apple, when this happens, iPhoto thinks that the size of one of the photos is several *billion* megabytes, which would fill up 100 million DVDs or the combined hard drive space of *all* the Macs Apple sells in a year. Obviously, iPhoto is incorrect here, the result of a bug—a programming error in the iPhoto code.

Apple says you can fix the problem by updating to iPhoto 4.0.1 or later via the Software Update pane in System Preferences. For the most part, the fix work, but the problem can pop up on random occasions. If you have an update installed, there are some simple ways of handling the problem:

- Quit iPhoto and launch it again. This usually does the trick.

- If that doesn't work, quit iPhoto and delete its preference file in your Home folder: ~/Library/Preferences/com.apple.iPhoto.plist.

- If that doesn't work, one of the photos may have a bad thumbnail image associated with it. First, you'll want to find out which one. Export half of the photos that you have selected; if the problem still exists, then export the other half. Keep trying to export a smaller and smaller batch of photos until you zero in on the problem. When you do, force iPhoto to create a new thumbnail by cropping the image (select an area and press the Crop button). Now select Undo Crop Photo from the Edit menu.

IMOVIE

UNDO CUTS WITH DIRECT TRIMMING

The Annoyance: It's annoying when I delete part of a clip from the timeline, and then I realize that I have cut too much or have cut the wrong part. Sure, I can reimport the footage from my camera, but that messes up the clip shelf with duplicate material.

The Fix: Use a feature called *direct trimming*, which was introduced in iMovie 4. (If you haven't upgraded to at least iLife '04, direct trimming, along with the audio improvements, are worth the $50 price tag for big iMovie users.) To shorten a clip using direct trimming, go to the timeline, grab the edge of a clip, and drag it towards the center. As you drag, iMovie's monitor displays the frames you cutting as you pass through them. If you change your mind, go back and drag the edge of the clip away from the center restore a portion or the entirety of the section you cut. This type of editing is known as *nondestructive*, at least until you empty iMovie's Trash—then it's gone for good. Therefore, it's a good idea not to empty iMovie's Trash until your project is nearly complete.

If the clip you've trimmed is in the middle of the timeline, iMovie fills the gap in time by moving all the clips that come after the edited clip to the left. This can be annoying if you'd rather have a blank space. To stop iMovie from moving the other clips, hold the ⌘ key while you directly trim. You'll get a blank space where you edited your clip. If you switch back to the Clip Viewer, you'll see a new black clip representing the portion you trimmed.

You can also use direct trimming to erase portions of a clip by dragging one clip on top of another. That is, if you hold the ⌘ key while dragging a clip along the timeline and place it on top of another clip, you erase the portions of the clip you are overlapping. If you drag without the ⌘ key, the other clips whill just move over instead of overlapping.

QUICKLY MOVE THROUGH FRAMES FROM THE KEYBOARD

The Annoyance: It can be tough to find the exact frame I want by dragging the little playhead along the scrubber bar. First, I drag too far right and pass it; then I miss it again by dragging too far left. Is there a better way?

The Fix: There sure is. To zero in on the frame you need, use the Right Arrow and Left Arrow keys to move forward or back one frame at a time. If you want to make bigger jumps of 10 frames at a time, hold the Shift key while you press an arrow key.

ADD A LOGO OR BORDER TO AN IMOVIE

The Annoyance: I use iMovie for my own business, and I want to put my logo in the corner of a movie. Unfortunately, iMovie doesn't offer any way to do this. Do I have to spend $300 on Final Cut Express?

The Fix: An upgrade to Final Cut will give you more editing power, but for a tenth of the price, you can add an iMovie plug-in called eZeMatte from eZedia ($29, *http://www.ezedia.com*). eZeMatte lets you overlay any still graphic image (known as a *matte*) from within iMovie. This can be a logo or a boarder that frames your movie. eZeMatte works with any graphics format that QuickTime supports—which is a whole bunch. You can use your own graphics, or use one of the borders, frames, and other graphics that come with eZeMatte.

After you install eZeMatte, you can apply a matte just as you would any other effect. In iMovie's clip viewer, click on the clip that will receive the effect. Next, click iMovie's Effects button; eZeMatte shows up as one of the options in iMovie's list of effects. Click on eZeMatte, and then click on the Configure button. You can now browse for the graphic file you want to use. Once selected, set the position of the graphic in the movie window and resize it if necessary. You can also add transparency. The results are professional looking and can sharpen any presentation.

> **t i p**
>
> Ever find a single frame that is so good that you'd like to create a picture for iPhoto? With the frame in the iMovie 4's monitor panel, go to File → Save Frame As. Next, choose JPEG in the dialog and type a filename. You can then go to the Finder and drag the image into iPhoto. Of course, there's nothing stopping you from reimporting the frame as a photo to use under titles and for other effects.

USE ISIGHT TO RECORD VIDEO FOR IMOVIE

The Annoyance: I want to use my iSight camera for recording into iMovie 4, but it's not going very well. iMovie suddenly stops recording, and the iSight's autofocus isn't always the most accurate. If that isn't bad enough, the pictures sometimes have a blueish-green tint.

The Fix: iSight can actually produce much higher quality video than is needed for video chat, but it has no controls other than the rotating on/off switch. iMovie doesn't give you any iSight controls, either, but you can add software that does. Then you can use iMovie for what it was designed for—editing.

There are several free or inexpensive utilities to choose from, but my favorite is Boinx's iVeZeen (formerly known as iRecordNow; $15, *http://www.ivezeen.com*). iVeZeen offers the best user interface while giving you a high degree of control over the iSight camera. iVeZeen can capture video in several formats, including the DV video that iMovie uses. A gigabyte of hard disk space holds about three minutes worth of DV video, so you'll need some free hard disk space to work with if you're planning to "video-tape" your dog's birthday party.

What I really like about iVeZeen is that it lets you focus the iSight while you're recording, which is particularly useful for acquiring superior results while moving in on close-ups. You can focus with a slider bar or the more precise "advanced" control arrows that increase or decrease the focus values one step at a time. If you don't like the colors you're seeing in the iVeZeen window, you can manually adjust the hue, saturation, and brightness using the controls shown in Figure 5-16. The Calibrate White Balance button is another great way to get good colors out of the iSight. You can also adjust the volume of the sound being recorded; choose to use the iSight's built-in mic or an external microphone for sound. The controls even let you switch back and forth between multiple cameras connected to the Mac.

iVeZeen is a cheap and easy way to use your iSight as a digital camcorder for iMovie-formatted video. But I don't want to give the impression that iSight is a replacement for a digital camcorder. iSight isn't as flexible as a real camcorder. Most notable is the smaller range of light you can shoot in. Indoor shooting without lighting can yield grainy images.

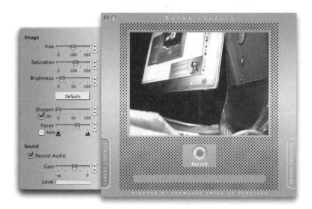

Figure 5-16. iVeZeen lets you control the focus and color of an iSight camera and outputs DV video that you can edit in iMovie.

Get Info

The Unofficial iMovie FAQ (*http://www.dan-slagle.com/mac/iMovie/*) is a good web site to begin your search for more information about tips and problems regarding the most recent version of iMovie.

KEEP KEN BURNS STILL

The Annoyance: I like the way the Ken Burns effect zooms in or out of a portion of a photo, but there are times when I just want the photo to stay put instead of panning and zooming. I'd also like to crop or enlarge a photograph from within iMovie.

The Fix: There is a way to use the zoom feature of the Ken Burns effect to get close up on a portion of a photo but without the motion. Basically, you tell the Ken

Burns effect to start and finish in the same place. To do this, you need to use a few tricks:

1. Click the Photos button (on the right side of iMovie's window).

2. Make sure the Ken Burns Effect checkbox is checked.

3. Select a photo to use from your iPhoto Library.

4. Slide the bottom slider to the left (to the Rabbit icon, as shown in Figure 5-17). This is just for convenience to keep your preview image from moving around.

5. Click on the radio button next to Start.

6. Drag your preview image to center it and use the top slider to adjust the zoom to where you want it.

7. Now here's the big trick: hold the Option key while you click the radio button next to Finish. The Start and Finish positions are now identical.

8. Use the bottom slider (or type a time in the box next to it) to indicate the length of time the photo will be on screen.

Figure 5-17. You can zoom in and crop a photo in iMovie using the Ken Burns effect.

9. Add the cropped photo to the movie by dragging it to a place in the timeline. An alternate method would be to position the scrubber bar on the timeline to where you want the photo inserted and click Apply.

LINE UP THE PLAYHEAD ON THE TIMELINE

The Annoyance: Getting the playhead exactly on the end point of a clip on the timeline can be a real pain, especially if you need to place a video clip, still image, or audio at an exact location in the timeline.

The Fix: In iMovie 4 or later, just hold the Shift key as you drag the playhead on the timeline. When it comes to the edge of a clip, the playhead snaps in place with a little pop. To make this feature permanent (without the Shift key), select "Enable timeline snapping" in iMovie's Preferences. If you don't like the pop sound, deselect "Play snap sounds."

iDVD

DISSOLVE iDVD INSTALLATION WOES

The Annoyance: When I ran the iLife installer DVD, it didn't install iDVD. I have a 1-GHz G4 processor, ample hard disk space, and the version of QuickTime that iDVD requires, so I don't understand what's going on.

The Fix: The problem is that the iDVD installation procedure is a bit different if your optical drive is not both a DVD burner (SuperDrive) *and* internal.

There are two types of drives you could have:

- An internal ComboDrive, which burns CDs but only reads DVDs.

- An external, FireWire, or USB 2 DVD burner.

To install iDVD 4 on a Mac with either a ComboDrive or an external DVD burner, complete a custom install as follows:

1. Insert the iLife '04 DVD (not the CD).

2. Launch the iLife installer and click through License Agreement and Read Me screens.

3. Select the hard drive to install on and click Continue.

4. Click the Customize button.

5. Click the checkbox next to iDVD in the list of applications to install. (If you've already installed the other iApps, uncheck their names.)

6. Click either the Install or Upgrade button.

Keep in mind, however, that iDVD won't let you burn discs unless your DVD drive is both a DVD burner and internal. If not, you can use iDVD 3.0.1 and later to create your DVD project on your Mac; to burn a disc, you'll have to copy the iDVD project file to another Mac that has an internal SuperDrive. (See the sidebar Moving an iDVD Project for further details.) If you have an external DVD burner, you can avoid iDVD altogether and use different software, such as Apple's top-end (and top-priced) DVD Studio Pro ($500) or Roxio's Toast 6 ($80, *www.roxio.com*).

That's the official word. Unofficially, there's a hack floating around the Internet that enables iDVD to burn to at least some external DVD burner drives. It's called HPfurz, two very small files that sit in your Home folder. When you hold the Control key as you click iDVD's Burn button, you can burn to certain external DVD burners. A Google search brings up HPfurz pretty quickly. If you want to try your luck with a URL, at publishing time, you could find it here:

http://forum.firmware-flash.com/viewtopic. php?t=23370

At this page, do a text search for "HPfurz.sit.hqx;" you'll find a download button at the second instance of the file name.

INSTALLING IDVD ON A MAC WITH A SUPERDRIVE UPGRADE

The Annoyance: I replaced my Mac's internal optical drive with an internal Pioneer DVD-R drive. I thought this would allow me to burn DVDs from iDVD, but iDVD tells me that my Mac "does not have a supported SuperDrive."

MOVING AN IDVD PROJECT

Need to burn your iDVD project on another Mac? Make sure that you copy over the right files. The first thing you need is the iDVD project file, which you'll find in your Documents folder (why iDVD doesn't create projects in your Movies folder is another annoyance, but we'll let that one go for now). The filename has the name of the project, ending with a *.dvdproj* file extension (as in *Sue and Bob's wedding.dvdproj*).

You also need to copy over the source material, which includes the video, still photos, and music you've used in the DVD project. If you're using photos from iPhoto and music from iTunes, these files can be all over the place. Fortunately, iDVD tells you where they are when you select Project → Project Info from iDVD's menu bar.

Collect all the source files and place them in a single folder on the other Mac. When you first launch your project, iDVD tells you that it can't find the source files and then lists them. You can select all the files in the dialog and click the Find File button. You can then browse to the folder that contains the source files to link them to the project. Once this little hack has been completed, you can continue to work on the iDVD project and eventually burn it to DVD on the other Mac.

The Fix: First, make sure you have the right drive. Drives that work include the Pioneer DVR-103, DVR-104, DVR-105, or DVR-107D (the latter requires Mac OS X 10.3.3 or later). Some drives, such as the DVR-106RD (the added R is the key in this case), are not supported by Mac OS X and iLife. If you've never been able to burn anything, including a CD, chances are you have an unsupported drive.

If you have been able to burn before but now receive this error message from iDVD, simply try restarting your Mac. I've come across an annoying problem with SuperDrive upgrades (which others have reported as well) in which the Mac seems to "forget" that the drive can burn. For some reason, restarting seems to straighten it out.

Finally, iDVD is a beefy application, so check to see if your Mac meets all the requirements. For iDVD 4, you need a 733 MHz (or faster) G4 processor, 4.3 GB of free hard disk space, Mac OS X 10.2.6 or later, and QuickTime 6.4.

KEEP IPHOTO ORDER IN IDVD SLIDE SHOWS

The Annoyance: When I make iDVD slide shows with an iPhoto album, iDVD randomizes the photos. I then have to rearrange them in iDVD to recreate the order I created in iPhoto. Shouldn't iDVD know better?

The Fix: To keep the photos in order, go back to iPhoto and select your album. Go to File → Export (Shift-⌘-E) and then select the File Export tab in the dialog that pops up. In the dialog, select "Use album name"; this exports the photos in the order you have them arranged in iPhoto. Save the exported folder. Now switch back to iDVD and import the Exported folder. (Keep the exported folder until after you burn the DVD.)

FILL YOUR SCREEN WITH SLIDE SHOWS

The Annoyance: When I create slide shows in iDVD, the pictures are displayed smaller than full screen, with a thick black border around them (as shown in Figure 5-18). It doesn't matter whether I export them from iPhoto or import them to iDVD, I still get this same effect. What is iDVD doing?

More Themes, Please

iDVD 4 comes with dozens of themes, but if you've used all of the themes that appeal to you, just add more.

Turn your attention to a web site called iDVDThemePak (*http://www.idvdthemepak.com*), which offers a variety of sets of iDVD themes, some for purchase, and some for free. The site also offers ButtonPaks, which are sets of DVD menu frames that contain your still images or movie clips.

IDVD FUN FACT

Have you ever wondered where iDVD stores its themes? You can see for yourself by Control-clicking on iDVD's application icon in the Finder. Select Show Package Contents from the contextual menu, and a new window called iDVD opens. Inside this window, open the Contents folder, and then open the Resources folder. Here you'll find files representing the themes (the *.theme* files), as well as graphic files representing various iDVD buttons and other interface items. Each of the .theme files is also a package that can be opened with a Control-click and the Show Package Contents option from their contextual menus. It's not a good idea to make any changes in here, though, as you can damage the way iDVD works. Apple hides all these files to keep them safe.

The Fix: iDVD defaults the display of slide shows to a setting called the TV Safe area. While movies are able to adjust to different models of TV screens, while slides can not. The TV Safe setting means that every television set can display the entire slide image. However, if you want the slides to be displayed at full-screen, go to iDVD's Preferences (⌘-,), click the Slideshow icon, and uncheck "Always scale slides to TV Safe area." Your slides will fill the screen and the Preview window, as shown in Figure 5-19.

Figure 5-18. TV Safe Mode causes the boarder to appear around this slide (shown here in iDVD's Preview window).

Figure 5-19. Turn off iDVD's TV Safe mode, and your slides will file the screen, but may get cropped on some television sets.

KEEP AUDIO IN SYNC

The Annoyance: Everything was just peachy with my project in iMovie 4. But since I moved it to iDVD 4 (using iMovie's iDVD button), the audio is out of sync with the video, so it looks like a foreign film dubbed in English. I can't find any iDVD commands to fix this.

The Fix: There aren't any fixes in iDVD. You have to go back to iMovie or even before to use one of several techniques:

- Extract audio in iMovie. Select all of the clips (⌘-A) in the project and choose Extract Audio from the Advanced menu. This creates a new audio track from the audio contained in the video. You'll have to wait a few minutes while iMovie crunches the digital audio numbers. Once it's done, click on iMovie's iDVD button. Finally, click the Create iDVD Project button to bring the movie into iDVD.

- Set your camcorder to use bit audio. Some camcorders default at 12-bit audio, but it's not the best for iDVD. The extra audio resolution not only gives you better sound quality, but also seems to help iDVD keep the audio in sync with the video.

At this point, you might say, "What! You expect me to reshoot all my footage! I suppose I should have the high school hold another graduation ceremony." Well, you'd certainly have a point there, but iDVD still prefers 16-bit audio. So here's what you can do to sweeten the audio if you've already shot video with 12-bit audio:

a) In iMovie, export the project to a digital camcorder that's set to bit audio. (In iMovie 4, select File → Share from the menu, and then click the Videocamera button. In iMovie 3, there's an Export command in the File menu.)

b) Create a new iMovie project (File → New Project).

c) Reimport the (16-bita audio) DV footage from the camera.

d) Extract the audio (as previously described).

e) Move the movie to iDVD. This could be a brand new iDVD project (using iMovie's iDVD button) or an existing iDVD project (using iDVD's Import command in the file menu).

f) If you've reimported the video into an existing iDVD project, go the Advanced menu and choose Delete Encoded Assets.

- Whip Mac OS X into shape. It also helps audio synchronization if Mac OS X is healthy. Use Disk Utility (*/Applications/Utilities*) to repair permissions, repair the disk, and run any other maintenance utilities you might have on hand, such as those described in Chapter 1.

Get Info

A good source of up-to-date iDVD information is the Unofficial iDVD 4.x FAQ web site (*http://www.kentidwell.com/idvd4/*). By the way, this site is not related to the Unofficial iMovie FAQ, previously mentioned.

DVD MEDIA: DVD-R VERSUS DVD+R

The Annoyance: I can't figure out which type of blank DVD discs I should get. In the store, there are DVD-R and DVD+R disks. I've also seen DVD-RW. Does it matter?

The Fix: DVD-R and DVD+R are two competing standards, as were VHS and Beta in the early 1980s. Most TV set-top DVD players can read both types of discs, but the important thing to know is which DVD format your drive supports.

For most Mac users, DVD-R is the format to use. That's because for many years, Apple used DVD-R burners inside of Macs. Apple only recently began shipping Macs with a DVD±R burner (the Pioneer DVR-107), which can use DVD+R media as well as DVD-R. Many external FireWire burners also support both formats.

Not all brands of DVD media work well with Macs, however. With some brands, iDVD might chug away for hours, only to have the Mac spit out the unfinished disc. Verbatim and Apple are two brands that usually work with all Macs. At this point, however, the only type of DVD media that Apple sells is DVD-R.

DVD-RW and DVD+RW are erasable formats. (The RW part means "read and write," as in CDs.) Like CD-RW, you can erase the entire disc to rerecord on it. DVD-RW drives usually support DVD-R, and likewise with DVD+RW and DVD+R. You can use the erasable formats for data storage, but they won't play in the DVD player connected to your television. Also, DVD-RW and DVD+RW take longer to burn than DVD-R and DVD+R.

DVD MEDIA: THE X FACTOR

The Annoyance: What about the various speeds of media—such as 2X, 4X, and 8X? Should I pay more for the higher X factor? Will it make burning in iDVD any faster?

The Fix: Anyone who has used iDVD knows that burning can take many hours for a big project. Most of this time is spent encoding the video, though, so the speed of your Mac's processor is much more important than the X factor of the media. Still, faster media can have some effect if your drive supports it. 1X means it will take an hour to burn an hour's worth of video (not counting the encoding). An 8X means that an hour's worth of video can be burned in 1/8th the time, or 12.4

minutes. However, there is no point in spending money on a media speed that your drive doesn't support. A 4X drive will burn 8X media only at a 4X rate. 2X drives are even worse. The 2X SuperDrive models write to 4X media at 1X speed—*slower* than 2X media.

So what speed is your Mac's internal DVD burner? Mac OS X won't tell you point blank, but will tell you the model of the burner you have. To find this information, launch System Profiler (*/Applications/Utlities*) and check under Devices and Volumes. To help you figure out what you have inside your Mac, here is a sampling of the DVD burners used in Macs for the past few years:

- The Pioneer DVR-103 (or DVR-A03) is a 1X drive. That's 1X in writing to DVD-R media.

- The Pioneer DVR-104 is a 2X drive.

- The Pioneer DVR-105 is a 4X drive.

- The Pioneer DVR-106 is a 4X drive.

- The Pioneer DVR-107 is an 8X drive, the first 8X drive used in Macs. (Requires Mac OS X 10.3.3 and later.)

GARAGEBAND

IMPROVE GARAGEBAND PERFORMANCE

The Annoyance: GarageBand runs so slowly on my 900 MHz iBook G3 that I can't use it. This is disappointing, because Apple says that a 600 MHz G3 is the minimum for GarageBand.

The Fix: Apple also recommends a G4 or G5 in order to use the software instruments in GarageBand. But even a G4 might not be enough. Fortunately, you can prevent your Mac from choking on GarageBand. Take a look at the following methods:

- Get a fast external hard drive. Much of what GarageBand does is read information from your hard drive— *a lot* of information, particularly if you are working with recorded audio (as opposed to the MIDI software instruments). A "fast" drive is one that spins at 7200 revolutions per minute (rpm). iBooks (even the newer G4s) come with 4200 rpm drives. PowerBooks

typically come standard with 4200 rpm, with an option for 5400 rpm. (New iMacs and Power Macs already have a 7200 rpm drive inside.) For $150, you can get a 7200 rpm FireWire or USB 2.0 drive with well over 100 GB of storage.

Once you plug in your new, faster hard drive, you need to move GarageBand's project files to it and tell GarageBand where they are. Copy the GarageBand folder (*~/Music/GarageBand*) to the new hard drive, and then delete the old GarageBand folder. When you launch GarageBand, it won't be able to find your project files and will tell you that no song is open. In the dialog, click the button called Open Existing Song and navigate to the song on your new external hard drive.

- Turn off FileVault (Mac OS X 10.3 and later). FileVault decreases the performance of your hard disk. FileVault is off by default, but if you've been using it, go to the Security preference panel (in System Preferences) and turn it off.

- Lower your monitor's color resolution. GarageBand expends a lot of effort drawing the scrolling tracks as you play them. If you lower your monitor's colors from millions to thousands, your Mac won't have to work as hard, and GarageBand can focus on producing music. If your Mac lets you, you'll get the biggest performance boost by using 256 colors, though things may look a bit strange. To change the color setting, open the Displays panel in System Preferences and choose Thousands (or 256) from the Colors pop-up menu.

- Change optimization setting. Go to GarageBand's Preferences (⌘-,), click the Audio/MIDI icon, and under "Optimize for", select "Maximum number of simultaneous tracks" (as shown in Figure 5-20). This loads more of your song into memory before playing

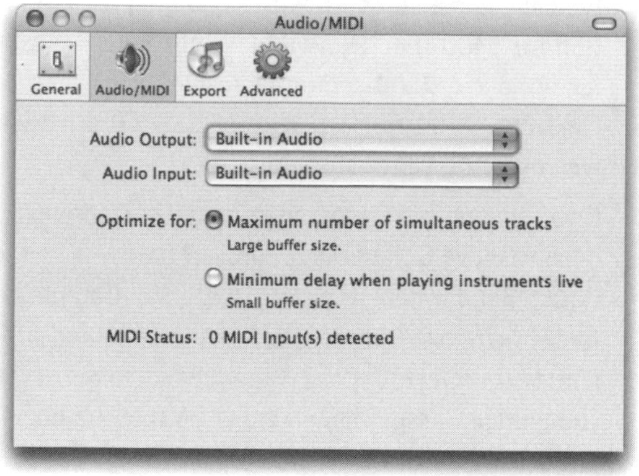

Figure 5-20. This "Optimize for" setting comes in handy, particularly if GarageBand is having trouble playing all of your tracks at the same time.

Keep an Eye on the Playhead

You can keep track of how much processing power your song is using by looking at the Playhead triangle as your song plays. If it stays white, the song is not using a lot of processing power. If the playhead turns yellow, the song is using a moderate amount of your Mac's processor. When it turns red, the song is placing a heavy load on the processor.

it, so you may see a slight (or long) delay after you click the play button.

- Reduce the permitted number of tracks and voices. You can lower the maximum number of tracks and synthesized sounds (voices) GarageBand allows. Go to GarageBand's Preferences (⌘-,) and click on the Advanced button. Now, set a lower number in the pop-up menus labeled Real Instrument Tracks, Software Instrument Tracks, and Voices per Instrument.
- Hide the Track Mixer. The Mixer column displays volume levels for each track as the song plays. These displays eat processor power, so if you don't need them, go to the Track menu and select Hide Track Mixer.
- Reduce the number of tracks in a song by mixing down. For this tip, see the next annoyance titled.

MIX DOWN TRACKS

The Annoyance: I have a G4 iMac with a 7200 rpm hard drive, but when I add several tracks, an error message pops up: "Part of the song was not played." It claims that my song has "too many tracks." I thought I was supposed to get 64 tracks?

The Fix: This message means that your song is placing a heavy load on your Mac's processor. In short, it just doesn't have the juice to play all of the tracks at the same time. Reduce the number of tracks in a song by *mixing down*, or combining several tracks into a single track. Unfortunately, GarageBand is not very versatile here, giving you just one option: to combine all of the tracks in a song into a single audio track. This means that every setting for every track—including the volumes and effects—becomes permanent and is no longer editable.

You don't have to mix down the entire song, however. You can mix down just a few tracks by creating copies of your song:

1. Create a copy of your complete original song as a backup. This lets you get back to your premixed tracks should you change your mind later.
2. Open a copy of the song (let's call it "My Song Complete").
3. Use File → Save As in the menu bar to create another copy of the project file. Use this copy to do the mixing and give it a descriptive name like "My Song Drum Tracks."
4. Delete the tracks that you don't want to include in the mix down. The remaining tracks are combined into a single audio track.

5. Choose File → Export to iTunes. This creates a new AIFF audio file in iTunes.

6. Open the copy of your song that contains all of the tracks ("My Song Complete") and delete the tracks that you exported to iTunes.

7. Go to iTunes and locate the mix down song. Drag it from iTunes into the GarageBand ("My Song Complete") window. GarageBand creates a new audio track, containing your mix down.

MUSIC SHARING, GARAGEBAND STYLE

Want to hear what others are doing with Garage-Band? Would you like others to hear your latest GarageBand masterpiece? Then check out iCompositions (http://*www.icompositions.com*), where you'll find great and not-so-great music in many different genres.

I like to start with the contests that iCompositions holds. Some of these tunes are truly exceptional, worthy of downloading to your Mac and iPod. You have to register in order to post your own music, but not to download music. After you register, iCompositions gives you 150 MB of free disk space on its servers to upload your music.

If you'd rather listen to GarageBand tunes as an uninterrupted stream, go to iCompositions's Internet radio station, MUGradio (*http://www.mugradio.com*). It plays nothing but the GarageBand-created music from iCompositions, all day and all night. To tune in, click Listen Now on MUGradio's home page, and iTunes should launch and start playing MUGradio. When this doesn't work, you can copy the long URL that appears (starting with "http"), go to the iTunes Advanced menu, choose Open Stream, and paste in the URL.

TRIM THE BEGINNING OF A MIDI LOOP

The Annoyance: There's an annoying editing problem with regions created by software instruments—that is, MIDI loops. You can easily shorten a loop by selecting its region in a track, placing the cursor at the end of the region, and clicking-and-dragging the end to the left. You can cut off as much as you'd like from the end of the track. However, this doesn't work when you try doing this at the beginning of a loop. You click-and-drag to the right but nothing happens.

The Fix: This bit of inconsistent behavior seems to be a hole in GarageBand's editing capability, but there is a way around it. First, delete the MIDI controller information (the notes or rhythm) in the portion that you want to cut. You can do this in the track editor, the portion at the bottom of the GarageBand window. Double-click the region you want to edit, and the track editor opens to your loop, as shown in Figure 5-21.

You can delete individual notes by clicking on each one and hitting the Delete key, or select multiple notes by

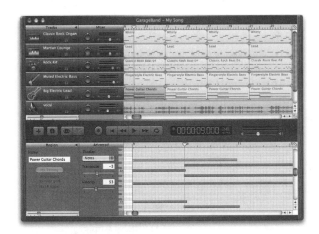

Figure 5-21. In this example, the object is to cut the selected loop to the left of the playhead. Before you can do this, you'll use the track editor to delete all of the MIDI data in this section.

Shift-clicking to delete. This procedure gets trickier when a note extends from the portion you want to cut into the portion you want to keep, as does the selected note in Figure 5-22. Like the whole region itself, a note doesn't let you drag the left end to the right to shorten it. You must drag the right end of the note to the left to shorten

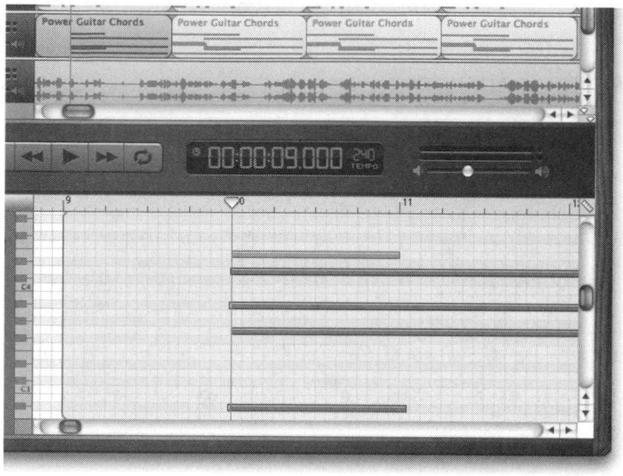

Figure 5-22. Now that you've removed all of the notes from the beginning of the loop, you can shorten it in the timeline.

Get Info

Just starting GarageBand and want to look at a manual? Apple's web site has several illustrated PDF files that can get you up and running:

http://docs.info.apple.com/article. html?artnum=93615

Another option is David Pogue's book, *GarageBand: The Missing Manual* (Pogue Press/O'Reilly). Not only is Pogue a Mac fanatic, he's also a former Broadway composer.

the note, and then drag the whole note to the right to move it to the location you want that note to play. Once all of the MIDI data is gone from the area you want to cut (as in Figure 5-22), you can go back to the timeline and drag the beginning of the loop to the right.

Although this workaround lets you trim the beginning of a software instrument loop, it does seem unnecessarily annoying in itself. Because of that, it's possible that Apple will eventually fix this in a later version of GarageBand. (Hint, hint, to anyone on the GarageBand team over there at 1 Infinite Loop.)

IMPORT MIDI FILES

The Annoyance: GarageBand is a MIDI sequencer, so I thought it would be a great place to use my vast collection of MIDI files. Much to my chagrin, GarageBand has no Import command. Is there any way to get GarageBand to wake up and smell the MIDI files?

The Fix: GarageBand doesn't yet have the ability to import MIDI files, but there is a free utility that converts MIDI files into a format that GarageBand understands. Bery Rinaldo's Dent du Midi (*http://homepage.mac.com/ beryrinaldo/ddm/*) is a simple utility that translates your MIDI files into GarageBand in minutes. Launch Dent du Midi and drag a MIDI file into its window. The utility creates a folder with each instrument as a separate AIFF file. Once it's complete, just drag the AIFF files into GarageBand's window; each one becomes a separate track.

These AIFF files aren't the standard audio files you may have used before. When you drag them into GarageBand, you'll see the little editable bars of MIDI, not the waveforms of an audio recording. That's because GarageBand keeps its MIDI information inside AIFF files. For instance, all of the Apple MIDI loops that come with GarageBand are AIFF files. (They are located in */Library/Application Support/GarageBand/Apple Loops/*, just in case you're interested.) After Dent du Midi converts your files, you can change the instruments, transpose, and do anything else you can do with MIDI in GarageBand.

MORE LOOPS

Need more loops in GarageBand? There are plenty of places to get them:

- ☒ Powerfx (*http://www.powerfx.com*) offers a variety of loop packages ranging in price from $10 to $200.

- ☒ For $100, Apple's GarageBand Jam Pack adds 2000 more loops.

- ☒ In addition to selling loop packages, Bitshift Audio offers a free package with 40 MB of drum loops (*http://bitshiftaudio.fileburst. com/free_bee.html*).

- ☒ Tuneup for GarageBand (*http://www.tuneuploops.com*) contains 500 loops for $35. TuneMedia also has a free version called Pack One Demo that has 10 MB of loops, no strings attached.

- ☒ The iCompositions download page (*http:// www.icompositions.com/downloads*) has collections of free loops available, as well as links to even more loops web sites.

- ☒ If you happen to have Apple's Soundtrack, you can use those loops in GarageBand. However, many of them are the same loops already in GarageBand and in Jam Pack.

iPod
ANNOYANCES

The iPod has changed the way people listen to music. For many, the iPod is the main reason to use iTunes. With an iPod, you can carry around your own personal radio station, playing the music you prefer, without the interruption of commercials and annoying jocks. The appeal of the iPod has caught on—it's as big as the Sony Walkman was a generation ago. Whenever you find yourself on a subway in any American city, you're likely to see one or more riders plugged into an iPod.

When a top-end iPod costs as much as a low-end Windows PC, you expect it to be trouble free, and for the most part, it is. Still, there are hassles—dealing with music formats, working with nonmusical data, and troubleshooting a rare problem. It's also no fun when the battery dies when you least expect it, or worse, won't recharge.

This chapter exposes some iPod annoyances that you may have run into or may experience in the future, and gives you the solutions to make your ears happy again. After all, there's no going back to transistor radios and cassette players once you have experienced the iPod.

COPY IPOD MUSIC BACK TO YOUR MAC

The Annoyance: iTunes copies data one-way only, from the Mac to the iPod. The music and playlist files are hidden on the iPod, so there is no way to manually move them back to my Mac. In fact, after my hard disk failed and I reformatted it, iTunes wanted to erase my iPod instead of moving the files back to the Mac. This is a real shame, because the iPod is *would be* a natural backup device for the gigabytes of music stored on my Mac.

The Fix: Blame this one on the lawyers. Apple needed the music industry's permission to sell their songs online; the music industry doesn't want people to be able to share music files. Lawyers met. The result is that you can't use your iPod to copy music to all of your friends' Macs or PCs. This made the lawyers happy, but it means that you—the person who actually *paid* for the music—can't restore your music library or playlists to your Mac after a hard disk failure—at least, not without the assistance of some third-party software.

The most complete of these is iPod.iTunes ($35, *http://www.crispsofties.com/i.i/*), which synchronizes both the music and the playlists between your Mac and the iPod. If you've accidentally deleted a song from iTunes, iPod.iTunes can restore it to the Mac, along with its ratings and playcount information. The ability to restore playlists is even more of a timesaver than restoring music files in the case of a hard-disk failure. You can also choose to have iPod.iTunes restore only playlists or only music (in the Settings tab, select the "Synchronization of" pop-up menu, as shown in Figure 6-1). Then, with the click of a button, iPod.iTunes checks each machine and synchronizes (see Figure 6-2).

If you have two Macs, such as a PowerBook and an iMac, you can use iPod.iTunes to keep identical music libraries and playlists on both Macs. Is this illegal? Not if you are copying music files that you own from one Mac to another—this is considered "fair use." It would not be kosher, however, to move files to someone else's Mac.

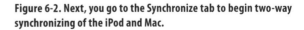

Figure 6-1. iPod.iTunes lets you move files from your iPod back to a Mac. First, use the Settings tab to set the data you want to synchronize.

Figure 6-2. Next, you go to the Synchronize tab to begin two-way synchronizing of the iPod and Mac.

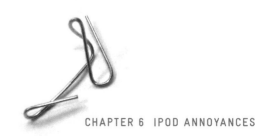

VIAGRA FOR YOUR IPOD'S BATTERY

The Annoyance: There is nothing more annoying about the iPod than to have the battery die right in the middle of a good song. How can I make the charge last longer?

The Fix: How you use your iPod greatly affects how long the battery charge will last. If you follow these battery-saving tips, you'll get the most out of a charge:

- Charge your iPod frequently. The iPod battery loses power when you aren't using it. If you haven't charged it in a few days, you aren't going to get the full eight hours of operation.

- Fully charge your iPod. It takes three to four hours to fully charge, even if the power meter indicates it's full before that.

- Don't use big song files. Apple says that files bigger than 9 MB use more battery power than smaller song files. The reason has to do with the iPod's hard drive. During normal playing mode, songs are played from a cache chip, not directly from the hard drive. A spinning hard drive uses a lot more power than reading data from a memory chip. If a music file takes up too much of the cache, the iPod needs to spin up the hard drive more frequently to move data into the cache.

To keep your file sizes small, use the compressed AAC or MP3 formats instead of the uncompressed AIFF or WAV formats for your music files. The AAC and MP3 formats are much smaller, which means more songs fit into the cache. This translates into less frequent access of the hard drive, which means a battery charge lasts longer. Of the later two compressed formats, AAC is slightly better, as it uses less hard disk space than MP3 to produce the same audio quality.

Another factor that can make file sizes big is song length. AAC files take up just under 1 MB per minute of playing time, which means Benny Goodman's 1939 performance of *Sing, Sing, Sing* is going to be a drain on the battery. The same is true with the movements of Mahler's symphonies. So if you are trying to conserve battery power, stick to playing shorter pieces of music.

- Lay off the Previous/Rewind and the Next/Fast-Forward buttons. Manually changing songs or rewinding or fast-forwarding through a song can cause the hard drive to spin up. Remember, you use less battery power if that puppy stays asleep.

- Turn off the equalizer in the iPod's Settings menu. Select EQ, and then set it to Off.

- Turn off the alarm. This is also found in the Settings menu.

- Keep the iPod at room temperature. Batteries operate less efficiently in cold winter temperatures and hot summer temperatures. The iPod battery's optimum operating temperature is 68°F (20°C).

- Avoid backlighting. It's probably a no-brainer that using backlighting takes up battery power. But if you know you must use backlighting, go to the Settings menu, select Backlight Timer, and select a short interval, such as two or five seconds. This way, the backlight turns itself off if you forget.

UNENDING IPOD POWER

The Annoyance: I sometimes need my iPod battery to last much longer than it does. No matter how many power-saving tips I use, I can't prevent the iPod battery from dying midway through a flight to Timbuktu. I'd love to take my iPod on a three-day backpacking trip, but my girlfriend tells me there aren't any AC outlets in the Grand Canyon.

The Fix: Whether you are jetting around the world's capitals or getting away from it all in a wilderness retreat, an external iPod battery pack will keep the tunes playing. One such pack, the Belkin Backup Battery Pack ($70, *http://www.belkin.com*), uses 4 AA batteries and gives you an extra 15 hours of playing time, should you need it. Bring enough batteries with you, and you can keep playing your iPod indefinitely, or until your trip ends.

Figure 6-3. The replacement battery for the docking iPod models is small, thin, and easy on the wallet.

REPLACE YOUR BATTERY

The Annoyance: Over the past few years, my iPod battery life grew shorter and shorter—now it barely holds a charge at all. Although I do like the new colors of the iPod mini, I don't really want to shell out the big bucks for a new iPod. If I can buy a replacement battery for my PowerBook, why can't I do the same for my iPod?

The Fix: If the iPod is still under warranty, send it back to Apple. (Typical iPod warranty is a year—check your sales slip.) If not, then shell out some smaller bucks for a new iPod battery (such as the one shown in Figure 6-3). The costs vary depending on which model you have, but replacement iPod batteries can be had for well under $50. As more and more iPods are sold, replacement battery prices will continue to drop. Just be sure you get the right battery for your specific iPod model.

There are several web sites that sell iPod batteries, and more battery sources are popping up all the time. Laptops for Less (http://www.ipodbattery.com) and PDA Smart (http://www.pdasmart.com/ipodpartscenter.htm) both include instructions and tools for opening the iPod. Laptops for Less offers its instructions on its web site, letting you know what's in store before you attempt to crack open your iPod.

You may have noticed that your iPod has no screws—you have to gradually pry it open with a screwdriver or some other tool, pressing on internal clips to detach them. A metal screwdriver can dent and scratch the plastic, so be careful how you wield these tools. If your replacement battery didn't come with metal tools, try using two or three stiff plastic guitar picks.

Where you start prying is important. For the older iPods, you start at the FireWire port. For the docking iPods, you start prying on the either side, 6 cm from the top. The iPod Minis have a cover on the top that you must first pry off with a small screwdriver. Whichever iPod you have, be sure to read the directions before attempting to replace the battery.

If the idea of forcing open your iPod with a screwdriver gives you the willies, then pay someone else to do it. Apple will replace an iPod battery for $99, including the battery and labor (*http://www.apple.com/support/ipod/*). However, other battery vendors will install the battery for less than Apple charges, so check around.

Inside an iPod

If you crack open an iPod, you'll see three main components: the battery, the hard disk, and a circuit board (much like the one in your Mac, except much smaller). The circuit board contains (among other things) a processor and a small amount of cache memory—32 MB worth. This is 256 times the amount of memory in the original Macintosh of 1984.

MY IPOD CAN'T REMEMBER THE DATE OR TIME

The Annoyance: After not using my iPod for a while, I have recently recharged it. Now it shows the wrong date and time.

The Fix: It sounds like you have let the battery drain bone-dry, and then tried to recharge it from an AC outlet. The drain of the battery deleted the time setting, but iPod gets its time setting from the Mac. To reset the date and time, just briefly plug the iPod into a Mac before using the iPod.

BOOKMARK AUDIO BOOK FILES

The Annoyance: I like to listen to audio books on my iPod, but I often need to stop in the middle of a chapter. When I get back to it, I've forgotten where I've left off and have to move forward and backward to find the right spot. At least my old books on tape would pick up where I left off. Even the 650-year-old Gutenberg Bible had bookmarks.

The Fix: Although your iPod can't display the illumination of the first printed book, it does support digital bookmarks, if you are using iPod software Version 1.2 or later. For instance, files purchased from Audible.com have a bookmarking feature that works automatically. When you stop the iPod, it creates an electronic bookmark. When you restart the iPod and go to the bookmarked piece, the file starts playing at the bookmarked spot (even if you have listened to something else inbetween). Bookmarks also work in iTunes, and move back and forth between iTunes and iPod, letting you listen to a book on both. If you are stopping a file multiple times, the latest bookmark is used.

That's great for Audible.com subscribers, but what about books that you import to iTunes from CDs? No problem. With a little trick, you can make *any* AAC file bookmarkable. If the audio file is in another format, you must convert it with iTunes (Advanced → Convert Selection to AAC).

The trick is to change the file's type code, an invisible indicator that usually tells Mac OS X what kind of a file you have. In this case, the type code has a different function—changing the four-character *type code* of an AAC file to "M4B" (where the forth character is a space) turns on the iTunes/iPod bookmarking feature for that file.

There are a number of utilities that you can use to change the type code of a file, including some you may already have. You can use the free Quick Change (*http://www.everydaysoftware.net/quickchange/*), which has the sole purpose of editing type and creator codes. To use any of the tools, you have to go into your iTunes music folder

(~/*Music/iTunes/iTunes Music*) and open the artist and al-bum folders, and then open the music file with the utility. There is, however, an easier way.

You can use a free AppleScript from Doug Adams called Make Bookmarkable that works from within iTunes, so you don't have to open any folder or even type the "M4B" code (*http://www.malcolmadams.com/itunes/scripts/scripts07.php*). Place Make Bookmarkable in the iTunes Scripts folder (~/*Library/iTunes/Scripts*). (If you don't see a Scripts folder, just create one with Shift-⌘-N and change the name of the untitled folder to "Scripts".) Now ,in iTunes, select an AAC file and choose Make Bookmark-able in the Scripts menu (see Figure 6-4). The next time

Figure 6-4. Select an AAC file and choose Doug Adams's Make Book-markable AppleScript from iTunes' Script menu. This changes the type code, which turns on the bookmark feature for that file.

Resume Playing

There actually is a way to shut off the iPod in the middle of a track so that it will resume playing at the same spot—without a bookmarkable file. Just pause the track and wait a minute or so until the iPod puts itself to sleep. To resume play at the same spot, press the Play button. Of course, this method doesn't allow you to play other tracks and then come back to your spot, as you can by bookmarking a file.

you stop listening to the file, an electronic bookmark will be placed there. It's not the Gutenberg Bible, but it's a handy trick.

THAWING A FROZEN IPOD

The Annoyance: My iPod is frozen asleep—none of the buttons work, and it's been charging for a day. The battery was fine the other day, so I don't think it's dead. And no, the Hold switch is *not* on. Is my iPod toast?

The Fix: Probably not. At least, not until you've tried resetting it. Resetting an iPod is like rebooting a Mac—it reloads the operating system into RAM but doesn't delete the files (your songs) on the internal drive. To reset your iPod, follow these steps:

1. Connect the iPod to a power source, either your Mac or an AC outlet. If the Mac is in sleep mode, wake it up.

2. Move the iPod's Hold switch to the Hold position; then move it to the Off position.

3. Simultaneously press the Menu button and Play/Pause button. (For the iPod mini, press the Menu and Select buttons). Hold the buttons until the Apple logo appears; this can take as long as six seconds.

With the iPod mini, holding the buttons can be tricky—you must press the buttons at locations towards the end of the click wheel, so as not to press the wheel. I've found this works best using two hands, with the iPod mini lay-ing flat on a desk.

If the iPod still isn't responding, unplug it, wait 24 hours, and try again. Resetting an iPod isn't completely harm-less, as it will delete some settings that are supported in iPod software 2.0 and later. Resetting returns the main menu to the default and empties the on-the-go playlists you may have created. Resetting also turns on the alarm clock feature.

> **FIXING AN IPOD WITHOUT BREAKING IT**
>
> You should never use the Disk Utility (*/Applications/Utilities*) or any other hard drive utility to format the iPod's disk drive. If you do, the iPod goes from being a trendy music player to nothing more than a portable FireWire drive with a bunch of useless buttons.
>
> The utility to use is iPod Software Updater (*http://www.apple.com/ipod/download/*). It can clear the iPod and perform the equivalent of reformatting a hard drive. It can also correct the damage you caused by running a disk utility. The Restore function erases all of the music and other files and returns the iPod to factory settings. The application can then install the latest version of iPod software, allowing iTunes to move your music library back to the iPod.

WHY DOESN'T MY IPOD SHOW UP IN ITUNES?

The Annoyance: My iPod mounts on my Mac's Desktop, but for some reason, it doesn't appear in iTunes. I have tried reinstalling the most recent iPod software, but much to my surprise, the iPod Software Updater doesn't recognize the iPod either. Now what?

The Fix: There's nothing wrong with the iPod. These are the symptoms of a corrupt iTunes system file called *iPodDriver.kext*. When this file is corrupt, you may see other symptoms as well. For instance, the iPod Software Updater may freeze (lock up), requiring you to do a force quit (via Option-⌘-Esc).

Simply delete the bad file and replace it with a fresh copy by reinstalling iTunes. In Mac OS X 10.3 and later, simply drag the *iPodDriver.kext* file, located in */System/Library/Extensions* to the Trash. When you move *iPodDriver.kext* to the Trash, the system asks you for your password.

With Mac OS X 10.2.8 and earlier, however, the system doesn't let you delete this file from the Finder. Instead, you'll use a Unix command from Terminal (*/Applications/Utilities*). At the prompt, type this command exactly, observing all capital and lowercase letters, as well as spaces:

```
$ sudo rm -R /System/Library/Extensions/ ↵
iPodDriver.kext
```

When you hit Return, the Terminal asks you for your password. Type in the same password you use to log into your Mac, and then hit Return once more.

With all versions of Mac OS X, you now restart the Mac and reinstall the deleted file. You can reinstall iTunes from an iLife CD or, to get the latest version, by downloading it from Apple (*http://www.apple.com/itunes/download/*). After installing iTunes, restart the Mac once more and connect your iPod.

There is a shortcut, however, that lets you install *only* the deleted file. This shortcut works whether you have iTunes on CD or have downloaded the full iTunes installer from Apple:

1. Locate the iTunes installer file, named *iTunes4.mkpg*. Control-click this file and select "Show Package Contents" from the contextual menu.

2. In the Finder Window that opens, go to the Contents folder and open the Resources folder.

3. Inside the Resources folder, you'll find an installer package named *iPodDriver.pkg*. Double-click it, and you're in business.

MOVE DATA FROM ENTOURAGE TO YOUR IPOD

The Annoyance: I'm annoyed that Mac OS X wants me to use an inferior calendar program, such as iCal. I use Entourage and want to move my calendar and addresses to my iPod, but iSync supports iCal only.

The Fix: While this is true, there are workarounds. You can import Entourage's Calendar into iCal using iCal's Import command (File → Import). You can then use iCal's Export command (File → Export) to export a file to your iPod's Calendar folder, or you can use iSync to move it over.

If you think this procedure is a lot to go through every time you want to update the calendar on your iPod, you're right. A better method to use is to use iPod It (*http://www.zapptek.com/ipod-it/*), a $15 shareware program designed for iPod owners who use Entourage. iPod It is a synchronizing application that supports more types of data than iSync does (as shown in Figure 6-5). Use iPod It to move Entourage's latest calendar to the iPod, as well as to move Entourage's contacts, messages, notes, and tasks. If you happen to use Apple's iCal or Address Book along with Entourage, set iPod It to move data from those applications as well. If that isn't enough, iPod It moves email from Entourage or Mail over to your iPod, so you can read your messages while you sit through a dull meeting.

Figure 6-5. iPod It moves contacts, calendar, and email from Entourage, as well as from Apple's applications, to your iPod.

> **SYNC IPOD WITH ICAL AND ADDRESS BOOK**
>
> If you use iCal and Address Book, and you've never synced them with your iPod, you're missing out on a convenient use for your iPod. With your iPod connected, open iSync, go to the Devices menu, and choose Add Device. Double-click your iPod, and it appears in the iSync window. When you click on the Sync Now button, your calendars and contacts will be synced to your iPod, where you'll find them under the Extra's menu.
>
> This lets you use your iPod as a somewhat hobbled PDA. Sure, you can't add new calendar items or change someone's address directly on your iPod—for that, you must use iCal and Address Book, respectively, and then use iSync again to sync the changes to your iPod—but if you're already carrying around your iPod, you can use it to quickly find phone numbers or view your schedule without having to lug a laptop or paper calendar.

If you *really* want to use iSync to do the syncing with Entourage, try the $25 PocketMac iPod Edition from Information Appliance Associates (*http://www.pocketmac.net*). This utility acts as a plug-in to iSync, letting you specify Entourage data for your iPod. (Figure 6-6 shows that iSync's usual iPod icon is modified with the Entourage icon). Like iPod It, PocketMac iPod Edition moves email from Entourage and Mail, and can move all of the Entourage data that iPod It does. It also converts Word and PDF files for viewing on your iPod. However, PocketMac iPod Edition does not support iCal or Address Book; if you are using one of these along with Entourage, iPod It is the utility for you.

Figure 6-6. PocketMac iPod Edition enables iSync to move Entourage data to your iPod.

AN EASIER WAY TO ADD NOTES

The Annoyance: iPod It can add Entourage Notes to my iPod, but what about text notes from other sources? The only way I've found is to create a text file with TextEdit and save it to the Notes folder on the iPod when the iPod is mounted in the Finder. Not only is this a tedious procedure, but the iPod truncates files larger than 4 KB. This works for quick reminders or driving directions, but not much else.

The Fix: There is a more effective way to get notes onto the iPod: copy text from any document running in any application, and then run an AppleScript. The script, Clipboard to Note, is a free download from Apple (*http://www.apple.com/applescript/ipod/*). The script strips out the raw text that you've copied, creates a text file, and stores it in the Notes folder of your iPod (as long as it's mounted). Not only that, but it divides the text into multiple notes if your clipping exceeds 4 KB.

By the way, the Notes feature works only with iPods with docking connectors and the iPod mini—not with older iPods.

DRIVING DIRECTIONS ON YOUR IPOD

An iPod can make any car trip seem shorter, but did you know it can also help you get to your destination? That's if you use PodQuest ($10, *http://www.mibasoft.dk*) to download driving directions from MapQuest and load them to your iPod.

PodQuest opens your default web browser to *MapQuest.com*, where you enter your starting point and destination. When MapQuest provides the directions, you can select a PodQuest menu command to download the directions to your iPod. PodQuest moves the directions to your iPod's Notes menu for newer iPods or to the Contacts menu for pre-docking iPods.

PodQuest installs the directions as a VCF file, which you can delete with the Finder when you get back from your trip.

KEEP PLAYLISTS ORGANIZED YOUR WAY

The Annoyance: Now that I have dozens of playlists, I wish the iPod had some other options for displaying them besides alphabetically. For instance, I'd like to have all of my Aerosmith playlists come first, followed by playlists containing twentieth century atonal chamber music.

The Fix: You can change the order of iTunes's playlist by using an old Macintosh trick: add characters to the front of playlist names. Just click the playlist name once to select it, click before the first character to place the curser, and type a character. A space before a playlist name won't work to move a playlist—iTunes and the iPod just ignore a space. However, you can bring a playlist to the top of the list by adding a dot (.) in front of the playlist name. If you want another playlist in front of that, use a hyphen (-). Hyphens come before dots alphabetically, don't you know.

Dots and hyphens are the best characters, because they are unobtrusive and are usually enough. However, there are dozens of others you can use as well. Here are some, in "alphabetical" order: - ! . @ * & # % $.

STORE MORE MUSIC THAN IPOD CAN HOLD

The Annoyance: My iPod is full, but my Mac's hard disk has plenty of space. What happens if I rip another CD? Do I now have to delete files from iTunes?

The Fix: Go ahead and burn more CDs. You can continue to use iTunes as your digital music library while keeping a subset on your iPod. You have two options, neither of which involves deleting music from iTunes:

- Manually tell iTunes which songs to keep on the iPod. You get exactly what you want, but this can be a real chore if you have 10,000 songs to manage.

- Let iTunes decide what will be on the iPod based on average play count and your ratings. iTunes will create a special playlist that determines what goes on the iPod, which you can then edit. (You'll need iTunes 4.2 or later for this trick.)

When you've loaded up your Mac past your iPod's capacity, iTunes will tell you when you connect the iPod to your Mac. You'll receive a message (see Figure 6-7) that asks if you want iTunes to select the songs. If you click the No button, iTunes will not update the iPod, and you can then proceed to the first option (manually selecting songs for your iPod). Here's how:

1. Select your iPod in the Source list on the left.

2. Press the iPod icon on the bottom right of the iTunes window. This brings up the iPod Preferences dialog, as shown in Figure 6-8. (You can't get to this window from iTunes Preferences.)

3. Click on the radio button next to "Manually manage songs and playlists."

4. Click the OK button.

5. Notice that songs on your iPod, which are usually grayed out, are now selectable. To remove a song from the iPod, select it from the iPod's list and press

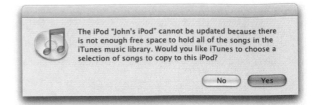

Figure 6-7. This message appears if you have more songs in iTunes than can fit in your iPod.

Figure 6-8. The iPod button at the lower-right corner of iTunes brings up the iPod Preferences dialog, where you can tell iTunes that you want to manually choose the songs.

Delete. To add a song, click Library in the source list and drag a song to the iPod icon.

If you want iTunes to take a crack at deciding what goes on the iPod, just click "Yes" in the dialog of Figure 6-7. iTunes will create a new playlist with a name like John's iPod Selection, which will be synced with your iPod every time you connect it to your Mac.

iTunes creates the iPod Selection playlist based on your listening habits. It calculates the average play counts and user ratings for each album in the library. iTunes first adds those albums with the highest scores to the iPod Selection playlist. Next, iTunes adds songs (again, by the album) that were most recently played or added to the library. If there is still some room on the iPod, iTunes randomly adds additional albums to the list.

You can edit the iPod Selection playlist just as you would any other playlist, by clicking and dragging songs to add and remove them from the playlist. (Note that you edit the iPod Selection playlist, not the actual iPod, whose songs remain grayed out.) This easy editing capability makes iPod Selection playlist a good starting place.

EARBUDS THAT STAY IN YOUR EARS

The Annoyance: The earbud headphones that came with my iPod are always falling out of my ears—especially when I'm working out. When I go running or hit the stair machine at the gym, I'm constantly pushing the earbuds back in.

The Fix: Just as everyone doesn't wear the same sized shoe, one earbud does not fit all. Heck, the iPod's earbuds fit my left ear better than my right ear. The solution for the active iPodder is to replace the earbuds that came with your iPod with something that fits better. There are two main factors to consider:

- Internal or External Speakers? Are you interested in sticking the headphones in your ears? For some people, old-fashioned, over-the-ears headphones are more comfortable. However, a more active person may prefer the earbud headphones because they tend to stay put if they fit your ear well.

- Cost. Think about how much you want to spend. You can go from cheap-and-easily-replaceable headphones to expensive and break-my-heart-if-I-lose-them headphones.

Whether low-cost or expensive, earbuds that stay put tend to be seated deeper into you ear than the standard iPod pair. They also come with multiple end-pieces for different sized ears. This is the case with the optional Apple Pod In-Ear Headphones ($39, *http://www.apple. com/ipod/accessories.html*), which come with three different pairs of end-pieces. For some people, however, these end-pieces don't keep the earbuds in place very well; they don't go deep enough into the ear canal.

Contrast this to the The Plug, by Koss (*$15, http://www. koss.com*), a headphone that goes deeper into the ear canal and stays in place better than either of Apple's earbuds. The Plug comes with four pairs of foam covers of different sizes and shapes, including cones, tubes, and a hexagon.

On the high end (but not too high) is the Etymotic ER6i Isolator ($139, *http://www.etymotic.com*). It goes deep into the ear and also comes with a pair of flexible silicon tips and a pair of foam tips, which are interchangeable. If you are interested in the ultimate fit, you can use the Etymotics with custom eartips made by an audiologist (the same kind of eartips that are made for a hearing aid). Another company, Future Sonics, can build a set of custom fit earpieces ($135, *http://www.futuresonics.com*), based on a mold of your ear, for its own line of headphones. Extravagant, yes, but they won't fall out of your ears.

HEAR MUSIC IN NOISY PLACES

The Annoyance: Even with the iPod volume turned up all the way, I can't hear the audio very well on airplanes, subways, or when I mow the lawn. If I press the standard iPod earbuds into my ears, the music gets louder and the noise is less noticeable. But this is only a short-term fix.

The Fix: One way to deal with noisy places is to go to iTunes and turn up the volume of all of your songs. This option provides you with louder volume than you currently have on your iPod. However, the better solution may be to invest in a better set of headphones specifically designed to cut out the noise.

To turn up the volume, click on Library in iTunes's Source list. Select all of the songs with ⌘-A. Bring up the information dialog with ⌘-I. Now drag the Volume Adjustment slider (as shown in Figure 6-9) to the right and click OK. This might help with quiet musical passages, but this approach has its own set of problems. It may not be loud enough for some passages. For other passages, simply cranking up the volume to drown out the noise can be dangerous to your hearing. You also lose any individual volume settings you may have previously set.

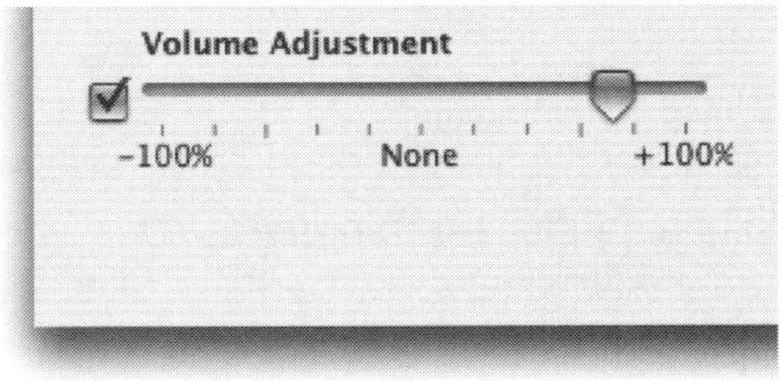

Figure 6-9. Using iTunes to raise the volume for all songs can help you hear music in noisy places.

A better solution is to try to keep the noise out of your ears by spending some cash on a set of earbuds or headphones designed to do just that: cancel out the noise. There are two approaches:

- Passive noise reduction. This is a low-tech approach that tries to block out sound by fitting snuggly around your ear or, in the case of an earbud, forming a tight seal in your ear canal. The earbuds are not as comfortable as headphones, but they tend do to a better job of passively blocking out noise. Passive noise reduction doesn't quite block out as much noise as active reduction does, but it also doesn't use batteries and produce a hiss. Some of the better models include the Etymotic ER6i Isolator ($139, *http://www.etymotic.com*), a lower priced but highly rated ver-

sion of the ER•4 MicroPro earbuds ($330). It takes some practice to situation these earbuds in your ear canal so that there is a good seal, which is required in order produce the deep bass frequencies. A similar pair is the Shure E3c ($179, *http://www.shure.com*). Sony's MDR-EX71SL ($50, *http://www.sony.com*) can also block noise and produce good audio.

- Active noise reduction. Also referred to as noise-canceling technology, active noise circuitry measures the ambient noise with a microphone and tries to produce sound that is 180 degrees out of phase, thus canceling out background noise. However, many of these active noise circuitries also add an audible hiss. One pair that doesn't is the Bose QuietComfort 2 Acoustic Noise Cancelling Headphones ($300, *http://www.bose.com*). These are comfortable over-the-ear headphones, which you can listen to at most Apple Stores (find them at most iPod and Mac stations). If you are wary of wearing a pair of $300 headphones on the subway, you might consider Sennheiser's PXC250 headphones ($150, *http://www.sennheiser.com*), which produce active noise canceling close to that of the Bose headphones. However, unlike Bose, the Sennheiser's PXC250 has a separate battery pack that you must carry around. If you're interested in earbuds with active noise reduction, check out Sony's Fontopia MDR-NC11 ($150, *http://www.sony.com*). At 1.7 ounces including the battery, this pair won't weigh you down.

FIND A PLACE TO CARRY EARBUDS

The Annoyance: Apple's iPod case (and many others) ignores the earbuds, as if the iPod were just another handheld PDA. When I carry my iPod around town—on the bus, in the taxi, and when hiking nearby trails—I usually slip the iPod (and its case) in my pocket. But when I stick the earbuds in a pocket, they always come out in a tangled mess.

The Fix: This annoyance is not just an inconvenience; if the earbud wires crimp or bend, you may find

Figure 6-10. The Marware SportSuit Sleeve gives you a pocket for your earbuds. There's also a hole at the top so you can leave the earbuds plugged in with the flap closed.

STANDARDIZE ARTISTS' NAMES

The Annoyance: The same artist sometimes has slightly different names on different tracks, based on the source. The iTunes Music Store might use "The Jimi Hendrix Experience" while the information iTunes receives when ripping a CD might provide "Jimi Hendrix." Sometimes, albums by the same artist differ, as in Miles Davis, the Miles Davis Trio, Quartet, Quintet, and so on. Other times, an ampersand (&) is used in the artist name (such as Simon & Garfunkel) while other times the artist name contains the word "and." It's even worse with classical music, in which the artist is sometimes the composer, sometimes the orchestra, and at other times the conductor.

iPod considers all these different spellings to be different artists, so I can't use the Artists category to listen to everything by one artist. It's a real pain to change the names in iTunes one at a time.

The Fix: Of course, you can always make a playlist, but that sort of defeats the purpose of the iPod's Artist category. A better approach is to standardize the artists name in iTunes, an action that you can complete in one swift move:

yourself with one or two dead earbuds before too long. Some strategies for carrying earbuds:

- Buy a new iPod case with a pocket for earbuds. Marware (*http://www.marware.com*) offers cases with earbud pockets in the $20 to $40 range (one is shown in Figure 6-10). It's a convenient solution, particularly if the case allows you to have the earbuds plugged into the iPod while they are in the pouch. Just be sure you get a case for your model iPod.

- Buy new earbuds that come with a case. These aren't difficult to find, as even low-cost earbuds are offering carrying cases. However, an earbud case is just one more item to carry around and keep track of, and eventually lose.

- How about retractable earbuds? Digital LifeStyle Outfitters offers the Zip Cord Retractable Earbuds ($20, *http://www.everythingipod.com*), which comes on a retractable spool that serves as the case. You can then stick it in the pocket of your iPod case.

1. In iTunes, search for a common word in the artist name, such as "Jimi."

2. Use the ⌘-A shortcut to select all of the items that show up in the search results.

3. Use the ⌘-I shortcut to open the Multiple Song Information window.

4. iTunes displays an alert message, saying "Are you sure you want to edit information for multiple items?" Click "Yes."

5. In the Artist field (see Figure 6-11), type a name that makes sense to you.

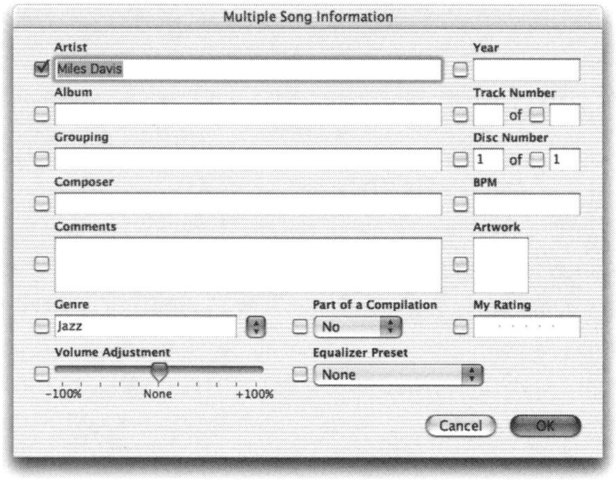

Figure 6-11. By selecting a group of songs in iTunes and hitting the Get info (⌘-I) command, you can standardize the artist name.

Remember, a shorter name fits better on the iPod screen. So you might change "Michael Tilson Thomas and the San Francisco Symphony" to "MTT & SFS."

FIND INEXPENSIVE IPOD CABLES

The Annoyance: Why are cables to connect the iPod to stereos or other devices so expensive?

The Fix: Here's a secret: there are no "iPod" connectors and cables. The iPod uses a standard 1/8-inch mini headphone jack, outputting the standard signal. It can

The Source of iTunes's CD Knowledge

When you import a CD, iTunes gets the song information that it moves to your iPod from the Gracenote CD Database (CDDB) (*http://www.gracenote.com/music*). Of course, you don't need to know the URL. Just have "Connect to Internet When Needed" selected in the General pane of iTunes Preferences.

use the standard converters and cables that you can find at your local hardware and electronics stores. For instance, a $3 connector from RadioShack does the job of the fancy "iPod headphone splitters," which cost four or five times as much. To plug an iPod into your home stereo, you typically need a cable with an 1/8-inch stereo male connector on one end (to plug into the iPod) and two mono RCA plugs on the other end. If you don't find a connector with that exact configuration, you should find converter connectors that you can string together to get you there.

Your friend, the audiophile, may argue that expensive cables with gold-plated connectors and extra shielding are less troublesome, which is true. But these cables aren't going to sit behind your entertainment console for years. If you start to get static from a bad cable after a few years, you can easily and inexpensively replace it.

Hardware
ANNOYANCES

Apple controls both the horizontal and the vertical on the Mac—designing the operating system as well as building the hardware. The result is that the hardware and software engineers at 1 Infinite Loop can cooperate or, at least, have access to each other's specifications. Compare this to your average PC, where the company building the operating system hides its family jewels from the people building the box (and vice versa). This is why the Mac generally serves up fewer hardware annoyances than your average PC.

This doesn't prevent hardware glitches, some of which have been almost Shakespearian in nature—spectacularly fatal flaws in otherwise great hardware, such as the spotted displays of the iBooks of 2002 and the famous exploding PowerBook of 1995. (It was actually Sony's battery that exploded, causing Apple to recall the PB 5300.)

Fortunately, most issues with Mac hardware and peripherals are not spectacular, simply annoying. This chapter helps you fix, avoid, or otherwise circumvent these problems.

receive higher quality sound with less noise than with a built-in audio port.

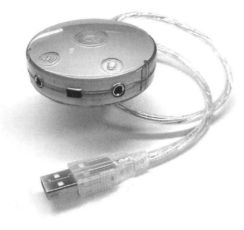

Figure 7-1. Griffin's iMic gives you a headphone port, as well as an audio-in port, that you can keep in front of your Mac.

GENERAL HARDWARE ANNOYANCES

BRING THE HEADPHONE PORT TO THE FRONT

The Annoyance: I like to listen to tunes when I'm at my Mac. Often I do so with a pair of headphones, but with the audio ports at the back of the Mac, it's a big production to plug and unplug the headphones. I have to move the Mac to where I can reach (and see) the audio port, which means moving the lamp, phone, and my collection of Star Trek snow globes. Is there any way to avoid doing the desktop shuffle just to plug in a set of headphones?

The Fix: Today's Power Mac G5's have a front-facing headphone jack, but many Macs have audio ports at or near the rear. One solution is to add your own up-front headphone port via a 1/8-inch headphone extension cable. However, a USB-to-audio interface gives you options that may surprise you in their usefulness. You can spend more than the cost of the Mac itself on audio interfaces; however, $40 buys you Griffin's iMic USB audio converter (*http://www.griffintechnology.com/products/imic*), shown in Figure 7-1. Plug the 2.5-inch iMic into any USB port and plug your headphones into the iMic, which you can keep in front of your Mac. The cable is 18 inches long, so you can plug it into a USB port at the back of your Mac, or coil the cable and plug it into your keyboard's USB port.

You can also use your new headphone port to connect external speakers or to feed audio to a tape recorder. The iMic (and other USB-audio interfaces) also has an audio-in port, which you can use to plug in your guitar for use with GarageBand. With an external audio interface, you

---

TWO, TWO, TWO HUBS IN ONE

Want to bring some of your other ports to the front of the Mac as well? Look for combo hubs that include both USB 2.0 and FireWire ports in one box. Both the D-Link DFB-H7 (*http://www.dlink. com/products/?pid=225*) and the Macally Hub-UF (*http://www.macally.com*) give you four USB 2.0 ports and two 400 Mbps FireWire ports. These are both powered hubs, meaning that the ports supply power to the peripherals (such as the iPod) without stressing out your Mac's internal power supply.

A combo hub doesn't have to take up room on your desk—if you own a hemispherical iMac. The UFO Hub from XtremeMac (*http://www.xtrememac. com*) also brings four USB 2.0 ports and two 400 Mbps FireWire ports to the front, with one important difference—the hub is a flat, white disk that fits under the iMac.

GIVE YOUR MAC A SPEED MAKEOVER

The Annoyance: My Mac is slow. Ultra slow. Molasses-in-winter slow. I thought it was fast five years ago, but today's applications, such as GarageBand and iMovie, seem to make beach-ball spinning more frequent than anything else. Apple says that Mac OS X doesn't work with non-Apple processors, yet I see processor upgrades for sale all the time. Can I upgrade my old Mac, or do I have to buy a new one to improve my performance?

The Fix: Apple would rather you buy a brand-new Mac, so it doesn't officially "support" (as in "provide tech support for") third-party processor upgrades. However, these faster processors do indeed run Mac OS X, allowing you to extend your Mac's useful life for a few more years. Manufacturers offer processor upgrades for most Mac models and guarantee that Mac OS X will run on them. You can get a processor upgrade card for as little as $200 or as much as $1000. How much should you spend? Well, that depends on how old your Mac is and how much it would cost to replace it. If your Mac didn't come with at least a G3 processor, it's also hampered by a slow system bus and may not be worth upgrading to Mac OS X readiness. Also, factor in the cost of other hardware upgrades you might want to make, such as a DVD burner, a bigger hard drive, and more RAM. If the total cost of your proposed makeover is close to the cost of a new equivalent Mac, go for the new Mac. Just as you wouldn't want to put a brand-new transmission in a 1988 Yugo, you may not want to sink $1000 into an eight-year-old Mac.

If your Mac is worthy of a makeover, there are several reputable companies that make processors upgrades. Fast Mac (*http://www.fastmac.com*) offers upgrades for the widest variety of Macs, including Power Macs (as shown in Figure 7-2), PowerBooks, and the original-style iMacs. Other companies include Sonnet (*http://www.sonnettech.com*), PowerLogix (*http://www.powerlogix.com*), and Giga Designs (*http://www.gigadesigns.com*). On most Macs, you can install the processor upgrade yourself. If you want to see what's involved before you buy, check the support page of the manufacturer's web site for installation instructions.

Figure 7-2. Processor upgrade cards are available for just about all Macs, including Power Macs, certain iMacs, and PowerBooks, even the short-lived Cubes. This is FastMac's upgrade for a Power Mac G4.

> **t i p**
>
> Not sure whether you need a processor upgrade? One way to check is to open the Activity Monitor utility (*/Applications/Utilities*) in Mac OS X 10.3 (which was called CPU Monitor before Version 10.3) and work with the software you use every day. Activity/CPU Monitor displays a graph of how much of your Mac's processing power your applications use. If the bars in the graph consistently peg at or near the top (near 100 percent utilization), then you would benefit from a faster processor.

TROUBLESHOOT A PROCESSOR UPGRADE PROBLEM

The Annoyance: I upgraded my Mac's processor, and the speed boost is *amazing*. The only problem is that, ever since the upgrade, the Mac's screen freezes from time to time—the cursor and everything on screen stops responding. My only option is to hit the Power button to turn the Mac off and on again, which can damage a file that is open at the time.

The Fix: Chances are this is a hardware problem, most likely related to the new processor or possibly with RAM. Unlike in Mac OS 9, freezing is usually not a typical symptom of a software problem in Mac OS X. You may need a new processor upgrade card. But before you call the manufacturer asking for a replacement unit, do a little troubleshooting to try to identify the problem:

1. Check that you've made the correct jumper settings on the card. Not all processor upgrade cards have jumper settings, but some do, so you should make sure they're set correctly in accordance with the manufacturer's directions.

2. Run Disk Utility (*/Applications/Utilities*) and any third-party disk repair program you may have. This is the first thing most tech support personnel will tell you to do, so you might as well get it out of the way.

3. Check to see if something is wrong with Mac OS X. Start up the Mac from another partition or hard drive, or from your system installation CD. (To do the latter, hold the C key down while restarting.) If you have an older dual-boot Mac, you can start up from Mac OS 9. Now run the Mac for a while. If the problem still occurs, then it is a hardware problem.

4. Check to see if the RAM is defective. If you have added RAM since you bought the Mac, it is possible that a RAM module that worked fine at slower speeds won't work well with the faster processor. Pull out the RAM module you previously added and run the Mac. If you've added more than one module, pull each one out, one by one, and try running the Mac. If your Mac is still freezing, then it's probably not the RAM.

Armed with these troubleshooting results, you can now call the manufacturer's customer service line. Be sure you make the call before the warrantee expires. When asking for a replacement, be firm but polite—being obnoxious to a telephone support rep won't get you anywhere.

BACK UP AND RESTORE PAINLESSLY

The Annoyance: Mac help books always talk about how important it is to back up your hard drive data, but the backup software is about as easy to understand as a Greek translation of *Finnegans Wake*. I'm also not sure which folders need to be backed up, or where to back them up to. I know iTunes and iPhoto can back up music and photos to CDs, and I could then reinstall Mac OS X from the system CDs. But restoring from multiple CDs in the event of a catastrophe would be even more confusing than making a backup. Is there a kinder, gentler way to safeguard my data?

The Fix: Consider this dream backup scenario: you plug a tiny FireWire hard drive into your Mac. Suddenly, without even a twitch of your mouse finger, everything on your internal hard disk is automatically copied to the external drive. And I mean *everything*—the invisible files, the Unix directories, every preference and configurations file, and all your data. On the backup FireWire drive, instead of some proprietary compressed archive, you get an exact working copy of your internal hard disk. If your internal drive turns to toast, you can immediately boot the Mac from the FireWire drive to restore your internal drive or to continue to work—check your email, connect to the company network, and finish that report that needs to be on your boss's desk by 5 p.m.

This scenario is no dream—it's real, thanks to the ABSplus Automatic Backup System from CMS (*http://www. cmsproducts.com/products_backup.htm*). The system consists of a CD, a FireWire cable, and a FireWire hard drive in one of two physical sizes. The portable model (as shown in Figure 7-3) is slightly bigger than an iPod and weighs only seven ounces, making it easy to carry with your PowerBook or iBook. At publishing time, it came in 20- to 80- GB capacities. A desktop model called the Velocity series is also available with a top capacity of 200 GB. If you have room on the ABSplus, you can back up several drives to it.

Figure 7-3. The Portable ABS backup drive weighs seven ounces.

Plug in the drive, and the ABS Backup software (as shown in Figure 7-4) launches and starts backing up. If you've previously backed up, it copies only files that have been changed or added since the last backup. A reminder program tells you to plug the drive back in when it's time for another backup. If you keep the drive plugged into the Mac all the time, you can schedule automatic backups with the included ABS Settings software. This utility also lets you exclude items from backup; if your ABSplus drive is close to filling up, you can exclude folders that you don't deem essential or that you have backed up elsewhere.

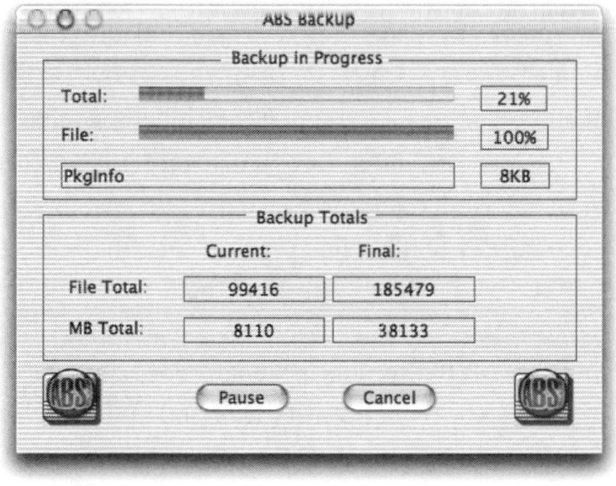

Should you need to restore a file or folder, simply drag it from the ABSplus drive to your internal hard drive. To completely restore your internal hard drive, just boot the Mac from the ABSplus drive and run another utility called ABSRestore from the ABSplus drive.

DOUBLE-SIDED PRINTING

The Annoyance: I need to print double-sided documents (known as *duplex printing*), but my printer can print single-sided sheets only. This means that the Two Sided Printing feature in Panther's Print dialog is grayed out. I have no choice but to take my printout to a copy shop to get it recopied as double-sided, and they don't even validate parking. Is there some kind of attachment I can get to enable double-sided printing, or do I need a new printer?

The Fix: If you have Mac OS X 10.3 or later, which offers another way to do double-sided printing in the Print dialog, you don't have to buy a new attachment nor a new printer. First, print the even-numbered pages, flip the printouts around, and then print the odd-numbered pages. Here how:

1. In the Print dialog, go to the Copies & Pages pop-up menu and select Paper Handling (see Figure 7-5).

2. Check the box next to Reverse Page Order.

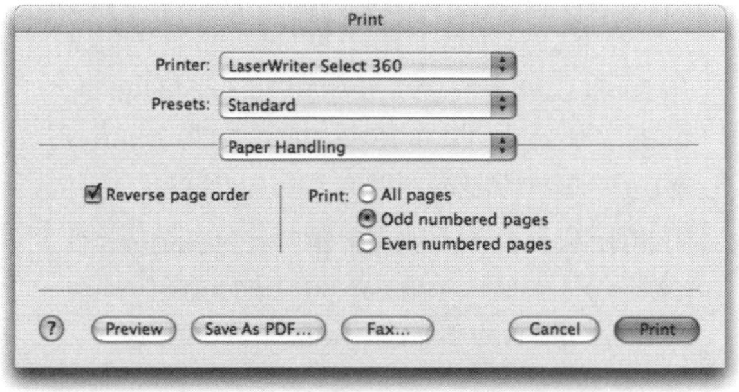

Figure 7-4. The ABS Backup software automatically launches and backs up everything on your internal hard drive when you plug in the external ABS plus FireWire drive.

Figure 7-5. This setting in Panther's print dialog allows you to print the even-numbered pages, flip the printouts around, and then print the odd-numbered pages.

3. Choose Even Numbered Pages as the Print setting.

4. Hit the Print button to print your pages.

5. Take the printout and place it into your printer where the paper supply usually is. Make sure you arrange it so that you print on the blank side.

6. Bring up the Print dialog again, and select Odd Numbered Pages.

Whether or not you use Reverse Page Order in Step 6 depends on how your printer feeds in paper. Try it out with a test run of six pages (three sheets) before you print large documents.

TECH TIP
PRINT TO PC PRINTERS WITH
PRE-PANTHER MAC OS X

Mac OS X 10.3 (and later) lets you print to a variety of printers connected to Windows PCs on a network and to PC printers connected directly to your Mac. You can add this same ability to Jaguar by installing a Free Software package called Gimp-Print (*http://gimp-print.sourceforge.net/MacOSX. php3*).

Gimp-Print is a set of printer drivers for PC printers designed to work with the Common Unix Printing System (CUPS), which is included with Mac OS X 10.2 and later. Mac OS X Version 10.3 and later includes the Gimp-Print drivers by default, which is why you need this download for Jaguar only.

If, after you download Gimp-Print, you are still having problems setting up printing to a PC printer, check this web page at the Gimp-Print site:

http://gimp-print.sourceforge.net/p_FAQ_OS_ X.php3#generalSetup

---

FLEXIBLE STAND FOR YOUR ISIGHT

The Annoyance: The little, toy plastic stand that came with the Apple iSight camera just aren't working for me. It's tough to aim the iSight at what I want to shoot, and when I do get it positioned, the darn thing just won't stay put. The idea of gluing an iSight stand to the back of my display with the included adhesive pad is not at all appealing.

The Fix: Sounds like you could use a flexible stand made especially for the iSight. MacMice (*http://www. macmice.com*) has a couple of flexible stands made from a bendable metal "gooseneck" tube with a FireWire cable inside. The 18-inch-long iFlex ($20) plugs right into a FireWire port of a notebook or iMac. For other Macs, a better option is the SightFlex ($30), which sits in a weighted desktop stand. With either, you can bend, twist, and shape the stand to firmly hold the iSight in any position or shooting angle.

KEYBOARDS AND MICE

EJECTING WITHOUT AN EJECT KEY

The Annoyance: My non-Apple keyboard doesn't have an eject key. I like the keyboard, but dragging and dropping CDs to the Trash is a pain. Yes, I know that discs get an eject icon next to them in the Finder's sidebar with Mac OS X 10.3 and later, but that means I have to first switch to the Finder and open a Finder window, then open the sidebar, and finally click on the icon. That's not any easier than the old drag 'n trash method.

The Fix: Actually, your keyboard does have an eject key—the F12 key, which ejects CDs and DVDs on third-party keyboards, and on older Apple keyboards that don't have an eject key. (In fact, the F12 key on PowerBooks and iBooks is labeled with the eject icon.)

If you want to eject with your mouse, there is an easier method than using Panther's sidebar eject icon—and it works in every version from Mac OS X 10.1 and later. You can add an Eject menu to the right side of the menu bar; this menu will always be there, so you can eject from any application without going to the Finder.

To install the Eject menu, bring the Finder to the front and hit Shift-⌘-G to bring up the Go to Folder window. Type this path:

/System/Library/CoreServices/Menu Extras

This brings up the Menu Extras folder, which is filled with, well, extra menus that you can add to the menu bar. Find the item called *Eject.menu*. (In Mac OS X 10.3 and later, Menu Extras items have generic document icon, as shown in Figure 7-6. Versions before Panther, the icons look like a folder.) Now double-click *Eject.menu* to install the menu in the menu bar (see Figure 7-7). To remove the menu, hold the ⌘ key while you drag it off of the menu bar.

Figure 7-6. Double-clicking Eject.menu here...

Figure 7-7. ...installs an Eject menu in the menu bar.

EJECT PROBLEMS

If the eject key or other standard methods aren't working to eject a disc, you may have a temporary software problem. Restarting the Mac often resolves these types of problems. If you are running Mac OS X 10.3 and later, hold the mouse down while restarting the Mac. The disc should eject.

In some cases, you may need to boot the Mac into Open Firmware—a command-line version of the operating system that is contained in a chip on the motherboard. This is the procedure:

1. **Restart the Mac. As soon you hear the startup sound, hold the Option-⌘-O-F keys.**

2. **You will see a screen that says, "Welcome to Open Firmware." You can release the keys at this point.**

3. **A command-line prompt appears; type the following:**

   ```
   eject cd
   ```

4. **Press Return; the disc ejects after a few seconds. The word "okay" appears at the prompt to let you know that the disc has ejected safely.**

5. **To reboot into Mac OS X, type** `mac-boot` **and press Return.**

POWER FOR YOUR WIRELESS KEYBOARD

The Annoyance: I go through batteries in my Apple Wireless Keyboard and Wireless Mouse like peanuts in an elephant house. I'd rather spend the money on buying songs from the iTunes store. It's also annoying to have to run to the store to buy batteries when I need to get some work to do.

The Fix: Try to get into the habit of turning off the keyboard and mouse (with the switch on the bottom) when you're not using them. You may think that Apple Wireless Keyboard and Mouse turn themselves off after a minute or two of non-use, but they actually go into a sleep mode that does use a little power. Over a period of weeks, this sleep power can drain your batteries.

You may also be able to get longer life from a different type of battery. Lithium batteries are expensive, but they last longer than standard batteries. Shops often refer to lithium batteries as *camera batteries*, but as long as they are AA-sized, they work. Lithium batteries also have a very long shelf life (up to 10 years), which means you can keep a supply of them on hand without worrying about loosing power in your drawer.

You could also consider using rechargeable batteries, which are better both for your wallet and the environment. Rechargeable batteries don't hold a charge as long as non-rechargeable batteries, but they can give you greater coverage if you buy two sets, one for the mouse and keyboard, and another to keep charged. Apple's Wireless Keyboard and Mouse can use rechargeable batteries that are nickel-metal-hydride (NiMH) or (NiCad); NiMH batteries have a longer service life than NiCad. (There are also rechargeable Lithium batteries, but Apple says they don't work in its keyboard and mouse.) Whichever batteries you use, stick to one type. Don't mix battery types in these devices, or you may damage the device.

CLEANING UP KEYBOARDS

Keyboard cleanliness may not be next to godliness, but it can prevent annoying problems. Over time, the dust, hair, and muffin crumbs that accumulate in a keyboard not only make it look unsightly, but can cause the keys to malfunction.

The best tool for cleaning a keyboard is a vacuum cleaner with the smallest brush attachment. With the Mac turned off (or the keyboard disconnected), run the bristles between the keys, both in a left and right and up and down motion.

If you spill liquid on your keyboard, immediately turn it upside down and shake as much it off as you can. (If it's a PowerBook or iBook, turn the entire unit upside down first.) Tilt the keyboard and try blowing a hair dryer set to cold over it. Next, run to the hardware or electronics store and buy a can of compressed gas, also know as compressed air. The aerosol can usually comes with thin straw that fits in the nozzle. Use this to blow between the keys. Tilt the keyboard and blow from the top down. (In a PowerBook or iBook, open the keyboard to check for liquid in underneath. It's also a good idea to remove the battery.)

If the keys are acting oddly or are producing the wrong characters, there is probably liquid trapped underneath. Pry off some keys with your finger or with a plastic fork or knife (not something that can cut into the plastic keys). Start with a key on the end, such as the F keys, and work your way over to the affected key. If you can, avoid removing the bigger keys, such as the Shift keys, as they use wire connectors that are more complicated to get back on. Now blow the compressed gas into the center well of affected key. When you're done, you can snap the keys back on.

Never spray a cleaning agent (or anything else) on the keyboard. If you want to remove coffee stains from your nice white keys, use a damp cloth.

WHERE'S THE POWER KEY ON THE KEYBOARD?

The Annoyance: I just purchased a new iMac and was disheartened to discover that there's no Power button on the keyboard. My older Apple keyboard has a Power button, so why doesn't this one? Now, I have to reach behind the iMac to turn it on. I'm sure Apple saved some money by removing the Power key, but I'd gladly pay the extra two bucks to get it back.

The Fix: If you have an older Mac USB keyboard, you can use it on the new Mac—the old Power key will work to turn the Mac on and will bring up the Shutdown Options dialog, just as it did on your old Mac.

Although you can't buy a power button, you can spend a bit more to buy a USB keyboard that includes a Power button. For instance, Macally's iKey ($45, *http://www.macally.com/spec/usb/input_device/ikey.html*) has a Power button. If you liked the old Apple Extended keyboard, the Matias Tactile Pro Keyboard ($100, *http://halfkeyboard.com/tactilepro/index.php*) is a near exact copy, including a Power key.

On your new Apple keyboard, there are a few keyboard commands that activate some of the functions that used the Power key, as well as the old Reset button that Macs used to have:

- Bring up the shutdown option dialog: Control-Eject. This bring up the "Are you sure you want to shutdown your computer" dialog, offering options for Restart, Sleep, Shutdown, and Cancel.

- Reset: Control-⌘-Eject (or F12). This command does the same thing the Reset button on older Macs did: restart the Mac immediately without quitting anything. You're not supposed to need it with Mac OS X, but occasionally, you may find yourself in a bind that you want to get out of.

- Shut down immediately: Control-Option-⌘-Eject. When you add the Option key to the mix, your Mac is forced to shut down without quitting any open applications or saving changes in any open documents.

Swift Scrolling

Want to speed up scrolling through a huge document or heavily populated Finder window? You can greatly accelerate scrolling by holding the Option key while you scroll, which causes the cursor to jump from paragraph break to paragraph break, rather than sentence to sentence. This trick also works whether you click the scroll arrow or use a scroll wheel on a non-Apple mouse.

DITCH THAT SINGLE-BUTTON MOUSE

The Annoyance: I recently swithced to a Mac from a Windows PC. I'm glad I made the transition, except for one annoying thing: the Apple one-button (or no-button) mouse. I was a real whiz with scroll wheel, and the second button saved me lots of time; the no-button mouse is a giant step backwards.

The Fix: Apple's tradition of a one-button mouse goes back to a decision made by Jef Raskin, whom author Owen Linzmayer dubbed "the father of the Macintosh." Several years before the first Mac shipped, Raskin persuaded Apple not to go with a three-button mouse for the sake of simplicity. That is, it is easier to teach beginners to use a one-button mouse. (By "beginners," think of a roomful of first graders or your doctor.)

A few years ago, however, Apple realized that not everyone was a beginner, which is why Mac OS X has built-in support for mice with two buttons and a scroll wheel. If the mouse you used with your PC was a USB mouse, simply plug it into your new Mac and start mousing around.

Mac OS X supports several functions of the second mouse button and the scroll wheel:

- The right button brings up a contextual menu—the Mac OS X equivalent of the Windows shortcut menu.
- The scroll wheel scrolls the selected window in the Finder and in many applications.
- Hold the Shift key while you move the scroll wheel to scroll horizontally.
- Use the scroll wheel to move up and down an open menu to highlight a command.

To get beyond the basic features, such as the using a third or forth mouse button, you'll probably need to install drivers from the manufacturer. Check your mouse manufacture's web site for a Mac OS X driver. You'll also find Mac OS X drivers for a number of third-party mice at this Apple web page:

http://www.apple.com/downloads/macosx/drivers

This Apple page even has drivers for Microsoft's IntelliMouse, both the Optical and Explorer versions. Microsoft posts Mac OS X drivers for its mice and keyboards at *http://www.microsoft.com/mac*. Once you get there, click the link for Other, and then follow the links for Mice and Keyboards.

Get Info

You'll find the story of how Jef Raskin came up with the idea for the Macintosh in *Apple Confidential 2.0* by Owen Linzmayer (No Starch Press, *http://www.owenink.com/ac/contents.html*). The chapter titled "The Making of Macintosh" describes Raskin's choice and reasoning for a one-button mouse.

DISPLAYS

MAKE SECOND MONITORS WORK WITH PANTHER

The Annoyance: When I upgraded my Power Mac to Panther, my second monitor stopped working. I really like having two monitors for all the palettes and windows I use. Was it something I said?

The Fix: If you have an older graphics card in a PCI slot supporting the second monitor, then Panther may simply be ignoring it. Fortunately, you can show Mac OS X who's the boss by launching Terminal (*/Applications/Utilities*) and typing this Unix command:

```
$ sudo nvram boot-args="romndrv=1"
```

Hit Return. You'll be prompted for your password; type it and hit Return again. You can now quit Terminal and restart your Mac. This command changes a setting in your Mac's parameter RAM chip (or PRAM), allowing the Mac to recognize the older graphics card and enabling the second monitor to work. This doesn't work with every video card, but it does work with a lot of old models. If it doesn't work, replacing the card with a newer model will get your second monitor running again.

Oh, yes, there is one more think you should know: there's a small chance the sudo nvram command will prevent your Mac from booting. Annoying, yes, but there's no need to panic, as you can easily reset the PRAM back the default settings (that is, with one monitor working). Just hold down the Option-⌘-P-R keys at startup until you hear the startup chime two or three times. This is known as "zapping the PRAM."

ACCELERATE AN OLDER GRAPHICS CARD

The Annoyance: I got my old graphics card to work with my second monitor, just as you described earlier, but it doesn't seem as fast as my main monitor. Window resizing, Panther's cube-rotation feature when changing users, and other effects are slower and not as smooth as on my main monitor.

The Fix: Picky, picky. The problem here is that your old card doesn't support the hardware acceleration provided by Quartz Extreme, the graphics software that is part of Mac OS X 10.2 and later. If your old card is a PCI Radeon from ATI or an 8 MB Radeon card in a notebook, you're in luck. A developer known as Zacks offers the free PCI Extreme! (*http://pages.cthome.net/zacks*), which enables older PCI Radeon cards and 8 MB Radeon cards in notebooks to use Quartz Extreme.

This won't work with other older cards, such as the Rage 128 Pro that shipped in many old Power Mac G4 models. If you have one of these, you can pickup a new card that supports Quartz Extreme, such as the ATI Radeon 9000; this will only set you back by $150.

CHECK FOR QUARTZ EXTREME

The Annoyance: I'm not sure whether the video card in my older Power Mac supports Quartz Extreme. Some 3D games run just fine, but I have one game that has very unsmooth graphics. The System Profiler (*/Applications/Utilities*) tells me that my graphics card has MB of video RAM (VRAM). Is this enough for Quartz Extreme? Should I buy a new graphics card? Or is something wrong with my system?

The Fix: Graphics cards need at least MB of VRAM in order to use Quartz Extreme, but some older cards with MB RAM still won't support Quartz Extreme. To find out whether Quartz Extreme is running on your Mac, there are a couple of tests you can run. If you have Mac OS X 10.3 or later, check its ability to automatically change Desktop pictures. To do this, launch System Preferences and click the Desktop & Screen Saver icon. At the bottom of the screen, click the checkbox next to Change Picture and set the pop-up menu to "every 5 seconds." If the Desktop pictures change by fading one into the other, then your graphics card supports Quartz Extreme. If each new desktop picture appears abruptly, without a transition, then your graphics card does not support Quartz Extreme.

> ### CLEANING A DISPLAY
> As with keyboards, you should never spray any liquid directly on a display. You don't want to risk dripping liquid into the electronics; cleaning fluid is no better than the spilt coffee.
>
> Whether it's on a notebook, an iMac, or a separate LCD or CRT monitor, or the built-in eMac display, the cleaning recommendation is the same. Use a dry soft cloth to wipe, or use a cloth slightly dampened with water.
>
> Never use solvents or cleaners with ammonia on a display. LCDs are made of plastic that can react to chemicals by discoloring or drying and cracking over time. And while CRTs are made of glass, they aren't windows—they often have a coating that can be damaged by chemicals, including the ammonia in window cleaner.

If you're running a version of Mac OS X before 10.3, there is a free utility called Quartz Extreme Check (*http://www.versiontracker.com/dyn/moreinfo/mac/15911*) that can tell you whether your video card supports Quartz Extreme. Double-click the utility and a dialog appears, telling you whether or not your Mac is "hardware accelerated." If it is, you're good to go; if not, no dice.

FIXING FUZZY FONTS

The Annoyance: I have an older Mac with a CRT display. I recently upgraded from Mac OS 9 to Mac OS X. Now all the text looks fuzzy. Has Mac OS X made my eyes go bad, or isn't my monitor good enough for the new OS?

The Fix: Fuzzy is often in the eye of the beholder, but the culprits are Mac OS X's font smoothing and your CRT display. Mac OS X and Mac OS 9 handle font smoothing very differently. Mac OS 9 uses *antialiasing*, a technique that adds various shades of gray around a character to make it appear smooth. Mac OS X (and Windows XP) uses a superior font-smoothing method called *sub-pixel rendering* that is specifically designed to take advantage of flat-panel displays. Sub-pixel rendering actually displays higher resolution characters than font smoothing. However, if you are viewing Mac OS X on a CRT display, the effect just doesn't work as well. Additionally, older CRTs have an inherent fuzziness; they aren't nearly as sharp as flat-panel displays or even newer CRTs. One option is to buy a new monitor. I recommend a flat-panel screen; once you use one, you'll never go back to a CRT.

If you don't want a new display or you have built-in display, as with an older iMac, you can use the font smoothing configuration tools that Mac OS X gives you. In System Preferences, go to the Appearance pane. At the bottom, set the Font Smoothing Style pop-up menu to "Standard—best for CRT." Under that, set the Turn Off Font Smoothing to 12. With this setting, only fonts that are bigger than 12 points are smoothed. (Figure 7-8 shows these two settings.)

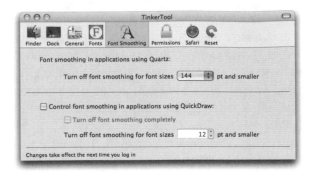

Figure 7-9. **TinkerTool lets you turn off Mac OS X's font smoothing for font sizes up to 144 points. This might give good results on an older CRT monitor, but you may not like it on a flat-panel display.**

Get Info

For a clear discussion on how sub-pixel rendering works, see *http://grc.com/ct-what.htm*.

Figure 7-8. These font-smoothing settings in Appearance Preferences minimize font fuzziness on CRT monitors.

To turn off font smoothing for fonts bigger than 12 points, you can use the free TinkerTool (*http://www.bresink.com/osx/TinkerTool.html*). As you can see from Figure 7-9, TinkerTool lets you turn off font smoothing for all fonts up to 144 points in size, which is just about everything. It's a matter of opinion—and a matter of the condition of your CRT display—whether or not this setting is pleasing to you.

POWERBOOKS AND IBOOKS

IMPROVE EXTERNAL DISPLAY QUALITY

The Annoyance: I frequently use my PowerBook with an external VGA display. The picture isn't as sharp on the external display as on the built-in display. The external display is what my audience sees, which ends up making me look bad.

The Fix: Your PowerBook doesn't have enough video RAM (VRAM) for both the built-in display and the VGA monitor, so the PowerBook shortchanges the external display. The solution is to shut the built-in display off, so that all of the video RAM is devoted to the VGA display. You might be aware that you can close the PowerBook and still operate it with an external display and an external keyboard. That's no great trick, but did you know that you can shut off the built-in display while keeping the PowerBook lid open so you can access the keyboard? An open lid also keeps the heat from building up.

You need a USB mouse for this trick. Here's how it works:

1. Connect the VGA display to the PowerBook.

2. Set the PowerBook to mirror mode. In System Preferences, click Displays. Set both displays to the same resolution and color depth. Now click the Arrangement tab and select Mirror Displays.

3. If you are using a USB mouse, unplug it.

4. Close the lid to put the PowerBook to sleep.

5. Plug in the mouse to the USB port to bring the Power-Book out of sleep mode. At this time, an image should appear on the VGA display.

6. Open the lid; the built-in display is turned off, but the built-in keyboard is still functional.

7. Go back to the Displays preference panel. The built-in display option no longer appears. You can now change the pixel resolution of the VGA display.

To bring the built-in display back to life, just click the Detect Displays button in the Display preferences panel.

SET HARD DRIVE SPINDOWN TIME FOR POWERBOOK/IBOOK

The Annoyance: Starting with Version 10.2, Mac OS X's System Preferences removed the ability to set a time for spinning down the hard disk. Now there's just a checkbox to "Put the hard disk(s) to sleep when possible." I think I could save more battery power if I could set this myself.

The Fix: Although the Energy Saver preference panel doesn't give you a way to set the spindown time, you can change it with a text command in Terminal. You can use the pmset command (short for *power management settings*) to set the spindown time to, say, five minutes, with the following command:

```
$ sudo pmset -b spindown 5
```

You are then asked for your password. The –b argument means that this setting is applied when the battery is in use. A –c argument (for *charger*) works when the power supply is plugged in. To make a setting for any power situation, use the –a argument.

The *pmset* command can also make other power management changes, including those of set by Energy Saver preferences. To view these settings, type the following in the Terminal:

```
$ pmset -g disk
```

To learn more about the *pmset* command, enter man pm-set in the Terminal to view *pmset*'s manual page.

KEEP YOUR LAPTOP COOL

The Annoyance: I need to use my PowerBook on my lap a lot, but it can get uncomfortably hot. Not only does it toast my thighs, but on a warm day, my sweaty wrists sizzle.

The Fix: As PowerBooks have become thinner and the processors faster, they tend to put out more heat. The smallest model, the 12-inch PowerBook, gets the hottest. The heat buildup can actually be worse when you use it on your lap, as your body can block air that would normally flow underneath the PowerBook on a solid surface. Thus, Apple says a hard surface dissipates heat better than a soft surface, such as your thighs.

One simple solution is to insulate your lap by providing a hard surface such as a stiff hardcover book under the PowerBook. For a more stable surface, try the $30 Podium CoolPad (*http://www.roadtools.com/podium.html*). It also includes risers that lift one end of the PowerBook off of the board, letting more air circulate under the PowerBook, therefore keeping it cooler. Macally's IcePad ($30, *http://www.macally.com/new/new_icepad.html*) is a wedge-shaped pad that allows air under the PowerBook.

You can also find a pad that actively cools. The Antec NoteBook Cooler ($40, *http://www.antec-inc.com/us/pro_notebookcooler.html*) includes two fans that draw heat away from the PowerBook. It's not quite as efficient on your lab as when it's on a hard service, but you can position it to keep the fans clear. For power, the NoteBook Cooler plugs into a USB port. (It also includes a pass-through USB to allow you to use USB at the same time.) Two fans run on your battery power, but not as much as you might think. By reducing the PowerBook's temperature, the NoteBook Cooler increasing battery efficiency and enables the internal fan to run less often, both of which make a battery charge last longer.

POWERBOOK THERMOMETER

Just how hot is your PowerBook? You can find out with Temperature Monitor, (*http://www.bresink.de/osx*), a free program from Marcel Bresink. Temperature Monitor reads the built-in temperature gauge of the PowerBook G4 (and some Power Mac G4 models) to tell you how hot it's getting. These Macs use the temperature gauge to tell the Mac how to regulate the internal fan. You can use Temperature Monitor to determine which cooling technique (such as the position of a NoteBook Cooler) is most effective.

By the way, the same Energy Saver preference panel settings that conserve battery power also keep your PowerBook cooler. This includes reducing processor performance (the Options tab) and the option called "Put the hard disk to sleep when possible" (the Sleep tab).

SOLVE THE MYSTERY OF DISPLAY SMUDGES

The Annoyance: I think there's some kind of smudge goblin that messes up the display of my iBook G4 at night. I make it a point never to touch my screen, as I'm pretty fussy about fingerprints. However, the smudges don't look like human fingerprints, hence, it must be a goblin. At first I thought it was the infamous iBook "white spot" defect, but to my relief, the smudges disappear with a slightly damp cloth. I also discovered that the smudge goblin visits a friend of mine with a brand new PowerBook. Should I hang garlic around the iBook, or should I go with a silver bullet?

The Fix: Harry Potter isn't going to help, as it's the notebook's own keys that are smudging the screen. In these newer, thinner G4 models, the display gets very close to the keys when the lid is closed—so close, that the keys can just touch the screen. Your hands can leave a layer of oil on the keys, which gets transferred to the display when you close the lid. If you've just finished a long gaming session, notice the smudges line up with the arrow keys or the keys you use to shoot with.

The fix is to use the thin foam sheet that Apple shipped with your notebook. Place it on top of the keyboard before you close the lid. If you no longer have this sheet, a thin piece of soft cloth, such as felt, works well to keep the smudge goblins away. If you're inclined to blow some dough, RadTech (*http://www.radtech.com*) offers cloths of the right size.

Index

Colophon

Our look is the result of reader comments, our own experimentation, and feedback from distribution channels. Distinctive covers complement our distinctive approach to technical topics, breathing personality and life into potentially dry subjects.

Genevieve d'Entremont was the production editor and proofreader for *PC Hardware Annoyances.* Derek Di Matteo was the copyeditor. Patti Capaldi, Melanie Wang, and Genevieve d'Entremont did the typesetting and page makeup. Colleen Gorman and Claire Cloutier provided quality control. Mary Agner provided production assistance. Julie Hawks wrote the index.

Eric Heinman designed the cover of this book using Adobe Illustrator, and produced the cover layout with Adobe InDesign CS using Gravur Condensed and Adobe Sabon fonts.

Patti Capaldi designed and implemented the interior layout using Adobe InDesign CS. This book was converted from Microsoft Word to InDesign CS by Julie HawksThe text and heading fonts are Rotis Sans Serif, Lineto Gravur, and Myriad Pro; the code font is The Sans Mono. The screenshots and technical illustrations that appear in the book were produced by Robert Romano amd Jessamyn Read using Macromedia Freehand MX and Adobe Photoshop 7. The cartoon illustrations used on the cover and in the interior of this book are copyright © 2004 Hal Mayforth.

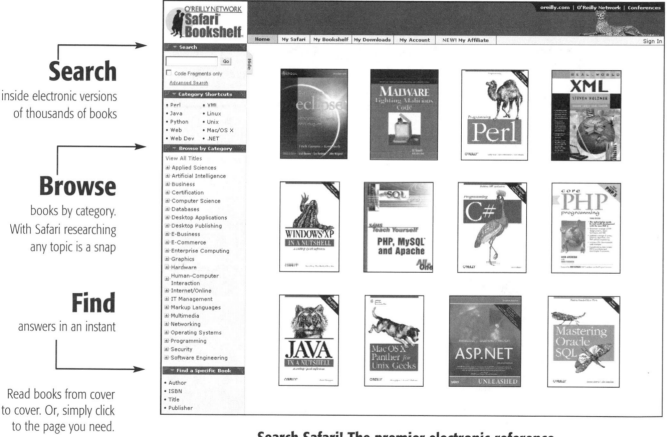

Related Titles Available from O'Reilly

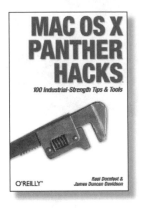

Macintosh

AppleScript: The Definitive Guide

Appleworks 6: The Missing Manual

The Best of the Joy of Tech

FileMaker Pro 7: The Missing Manual

GarageBand: The Missing Manual

iLife '04: The Missing Manual

iMovie 4 and iDVD: The Missing Manual

iPhoto 4: The Missing Manual

iPod & iTunes: The Missing Manual, *2nd Edition*

Mac OS X Panther in a Nutshell

Mac OS X Panther Pocket Guide

Mac OS X Panther Power User

Mac OS X: The Missing Manual, *Panther Edition*

Mac OS X Unwired

Macintosh Troubleshooting Pocket Guide

Modding Mac OS X

Office X for the Macintosh: The Missing Manual

Revolutionaries in The Valley: Their Incredible Stories of How the Mac was Made

Running Mac OS X Panther

Mac Developers

Building Cocoa Applications: A Step-By-Step Guide

Cocoa in a Nutshell

Learning Carbon

Learning Cocoa with Objective-C, *2nd Edition*

Learning Unix for Mac OS X Panther

Mac OS X for Java Geeks

Mac OS X Hacks

Mac OS X Panther Hacks

Mac OS X Panther for Unix Geeks

Managing & Using Mac OS X Server

Objective-C Pocket Reference

RealBasic: The Definitive Guide, *2nd Edition*

Keep in touch with O'Reilly

1. Download examples from our books

To find example files for a book, go to:

www.oreilly.com/catalog

select the book, and follow the "Examples" link.

2. Register your O'Reilly books

Register your book at *register.oreilly.com*

Why register your books?
Once you've registered your O'Reilly books you can:

- Win O'Reilly books, T-shirts or discount coupons in our monthly drawing.
- Get special offers available only to registered O'Reilly customers.
- Get catalogs announcing new books (US and UK only).
- Get email notification of new editions of the O'Reilly books you own.

3. Join our email lists

Sign up to get topic-specific email announcements of new books and conferences, special offers, and O'Reilly Network technology newsletters at:

elists.oreilly.com

It's easy to customize your free elists subscription so you'll get exactly the O'Reilly news you want.

4. Get the latest news, tips, and tools

www.oreilly.com

- "Top 100 Sites on the Web"—PC Magazine
- CIO Magazine's Web Business 50 Awards

Our web site contains a library of comprehensive product information (including book excerpts and tables of contents), downloadable software, background articles, interviews with technology leaders, links to relevant sites, book cover art, and more.

5. Work for O'Reilly

Check out our web site for current employment opportunities:

jobs.oreilly.com

6. Contact us

O'Reilly & Associates
1005 Gravenstein Hwy North
Sebastopol, CA 95472 USA
TEL: 707-827-7000 or 800-998-9938
       (6am to 5pm PST)
FAX: 707-829-0104

order@oreilly.com
For answers to problems regarding your order or our products. To place a book order online, visit:

www.oreilly.com/order_new

catalog@oreilly.com
To request a copy of our latest catalog.

booktech@oreilly.com
For book content technical questions or corrections.

corporate@oreilly.com
For educational, library, government, and corporate sales.

proposals@oreilly.com
To submit new book proposals to our editors and product managers.

international@oreilly.com
For information about our international distributors or translation queries. For a list of our distributors outside of North America check out:

international.oreilly.com/distributors.html

adoption@oreilly.com
For information about academic use of O'Reilly books, visit:

academic.oreilly.com